Urban Parks and Open Space

PRINCIPAL AUTHORS

Alexander Garvin

Gayle Berens

CONTRIBUTING AUTHORS

Christopher B. Leinberger

Martin J. Rosen

Steven Fader

Peter Harnik

Terry Jill Lassar

David Mulvihill

SPONSORED BY

Advisory Committee of ULI–the Urban Land Institute and the Trust for Public Land

John Baird
Baird & Warner
Chicago, Illinois

Cheryl Barton
Cheryl Barton Landscape Architects
San Francisco, California

William Behnke
Willoughby, Ohio

Mark Francis
University of California
Landscape Architecture Program
Davis, California

Beverly Griffith
Austin, Texas

James Hoyte
Lexington, Massachusetts

Fred Kent
Project for Public Spaces, Inc.
New York, New York

Franklin Martin
Hidden Springs LLC
Boise, Idaho

Robert McNulty
Partners for Livable Communities
Washington, D.C.

Patrick Phillips
Economics Research Associates
Washington, D.C.

Christopher Sawyer
Alston & Bird
Atlanta, Georgia

Additional Reviewers

Ned Baier, Jack Batman, Daniel Biederman, Kathleen Blaha, J. Blaine Bonham, Lloyd Bookout, Michael Bradley, Marrice Coverson, Mary Dahl, Dan Dailey, Richard Dattner, David Fisher, Robin Frye, Alexander Garvin, Cuma Glennon, Jerri Greene, Peter Harnik, Martha Ketterer, Laurie Lundy, Jill Manton, Patrick C. Moore, David Mulvihill, Rhonda Rae, Stanley Saitowitz, Michael Shiosaki, Michael Van Valkenburgh, Robert Weinberg, Charles Wells, Charles Wilt.

About the Authors

Gayle Berens

Gayle Berens is a director in the policy and practice department of the Urban Land Institute. In addition to directing and developing university-related programs for ULI, she is also responsible for development and implementation of ULI's inner-city program. Berens is the coauthor of *Real Estate Development Principles and Process*, first and second editions, as well as project director for *Graaskamp on Real Estate, Classic Readings in Real Estate and Development*, and the ULI *Directory of Real Estate Development and Related Education Programs*. She has written many articles for *Urban Land* and many case studies for the *ULI Project Reference File* series. Berens has organized several symposia and mayors' forums dealing with city revitalization, and for six years she directed ULI's Real Estate School. She earned an undergraduate degree from the University of Wisconsin at Green Bay and a graduate degree from Georgetown University.

Steven Fader

Steven Fader, AIA, is a project architect and senior associate at Levin and Associates, Architects, in Los Angeles, where he specializes in site and master planning. He has also worked as a project architect for Ellerbe Becket Architects and Rachlin & Rachlin Associates. Fader has been a contributing author for the *Business and Industrial Park Development Handbook, Value by Design: Landscape, Site Planning, and Amenities, Urban Land*, and the *ULI Project Reference File* series. He holds memberships in The American Institute of Architects, the Los Angeles Conservancy, and the Urban Land Institute. Fader's undergraduate degree is from Temple University, and he holds two masters' degrees: one in urban and regional planning from Cornell University, and the other in architecture from the University of California at Los Angeles.

Alexander Garvin

Alexander Garvin has combined a career in urban planning and real estate with teaching, architecture, and public service. He is currently a commissioner on the New York City Planning Commission and an owner, developer, and manager of New York City real estate. From 1970 to 1980, Garvin held prominent positions in New York City government, including deputy commissioner of housing and director of comprehensive planning. Before entering government, he pursued a career as an architect.

Garvin is adjunct professor of urban planning and management at Yale University. He is a fellow of the Urban Land Institute and has organized and taught ULI workshops on basic real estate development, the residential development process, and the role of design in real estate. Garvin is also the author of *The American City: What Works, What Doesn't*, published by McGraw-Hill, which received the 1996 AIA book award in urbanism.

Peter Harnik

Peter Harnik's writing career began in 1970 when he served as coauthor and assistant editor of *Earth Tool Kit*, an ecological handbook produced by the organizers of the first Earth Day. Since then he has served as editor of two periodicals, *Environmental Action* and *Trailblazer*, and has written two books on the rails-to-trails movement, *Converting Rails to Trails* and *Railroads Recycled*. Harnik has written widely on energy, transportation, and ecology issues and is currently working on a booklet on alternative vehicle fuels to be published by Public Technology, Inc.

Harnik cofounded the Rails-to-Trails Conservancy, initiated trail creation efforts in Washington, D.C., Maryland, and Virginia, and serves as president of the Washington Area Bicyclist Association. In 1987, the Friends of the United Nations Environment Programme named Harnik one of the "Global 500" environmental achievers. Harnik is a graduate of Johns Hopkins University.

Terry Jill Lassar

Terry Jill Lassar is a consultant and writer based in Portland, Oregon, who specializes in planning, urban design, and retail and residential development. For two years she headed a Portland transportation planning project aimed at encouraging compact, dense development next to the new Westside MAX light-rail stations.

Lassar was on the research staff of the Urban Land Institute for five years, where she focused on public/private development, land use and zoning, urban design, downtown development, and urban public policy issues. She is the author of *Carrots & Sticks: New Zoning Downtown,* the editor of *City Deal Making,* and a contributing author for *Remaking the Shopping Center* and *Flexible Zoning.*

Christopher B. Leinberger

Christopher B. Leinberger is managing director and co-owner of Robert Charles Lesser and Company, the leading independent real estate consulting firm in the country. He is also a partner in the Arcadia Land Company, an innovative development firm that combines town founding and land stewardship. Leinberger is a nationally recognized authority on metropolitan development trends and strategic planning for metropolitan areas and real estate companies.

Leinberger has written for numerous periodicals, including *The Atlantic,* the *Wall Street Journal,* and *Urban Land.* He is the author of *Strategic Planning for Real Estate,* published by the Urban Land Institute and the National Association of Industrial and Office Properties (NAIOP). An active member of ULI, Leinberger is also on the National Advisory Board, NAIOP, and on the National Council of the Conservation Fund. Leinberger is a graduate of Swarthmore College and holds an MBA from Harvard Business School.

David Mulvihill

David Mulvihill, a senior associate in the policy and practice department of the Urban Land Institute, has written more than 60 articles for *Urban Land* on a wide range of real estate development and land use topics. Mulvihill is also the editor of ULI's monthly newsletter, *Land Use Digest,* coeditor of the *ULI Project Reference File* series, and writer of ULI's academic newsletter, *Teaching Development.* As manager of ULI's InfoPackets, he is responsible for researching, compiling, and updating information on more than 85 topics related to real estate. Mulvihill has also assisted in the research and writing of several recent ULI publications and is closely involved in the management of ULI's annual Real Estate School. He is a graduate of Carnegie-Mellon University.

Martin J. Rosen

Since 1978, Martin J. Rosen has served as president of the Trust for Public Land (TPL), a national nonprofit land conservation organization based in San Francisco with offices throughout the United States. Working in places as diverse as Hell's Kitchen in New York City, the Columbia River Gorge in the Northwest, the Florida Keys, and Barton Springs, Texas, TPL has protected over $1.2 billion worth of land —almost 1 million acres of wild, scenic, and urban open space for people in 44 states and Canada.

Rosen has been honored with several awards for his contributions to land use: the Horace Albright Medal from the National Park Foundation; the I. Donald Terner Award from Lambda Alpha International–Golden Gate chapter; and the highest honor from the Landscape Architecture Foundation.

Rosen graduated from the University of California at Los Angeles and from Boalt Hall School of Law at the University of California at Berkeley. He has practiced law, primarily dealing with regulatory matters, for more than 25 years. Rosen serves on the boards and advisory committees of various environmental and educational institutions and is a frequent speaker at professional meetings.

Contents

Preface

ULI–the Urban Land Institute and the Trust for Public Land (TPL) are pleased to sponsor this book on urban parks and open space. This volume represents the first joint publishing effort of two institutions that have somewhat different missions but that share a common goal: responsible use of land.

While ULI is noted primarily for its work in real estate development, and TPL is noted primarily for its work in safeguarding land for conservation and public use, the marriage of these two forces in this publication signals the understanding that a thoughtfully implemented urban development plan should include more than great buildings; it should include great parks and open space because both buildings and open space benefit from each other.

The goal of this book is to strengthen understanding of the value—economic, social, communal, environmental, and aesthetic—that urban parks and open space add to our cities and neighborhoods. The book also stresses the importance of giving open space greater consideration in urban development and redevelopment plans. Well-planned open space can promote community investment, educate citizens about the environment, contribute to a city's unique character, and link surrounding buildings to create a sense of place. Manhattan is an example of a city

that is as well known for its dramatic open space as for its dramatic buildings. Each contributes something special to the fabric of the city and to the people who live and work in it.

While parks, trails, gardens, and other forms of open space alone cannot solve urban problems, they are crucial to the health and quality of life of our cities. Trends show that by the year 2000, 80 percent of Americans will live in metropolitan areas. In redeveloping our cities to accommodate this new growth, we can learn from 19th-century city development and from more recent suburban development. In both cases, parks and open space are often the primary organizing elements that shape development, create livability, and preserve property values.

We hope that the case studies in this book will encourage a variety of civic players to take a fresh look at open space. Private developers, for example, who are considering urban settings for future development projects need to think about how to use open space to enhance their projects.

Similarly, public agencies need to recognize the value of investing in parks and open space, which can play an important role in attracting private investment and securing the value of existing investment. In many cities, for example, the public sector owns derelict waterfronts that can

Enhancing the Public Realm

Alexander Garvin

Originally proposed as a "greensward" by its designers, Central Park today accommodates a wonderful variety of landscapes and built features that are cherished by visitors.

In 1850, the public realm in the United States consisted of unpaved streets, barely landscaped squares, rudimentary marketplaces, and vast territories of wilderness. Everything else was in the hands of property owners whose actions were virtually unregulated. There were, as yet, no large public parks acquired, developed, and managed specifically as recreational facilities.

Imagine Manhattan if public officials in the mid-19th century had chosen not to spend the money needed to acquire and develop America's first large public park. The New York of today would be without Central Park, an unusually beautiful recreational facility actively used by a quarter of a million people on a typical weekend. Equally important, the city would be collecting far less tax revenue.

Property values in Manhattan doubled during the 15 years after park development began. In the three wards surrounding Central Park, two-and-a-half miles north of most of the city's real estate activity, values increased nine times.[1] These park-generated tax revenues allowed the city to pay for municipal services that it could not otherwise have afforded and provided the stimulus for city officials to acquire the 26,369 acres of land that currently constitute New York City's extraordinary park system.

Now, imagine what life would be like today if cities across the nation had watched New York's rejection of park spending and decided to follow suit. Most cities would have continued to direct their resources to more pressing needs, such as police protection and public education. And the public realm would now consist primarily of streets, roads, and highways—rather than parks.

Fortunately, that didn't happen. Central Park initiated more than a century of governmental property acquisition and park development in the United States. City, state, and federal agencies now own and operate hundreds of millions of acres of streets and highways, bridges and tunnels, and a wide array of public buildings. Most of this public realm, however, consists of parkland that was acquired and developed to be a place of refuge from city life, a recreational resource for large numbers of people, a scenic treasure preserved for posterity, or a means of maintaining ecological balance. The very creation of this vast public realm allowed attention to be directed to the many other issues that have come to dominate the public agenda. If the country had not invested in a vast system of public parks, city and suburban residents would still be clamoring for parks.

After a century of sustained park development, post–World War II America shifted away from using appropriations to provide the public with additional open space; instead, public officials tried to accomplish the same result less expensively, through regulation. One result is that we have become mired in unnecessary political conflicts because community attempts to ensure privacy and security consistently clash with government efforts to guarantee public access to open space.

Such conflicts have deflected public attention away from the increasing demand for recreational facilities brought about by America's post–World War II population increase of more than 100 million. As most cities and suburbs continuously reduce appropriations for park acquisition, development, and maintenance, increasing numbers of people crowd into existing facilities. The result is a growing imbalance between the supply of public open space and the demands made on it by a growing population.

We have forgotten the reasons that Americans in the late 19th and early 20th centuries devoted so much energy and money to creating a vast array of public parks. They understood that judicious public spending on park development stimulates widespread and sustained private investment, alters settlement patterns, encourages social interaction, and reshapes the very character of daily life. If we are to supply open space to our growing population, we will have to stop trying to expand the public realm on the cheap, through regulation, and resume the program of property acquisition and park development that worked so well during the late 19th and early 20th centuries.

This essay examines some of the issues involved in locating and designing public parks that arose during the 19th century—issues that are every bit as significant today. What types of sites are best suited for park development? Where should they be located? What principles should determine their design? How should they be financed? Who should own and manage them?

Denver's Sixteenth Street Mall provides pedestrians with 13 blocks of landscaped open space free of cars, trucks, and taxis. Free bus service, carrying some 100,000 people a day, runs up and down the street, and the new light-rail system intersects with Sixteenth Street.

Parks are not the only form of public open space. Consequently, this essay also examines the role of other forms of publicly owned open space: squares, marketplaces, streets, and highways. A great deal can be learned from expansions of this portion of the public realm. Pittsburgh's Mellon Square, for example, has demonstrated how to use parking fees to cover debt service on the bonds that paid for the creation of the square. Denver's Sixteenth Street Mall has demonstrated what so many failed pedestrianized shopping streets do not—that properly located, intelligently designed, vehicle-free streets can provide a focus for downtown revitalization. The transformation of Washington's Chesapeake & Ohio (C & O) Canal into parkland has demonstrated that reclaiming commercial waterways for recreational purposes can stimulate private investment that completely alters land use patterns.

Finally, this essay reviews some recent approaches to park design, financing, and management that provide promising models for future action. Boulder, Colorado, enacted a sales tax earmarked specifically for parks. New York's Hudson River Park Conservancy uses lease and concession fees to pay for park maintenance. The Bryant Park Business Improvement District raises maintenance funds through a dedicated real estate tax paid by surrounding property owners and through revenue generated by restaurants and concessions. These and other examples throughout this book provide promising models that can be inserted into traditional public-sector models and adopted across the country.

Nineteenth-Century Park Development and Design

Writing in 1870, landscape architect Frederick Law Olmsted described Prospect Park in Brooklyn and Central Park in Manhattan as "the only places" in those cities where "vast numbers of persons [are] brought closely together, poor and rich, young and old . . . each individual adding by his mere presence to the pleasure of all others."[2] These parks had been open to the public for less than a decade when Olmsted described their role as social mixing valves. Yet merely the decision to acquire land for them had already spurred development of countless parks in other cities.

Today most city governments operate and maintain a large inventory of such mixing valves for their increasingly diverse populations. The New York City Department of Parks and Recreation manages 18 miles of beaches; 46 swimming pools; 16 golf courses; six skating rinks; and 1,570 parks, playgrounds, and public spaces. The Minneapolis Park and Recreation Board, serving a population less than 5 percent of New York City's, has a system of more than 6,000 acres containing 170 park properties, including 42 recreation centers, 61 supervised playgrounds, 21 beaches, and 22 major still-water lakes.

Park systems like these do not just happen. They are the product of myriad decisions made over decades by hundreds of public officials. Those decisions include where parks should be located; for whom they should be provided; how they should be designed; how they will be paid for; who should be responsible for management and maintenance; and how desirable spillover benefits will be maximized for surrounding communities.

From the beginning, there was controversy over such decisions. Public officials looked for ways to purchase properties at low prices. Land that was not easy to develop, either because of steep slopes, drainage difficulties, or some other problem, was usually the least expensive to acquire and was consequently appealing to budget-conscious public officials. Often these sites were no more appropriate for park development than for private construction, but they were acquired anyway.

In 1873, when Olmsted and his partner, Calvert Vaux, were asked to prepare designs for a park on the cliffs overlooking Harlem, they pointed out that the proposed Morningside Park would add "another public ground chosen without the slightest reference to any . . . requirements of the city, and [one that] happens to be singularly incapable of being adapted to them."[3] Worse still, they argued, "by no appropriate treatment could a ground having the natural features of Morningside Park be made a safe and reputable place of resort at night."[4] They succeeded in forestalling its development until 1887. Anyone from Columbia University, on the heights above the park, or from Harlem, on the flats below, can certify that Olmsted and Vaux were correct. Morningside Park is not "a safe and reputable place of resort at night."

The first parks proposed by George Kessler for Kansas City in 1893 were also located on steep slopes that were unattrac-

Figure 1 • America's 15 Largest City Parks

Park	City	Size (Acreage)
Cullen Park	Houston	10,534
Fairmount Park	Philadelphia	8,700
Griffith Park	Los Angeles	4,218
Eagle Creek Park	Indianapolis	3,800
Pelham Bay Park	Bronx (N.Y.C.)	2,764
Mission Bay Park	San Diego	2,300
Greenbelt Park	Staten Island (N.Y.C.)	1,778
Swope Park	Kansas City, Mo.	1,769
Rock Creek Park	Washington, D.C.	1,754
City Park	New Orleans	1,500
Forest Park	St. Louis	1,293
Flushing Meadows–Corona Park	Queens (N.Y.C.)	1,258
Lincoln Park	Chicago	1,212
Balboa Park	San Diego	1,203
Van Cortlandt Park	Bronx (N.Y.C.)	1,146
Central Park (for comparison)	Manhattan (N.Y.C.)	843

Note: All parks on this list (except Rock Creek) are wholly city owned, and size is based only on land acreage that is intended for passive or active recreation. It does not include water acreage or land intended simply for open space preservation. Because of Rock Creek Park's location in our nation's capital, Congress preserved it as one of our first national parks, but its function as a city park makes it eligible for this list.

tive for real estate development. Even so, the board of park commissioners faced opposition from citizens concerned about the loss of real estate tax revenues. Consequently, in 1899, the board eliminated from these sites the most easily developable land. Only when the remaining, relatively poor sites proved to be popular did the commissioners begin acquiring larger, more accessible properties that were more suitable for park development.

The romantic landscapes that Olmsted created on the sites of Brooklyn's Prospect Park and Manhattan's Central Park became models for most 19th-century parks. Landscape gardener Maximillian G. Kern copied their rolling meadows and curving pedestrian paths in 1876, when he transformed 1,372 acres on the outskirts of St. Louis into Forest Park.[5] Like so many of Olmsted's followers, however, Kern and his associates, Henry Flad and Julius Pitzman, believed that a sylvan setting was all that was needed. Consequently, they paid scant attention to the needs of the large numbers of people who used the park. By 1915, St. Louis had begun to alter this inadequate design because, as its department of parks explained, "The primary purpose of the park system has become the raising of men and women rather than grass or trees." None of Olmsted's parks required alteration because he always designed them for active use by large numbers of people.

Olmsted understood the inherent conflict between maintaining grass, bushes, and trees and accommodating the masses of people who use any successful park. As he explained in 1888, when he designed the park through which visitors would come to see Niagara Falls, the problem was to maintain a newly planted landscape while simultaneously protecting it from "the riotous actions of a mob unconscious of wrong purposes and indignant at obvious constraints upon what it regards as harmless conduct."[6] Conse-

quently, Olmsted always made sure to protect the natural environment while at the same time providing for the varied needs of the people who used his parks. Too many of his followers misunderstood this balance of interests and took only one of these objectives into account.

Some planners design each park only to meet the needs of nearby residents. Others ignore the needs of potential users and adjust each park design to the capabilities of the site. Olmsted believed it was a mistake to do one or the other exclusively. As he explained when designing the "Emerald Necklace" park system for Boston, one should not consider each site "independently of its relations to others of the system, as if it were to be of little value except to the people of the districts adjoining it."[7]

These 19th-century examples demonstrate that acquiring property and labeling it parkland is not enough to create facilities in which "vast numbers of persons [are] brought closely together." The property must be located in places easily accessible to vast numbers of people, and its topography must provide them with suitable gathering places. The arrangement of grass and bushes and trees must be capable of withstanding heavy pedestrian traffic. As Olmsted explained when designing the Boston park system, "A site for a park to stand by itself and be little used except by those living near it should be a very different one from that for a park designed for more general use, and especially for a park which is to stand in a series."[8]

Understanding the Public Realm

It is misleading to think of parkland as the only form of open space available to the public. Large numbers of people come together in other places that are publicly owned but that have not been acquired strictly for recreational purposes

Intended as a public meeting place, the New Haven Green is an early form of open space modeled after its European predecessors.

—streets, squares, and marketplaces. They congregate in places that are privately owned but that are widely used for recreation by the general public—building plazas, shopping centers, business parks. It is important to understand how such spaces work and to make them an integral part of a community's total open space strategy.

People also spend time in privately owned open spaces that are used in common by residents but that are not available to outsiders—swimming pools, sun decks, tennis courts, private country clubs. While such forms of open space bring together people who live near these facilities, most of the users are already acquainted with one another. Consequently, this is not open space where "vast numbers of persons [are] brought closely together, poor and rich, young and old." Nevertheless, many zoning ordinances offer bonuses to developers who include such "public open space" in their projects.

During the past two decades, huge territories have been designated as parkland that are not available to the public

—natural habitats, wetlands, environmental preserves. Such areas are usually private property set aside by developers to satisfy environmental regulations. The acreage may expand the public realm, but as long as the land is unavailable for public use, it is a misnomer to call these areas parks.

Squares, Marketplaces, and Thoroughfares

Squares, marketplaces, and thoroughfares, like parks, act as mixing valves for large numbers of people. Long before they began acquiring land specifically for public recreation, governments provided town greens, public commons, and squares. As a result, city residents became accustomed to strolling and gathering in places such as the Boston Common, the New Haven Green, and New Orleans's Plâce d'Armes (now Jackson Square). When competitive sports and more active forms of recreation became popular during the 19th century, city dwellers eagerly shifted their activities to the newly created public parks that offered the space and facilities they sought.

Just as public squares are often overlooked as recreation sites, so are marketplaces. For decades, Seattle's Pike Place Market and Los Angeles's Farmers' Market have played much more important roles as tourist destinations than as local shopping facilities. In Portland, Oregon, more than 200 craft vendors come together for Saturday Market, which continues throughout the weekend and attracts more than 10,000 people from all over the metropolitan area.

The least appreciated of our nonpark forms of public open space are thoroughfares. In ancient Rome, ordinary streets were understood to be settings for public recreation. The broad, tree-lined avenues that Haussmann developed in 19th-century Paris were specifically intended to be promenades. Olmsted understood this when he proposed that cities create landscaped

boulevards leading to large public parks and out to the suburbs. Such ample thoroughfares were intended to be places of recreation for the residents of the buildings that lined them, as well as to provide enjoyable settings for travelers journeying into the country. Olmsted and his partner, Calvert Vaux, initiated the creation of America's first such landscaped boulevards in 1867, when they provided plans for Eastern and Ocean parkways in Brooklyn. Richmond's Monument Avenue, Denver's Speer Boulevard, and Philadelphia's Franklin Parkway are a few examples of Olmsted and Vaux's influence.

Although this purpose has been largely forgotten, many limited-access parkways are designed to be settings for public recreation. Chicago's Lakeshore Drive, first proposed by Daniel Burnham in 1894 and again in his *Plan of Chicago* of 1909, was intended not simply as a traffic artery, but

In a downtown riverfront district that was once nearly abandoned, Saturday Market in Portland, Oregon, transforms a plaza and an adjacent parking lot under a freeway.

Alexander Garvin (1990)

also as a way of allowing city dwellers to "constantly seek the refreshment of the country."[9] The Bronx River Parkway, begun in 1907, had beautifully landscaped borders that gave motorists the illusion of driving through a public garden. During the mid-1920s, Robert Moses, the first chairman of the New York State Parks Commission, began creating a system of state parks connected by similarly landscaped motorways. These scenic parkways made the entire trip from home to park and back again a delightful form of recreation. A decade later, the federal government took the next step by making the entire Blue Ridge Parkway a scenic attraction. By then, Connecticut's Merritt Parkway and Virginia's Mount Vernon Parkway and Skyline Drive were already in operation; they were soon followed by the Arroyo Secco Parkway in southern California.

Privately Owned Public Open Space

After World War II, government action to increase the availability of public open space shifted from new park development to other strategies. Perhaps this was because most cities (though few suburbs) already had impressive parks, or because of the mounting cost of operating extensive park systems, or because there were other, more important demands for public expenditures. Whatever the reasons, an increasing number of cities chose to have private property owners provide the public with the additional open space that the cities were unwilling to purchase. Zoning became a favorite device in this effort.

From its inception in 1916, zoning had regulated the placement of buildings on privately owned land. One of the principles underlying zoning was that the public was entitled to adequate light and air on public thoroughfares. Thus, zoning limited the height of buildings, required them to be set back from the street, and forced them into an envelope that guaranteed sunlight on the sidewalk. In lower-density areas, this resulted in suburban subdivisions, such as Prairie Village, Kansas, which have houses with front-yards, side yards, and rear yards. In business districts, zoning produced office buildings that stepped back from the street, and the setback space became privately owned public space.

While it was appropriate for cities to regulate privately owned land, it was understood that government played no role in the management of the privately owned buildings lining public thoroughfares. Government agencies designed and managed the thoroughfares primarily as vehicular circulation routes. Property

New York's Taconic State Parkway is one of many scenic state parkways beloved by residents and visitors.

Alexander Garvin (1976)

Mandated front and side yards in this section of Prairie Village, Kansas, provide open space that enhances the community's appearance and creates places for neighboring homeowners to interact, but none of this open space is available to the general public.

Alexander Garvin (1994)

owners were responsible for maintaining sidewalks and providing pedestrian access to their buildings. Consequently, motor vehicles dominated the public realm, while pedestrians dominated the quasi-private open space between the streets and the buildings that bounded them. It was an uneasy relationship that had to change.

A similar situation was developing in the suburbs. Millions of new homeowners took pride in the lawns, bushes, and trees that occupied their government-mandated front, side, and rear yards. These yards provided open space and greenery, but they were available for use only by individual homeowners (and their guests), who had no responsibility for the public streets along which the yards were located. Streets were thought of primarily as vehicular circulation routes, without much consideration of their role as public open space.

Because so many residential subdivisions lacked public parks, suburbanites went jogging, bicycling, and picnicking on the grounds of office parks or "hung out" at the local shopping center. Children played in the street. When children were involved in traffic accidents, the usual

response was to install traffic signals. Neither the homeowners nor the government officials, who were responsible for these "dangerous" streets, recognized that the traffic artery was often the only public space in a subdivision.

This form of suburbanization causes more than just traffic accidents. When residents have no place in which to encounter people who are different from themselves, the result is an increasingly insular society.

Current Park Development Strategies

By the second half of the 20th century, most cities had invested in major park systems. Yet their residents were moving to the suburbs, where they believed there were better opportunities for recreation. In fact, the very suburbs to which city dwellers moved were seriously lacking public parkland. It was too late to create major public parks in these areas because the best sites had already been developed as residential subdivisions. While suburban areas had growing populations, most residents were unwilling to vote

Rotterdam was one of the first cities that attempted to spur metropolitan revival and increase the public realm by "pedestrianizing" when it banished cars from the Lijnbaan, its main shopping street.

owned property (especially land used by motor vehicles) and to require property owners to make increasing amounts of their land available for public use. Both approaches are fraught with controversy. The first increases competition among different groups who believe that they are entitled to use publicly owned property. The second sharpens antagonism between private property owners and the civic and government organizations seeking to increase the public realm.

Retrofitting Streets as Pedestrian Open Space

Almost half a century has passed since architect Victor Gruen proposed an obvious solution: banish motor vehicles from selected streets and retrofit them as public open spaces. Such "pedestrianized" streets can then be designed and managed in a manner that allows downtown merchants to compete with those in shopping centers.

Gruen based his proposal on Rotterdam's Lijnbaan, a 3,000-foot-long retail street that replaced the tangle of arteries destroyed by aerial bombing early in World War II. The Lijnbaan, which opened in 1953, looked more like a shopping center than a city street. Gruen recognized immediately that similar shopping precincts could be created in cities across the United States. He proposed to do so by removing the roadbed; installing appropriate paving; providing new lighting and street furniture; requiring consistent signage; and adding trees, flowers, and other landscape elements.

In 1958, Kalamazoo, Michigan, became the first American city to adopt Gruen's ideas. Within a few years, similar projects were underway in Miami, Knoxville, Fresno, Providence, Honolulu, and countless other cities. In some cities, like Providence, the creation of a pedestrian mall was not enough to keep shoppers downtown. But whether or not these retrofit-

for the increased taxes needed to pay for public parks.

City residents were as unwilling to pay for parkland as their suburban counterparts. With the exception of Minneapolis, Boulder, and a very small number of other cities, spending on parks has been steadily cut. In New York City, for example, during the 1940s and 1950s, when Robert Moses was parks commissioner, parks accounted for approximately 1.5 percent of the annual operating budget; by the 1990s, this figure had dropped to less than half a percent. In suburban areas, where recreation facilities consist of swimming pools, gyms, public golf courses, and school ball fields, spending levels are often still lower.

How can public officials satisfy the growing number of unhappy constituents demanding additional public open space if citizens are unwilling to spend additional sums to acquire parkland? The two most popular strategies used in recent years have been to make available for recreational purposes other government-

ted arterials were successful in attracting and retaining retail shoppers, they did substantially increase the amount of open space available to the public.

Pedestrianization is an attractive approach to increasing public open space because it does not cost governments much money. Nothing has to be spent on land acquisition; and construction, management, and maintenance can be charged to surrounding property owners. There is no cheaper way to provide citizens with additional public open space.

Once pedestrianization became popular, federal and state governments began paying most of the development cost. The city of Philadelphia, for example, paid less than $300,000 of the $7.4 million cost of pedestrianizing Chestnut Street: the federal government covered 80 percent and the state of Pennsylvania 17 percent.[10] Local governments were also able to transfer to the private sector a large portion of the cost of street maintenance. Properties within Minneapolis's Nicollet Mall special assessment district, for example, pay 90 percent of the maintenance costs.[11]

Nicollet Mall proved successful for several reasons: it takes less than ten minutes to walk from one end to the other; virtually all the city's office, retail, hotel, and convention facilities are within a block or two of the mall; and the mall was planned in conjunction with the city's skywalks and parking garages. A similarly critical mass of facilities is clustered along Denver's Sixteenth Street Mall. In this case, the city's main office, retail, hotel, and convention facilities are combined with the state capitol, a performing arts center, a university, and two suburban bus terminals. In many other cities, however, pedestrian malls have been dismal failures. They failed because public officials erroneously thought that success was merely a matter of removing motor vehicles, repaving, and adding glitzy street furniture—just as they had earlier erroneously thought that successful parks were merely a matter of acquiring property and planting grass and trees.

Pedestrianizing Nicollet Avenue in Minneapolis cost $3.8 million—three-fourths of which came from an 18-block special assessment district to which adjacent property owners contributed in proportion to the benefits they were to receive. Nicollet Mall opened in 1967 to 9,000 daily shoppers; ten years later, there were over 40,000.

Alexander Garvin (1996)

Transforming Highways into Parks

Reclaiming highways, another attractive way to increase public open space, also requires virtually no expenditures for acquisition and no lengthy land assembly process. Freeway Park in Seattle is the most imaginative example of this strategy. When Interstate 5 opened in 1965, it cut downtown Seattle in half, creating an unwanted division between the central business district and nearby commercial and institutional activity. More important, the interstate had a blighting effect along both edges of the highway. Public officials decided to knit

Frederick Housel

Frederick Housel

In Seattle, designer Angela Danadjieva created a master plan for Interstate 5 that resulted in one of the most extensive freeway air-rights development plans in the country. In essence, the project called for a 20-acre lid to be suspended over the freeway, linking downtown to the residential neighborhood of First Hill. The development ultimately included three projects: Freeway Park, Pigott Memorial Corridor (an extension of the park), and the Washington State Convention and Trade Center.

together the two sections of the city by building a park on top of the highway. They hired Lawrence Halprin & Associates, whose primary designer, Angela Danadjieva, created a park with a variety of places where children can play, parents can sit and gossip, downtown workers can stroll, and everybody can escape the hustle and bustle of the city. When this five-acre facility opened in 1976, it increased the attractiveness of sites for office buildings and retail stores in the business district to the west of the freeway and for residences and institutions to the east. Indeed, the project was so successful that in 1984, an additional two-acre section of the freeway was covered to extend the park.

Development costs for highway transformation can often be charged to federal and state governments. In Portland, Oregon, the federal interstate highway system paid for a multilane freeway encircling the business district. This ringroad rendered superfluous Portland's main highway bypass, six-lane Harbor Drive, which ran along the Willamette River. The removal of Harbor Drive in 1974 provided a unique opportunity to reclaim 2.75 miles of prime waterfront land as public open space—making it possible to create Tom McCall Park with-

out causing traffic problems or relocating residents or businesses.

Portland is not unique in reclaiming highway rights-of-way as public parks. To provide a site for a proposed "Inner Belt" highway, Boston cleared a wide swath of land running from the Back Bay and South End to Jamaica Plain and Roxbury. Eventually, the highway was abandoned and the 4.7-mile route became Southwest Corridor Park. The park is created on a platform over the relocated Orange subway line, which, in turn, replaced an old elevated transit line. The city is planning to create a similar linear park when it uses federal interstate highway funds to bury Central Artery, the elevated highway separating downtown Boston from its North End waterfront. This smaller, 20-acre linear park will be created by platforming over the highway, once it is buried.

When the 1989 Loma Prieta earthquake rendered the Embarcadero Freeway unusable as a highway, San Francisco decided not to rebuild it (see the case study on the Embarcadero Promenade). Instead, the city created an at-grade boulevard that includes a palm-lined tramway and a 25-foot-wide pedestrian promenade. This narrow, linear park is punctuated by artwork and provides space for jogging, bicycling, and other forms of recreation.

New York City is creating a similar linear park along Route 9A, which runs at grade along the Hudson River in Lower Manhattan (see the case study on Hudson River Park). Route 9A is on the site of the ill-fated Westway project, a 226-acre redevelopment project planned atop a 4.2-mile-long mapped section of the interstate highway system. When the Koch administration chose to trade in its interstate highway fund reservation ($1.7 billion), a portion of this money was earmarked to rebuild the highway at grade.

The Hudson River Park will be created along this right-of-way. If all goes as planned, the new Hudson River Park will include a 4.5-mile waterfront esplanade connecting 13 renovated public recreation piers, ball fields, playgrounds, boating facilities, and the Chelsea Piers (a privately financed and developed sports and entertainment complex). Unlike the proposed Westway project, Hudson River Park will not be built over the highway and will thus be separated from the rest of Manhattan by six to eight lanes of vehicular traffic.

The nearly $330 million capital cost of this new linear park will come primarily from city, state, and federal funds. That is the park's only similarity to a conventional public park, managed and maintained by a city parks department. The development of Hudson River Park is being managed by the Hudson River Park Conservancy, a nonprofit subsidiary of New York State's Empire Development Corporation.[12] Properties along the right-of-way of Route 9A, such as the Chelsea Piers, will generate lease and concession revenues to cover the park's operating expenses.

Using Parking Garage Revenues to Pay for Parks

Another way to minimize the cost of acquiring, developing, and maintaining public open space is to use it simultaneously for automobiles and people. San Francisco pioneered this strategy in 1940, when it opened a 1,700-car public parking garage under Union Square, a traditional, landscaped, 2.6-acre park that had been donated to the city in 1850. Los Angeles did the same in 1951 when it dug up Pershing Square, its five-acre downtown park, to provide 2,150 underground parking spaces.

While garage revenues defrayed the cost of maintaining Union and Pershing

Boston's five-mile-long Southwest Corridor Park was part of a $780 million transit project that combined an existing commuter railroad, a new subway line, and vacant and underused property.

Alexander Garvin (1994)

Inspired by Union Square in San Francisco, the park at Mellon Square in Pittsburgh was created on the roof of a six-level parking garage. Mellon Square was built in 1953 as part of the city's Renaissance I redevelopment effort and was considered at the time to be the centerpiece of the city's revitalization.

squares, these projects did not add one square inch of public open space to either city. Pittsburgh was the first city to use parking demand to provide an income stream that would cover debt service on the capital borrowed to pay the cost of developing and maintaining a new park. In 1948, Pittsburgh's public parking authority proposed building a six-story garage on the 1.37-acre site that is now Mellon Square. The following year, the Mellon family offered to pay for the construction of a park on this site. In exchange, the city agreed to build the garage underneath the park.

Mellon Square is a park that occupies a 230-foot by 260-foot block right in the middle of downtown Pittsburgh. The park is level with William Penn Place, at the top of the site. Underneath is a six-level, 896-car garage. Because of the steeply sloping site, garage entrances from the two side streets have been slipped in beneath the park. The project's designers, Mitchell & Ritchey (architects) and Simonds & Simonds (landscape architects), avoided leaving a blank wall at the bottom of the hill along Smithfield Street. Instead, they lined the street with retail stores that provide rental

revenue—and, more important, active street life.

The Mellons paid $3.65 million for land acquisition and demolition, plus $650,000 for construction of the surface park. Mellon Square Garage, Inc., initially leased the site from the parking authority for 38 years, later extended an additional 21 years. The authority financed the $3.5 million cost of building the garage from a portion of its parking fees and commercial rents. The remaining revenues cover operating costs and rent to the parking authority.[13]

A growing number of cities provide parking under public parks. The garages under Grant Park (Chicago), the Boston Common, and Market Square (Alexandria, Virginia) do little more than accommodate automobiles under parkland that would otherwise look very much the same. Other park/garage combinations actually enhance daily life in the surrounding city. Mellon Square does so by providing stores that enliven street activity. Post Office Square does so by including a café-restaurant, creating consumer traffic that integrates the park into the daily life of downtown Boston (see the case study on the Park at Post Office

The stores at the base of Mellon Square bring customers to the area, enhancing street life in downtown Pittsburgh.

Square). The planners of Post Office Square recognized that small, center-city parks have to be made a part of the complex mix of activities that take place in downtown locations and cannot simply be refuges from the city's busy streets.

Reclaiming Waterways as Public Open Space

Perhaps the most appealing way to recapture public open space is to make waterfronts accessible and attractive. Too many thousands of miles of oceanfront, lakefront, and riverfront land are currently hazardous, ill maintained, or occupied by land uses that preclude public use. Moreover, in some cases these waterfront areas have a blighting effect on neighboring communities.

Many sections of Minneapolis, for example, were regularly flooded when privately owned lakes and streams overflowed. Starting in 1883, the board of park commissioners began to purchase these properties, to landscape them as public parks, and to build vehicular roadways and pedestrian paths to make them accessible to vast numbers of residents. Under the inspired leadership of

Theodore Wirth, superintendent of parks from 1906 to 1935, the park board dredged wetlands and destroyed natural habitats —something that is currently precluded by federal statute. The flooding has been stopped. More important, these waterways are now available for sailing, rowing, canoeing, fishing, swimming, ice-skating, jogging, bicycle-riding, and casual strolling. Largely as a result of Wirth's efforts, Minneapolis has the most actively used urban waterfront open space in the country.

Many cities think of their waterfronts in the limited way that Olmsted warned against. Los Angeles faced the same serious flooding problems as Minneapolis. In 1914, when the Los Angeles River overflowed, causing $10 million in damage, engineers recommended channelization. Flooding caused 40 deaths in 1934 and 59 in 1938. The city's solution was, in 1939, to relegate 46 miles of the Los Angeles River's 58-mile route through the city to concrete culverts fenced off from the public. Los Angeles no longer experiences serious flooding, but by investing in a single-function capital improvement, the city missed its opportunity to create a rich and varied 58-mile public park that would also have solved an environmental problem.

The citizens of San Antonio were much wiser. From the early 1920s until the mid-1930s, they kept public officials from implementing an engineering solution to San Antonio's flooding problems. When the city government proposed relegating the horseshoe-shaped, downtown section of the San Antonio River to a concrete conduit and creating a new downtown street by paving over it, citizens demanded that the riverfront be transformed into a public park. Money for this project did not become available until 1939, when the Works Progress Administration (WPA) agreed to provide $300,000 if the city put up $75,000. The city raised the needed matching funds by issuing bonds.

Paseo del Rio, as this new park was called, opened in 1941. The city solved the flooding problems by dredging a bypass channel across the open end of the horseshoe and installing locks at either end. Whenever necessary, these locks are closed so that floodwaters can be channeled away from the riverfront park.

Waterfronts are often easy to retrofit for public use when contiguous land uses become obsolete. This is how the C & O Canal became available for use as a park.

The first leg of this 185-mile canal opened in 1830. It would eventually extend from Georgetown in Washington, D.C., to Cumberland, Maryland. By the time the canal was finished in 1850, it included 74 locks, 11 aqueducts, seven dams, and 190 culverts. The speed and low cost of shipping goods up and down the canal drew factories and warehouses to its banks. However, business along the canal began to decline with the rise of the railroads. When trucks began to replace rail as the favored method for moving freight, the utility of sites along the canal declined still further. In 1924, after a major flood, the C & O Canal ceased operations.

The U.S. government acquired the canal in 1938 and dedicated it as a public park the following year. After World War II, the park service proposed transforming the right-of-way into a scenic automobile parkway. This was opposed by Georgetown residents, who objected to the traffic, and, ironically, by preservationists, who appreciated the canal's new-found role as a public park. The controversy hit the press in 1954, when Supreme Court Justice William O. Douglas dramatized the issue by leading a well-publicized hike along the canal. Within seven years, Congress passed legislation designating the C & O Canal as a national historic park.

Like the Paseo del Rio in San Antonio, the canal's landscaped banks became a tourist attraction. And, like the Paseo del Rio, the park drew the attention of real estate developers, who saw a potential market in the tourists who came to the park. By 1970, Canal Square had become the first of many lofts and warehouses that would be replaced by retail shops, offices, residential buildings, and hotels. The most important change came in 1981, with the opening of the first section of Georgetown Park, an air-conditioned shopping mall. From then on, the canal was no longer just a national historic site; it had been transformed into just

When the city of Los Angeles eliminated serious flooding by relegating the Los Angeles River to a system of fenced-off concrete culverts, it missed an opportunity to create a 58-mile-long greenway. Private sector and nonprofit groups are currently working on a plan to create a greenway along the river.

Alexander Garvin (1996)

The C&O Canal towpath is a popular jogging, biking, and hiking path for residents and tourists. Destructive floods in January and September of 1996 brought out volunteers and financial contributions from many friends of the canal, enabling it to reopen in early 1997.

Alexander Garvin (1981)

the sort of social mixing valve that Olmsted admired.

Plaques now remind visitors that the C & O Canal once wound through a shipping district dominated by factories and warehouses rather than by hotels, restaurants, boutiques, and condominiums. The canal's significance, however, is not its "historic" character. The canal is a model for the adaptive use of waterfronts as active public parks that attract large numbers of people, who, in turn, attract developers. In abandoned sections of our cities, park projects can bring new life and generate real estate tax payments to cover both park operating costs and debt service on park development.

"Public" Open Space on "Private" Property

The least expensive way to provide public open space in developed areas is to have property owners create, manage, and maintain it. Although the Fourteenth Amendment to the Constitution explicitly forbids states (and therefore local governments) from taking property for public use without compensation, it

does not preclude local governments from encouraging owners to provide access to their property for public use. Consequently, local governments have enacted a variety of incentives to induce property owners to expand the public realm.

Once private property is open to the general public, its owner becomes responsible for maintenance and management of the public realm. Some of the resulting expenditures—insurance, for example—are quite costly. Imposing this financial burden is practical only when revenue is sufficient to cover the added expense. Thus, for many areas in need of additional public open space, mandating open space that is accessible to everybody is not an effective strategy.

Incentives, on the other hand, are neither unconstitutional nor financial burdens. No property owner needs to comply with them. Thus, they cannot be considered a taking, which requires government to compensate the owner. Since effective incentives provide benefits that exceed the cost of complying, the owner is more than compensated for any costs that are incurred.

New York City continues to add to its public realm by providing a bonus of additional rental floor area to developers who provide the public with access to outdoor and indoor space on their property. Pictured here is Sony Plaza.

New York City adopted the incentive approach in 1961, when it added to its zoning resolution an as-of-right incentive for property owners who provided publicly accessible open areas. In certain high-density residential or commercial zones, developers were permitted additional floor area in exchange for any sidewalk or plaza space added to the public realm.

Although the incentive arrangement included minimum design standards, these standards were not always sufficient to encourage the use and enjoyment of the new public spaces. Consequently, the city planning commission introduced a series of zoning changes that refined the design standards, established safety and maintenance requirements, allowed night-time closing, and increased the areas in which street-wall requirements precluded plaza development.

In 1996, after 35 years of experience, much of it unsatisfactory, the planning commission decided to eliminate outmoded requirements and upgrade others. It also consolidated the confusing array of piecemeal provisions into a zoning text amendment that simplified, reorganized, and improved regulations covering plazas, arcades, covered pedestrian spaces, and public galleries.

A similar effort to encourage property owners to supply open space is underway in the suburbs. Both the opponents of cookie-cutter suburban development and the supporters of open space preservation object to the monotonous pattern of single-family houses with identical front, side, and rear yards. Unfortunately, the preservation of the landscape greatly reduces the number of houses that can fit on any site, which, in turn, reduces profit from development. Moreover, the preservation of the landscape may be effectively rendered illegal by yard or setback requirements that dictate where houses must be placed on a site; often, such siting requirements cannot be met without the elimination of mature trees or the destruction of interesting natural features.

Currently two approaches to preserving suburban open space are being used. The first allows developers to build more than the ordinarily allowable number of houses, if the houses are arranged in a manner that protects attractive landscape features and provides common open space. This alternative to yard and setback requirements, called planned unit development (PUD), began to be added to zoning ordinances and subdivision regulations during the 1960s. The second approach is to require that site plans comply with state and local environmental legislation. This approach became prevalent during the 1970s and 1980s, as state after state enacted such legislation. Some more recent master-planned communities, such as Rancho Santa Margarita, California, and Kentlands, Maryland, include substantial areas for active recreation by large numbers of people.

Unlike large-scale master-planned communities, the PUD approach is based on simple economics. Small suburban subdivisions usually cannot afford to provide the amenities that are routinely supplied in large-scale master-planned communities. The PUD approach alters this situation by providing developers of smaller subdivisions with an economic incentive to create an improved site plan and provide community amenities. In exchange, the project is permitted to include a greater number of dwellings than would be permitted by conventional zoning. Developers readily adopt this alternative to standard subdivisions when the profit from selling these additional dwellings exceeds the additional cost of complying with PUD requirements. As a result, PUDs are often tailored to the natural features of their sites and provide amenities that are not available in conventional subdivisions.

Despite improved site plans and attractive open spaces that can be enjoyed by their residents, PUDs have provided little open space that is clearly earmarked for the general public. Unlike a city zoning bonus that requires public access to plaza space, a suburban PUD bonus has no such requirement. Most people are unaware of the open space because it is usually located behind private homes. Moreover, residents concerned with privacy and security routinely discourage strangers from intruding into their carefully planned environment. As a result,

by the 1990s, much of the open space provided by PUD developers was used primarily by PUD residents and their guests; and in the case of gated communities, such open space was unavailable to the public.

State and local environmental protection statutes have had a similarly limited effect on suburban open space development. Faced with litigation or the threat of litigation, most developers eventually negotiate site plans that are acceptable to environmentalists: they agree not to develop wetlands, steep slopes, sensitive habitats, and other problem areas, which they then generously designate as "open space." As a result, many new master-planned communities include vast amounts of open space that is specifically designed to be difficult for community residents to use.

Like the cheap land that was purchased for city parks during the 19th century, much of this "open space" is no more attractive for active public recreation than for construction. But unlike those early parks, many of these environmentally sensitive areas are closed to the public. Thus, residents of newly developing suburban areas whose environments have been "protected" have even less usable public open space than they left behind in the city.

New Directions

Many of the case studies in this book illustrate the continuing effort to adapt and reuse underutilized and abandoned city land for recreational purposes. There are still plenty of city streets and railroad rights-of-way that can be reclaimed as vehicle-free, public open space, just as there are miles of largely vacant waterfront that can become usable parkland. And these are not the only opportunities. Plenty of land once used for industrial manufacturing sits vacant because the costs of cleaning it up and retrofitting it for public use are high or because obsolete zoning prohibits use for nonindustrial purposes.

Similar opportunities exist in suburban areas, which harbor the same underused streets and railroad rights-of-way, abandoned waterfronts, and empty manufacturing plants found in cities. The suburbs also have opportunities that cannot be found in cities. Air-conditioned shopping malls and "big-box" retailers have forced many strip malls and open-air shopping centers out of business. Such areas could be purchased at relatively low prices and redesigned as public parks, depending on their surroundings, ease of access, and other factors.

The key to exploiting these opportunities, however, is not the creation of ever-more-inventive land use regulations. So far, regulation has often succeeded in producing a large number of unsatisfac-

tory open spaces, taking huge amounts of land out of public use, and triggering a property rights backlash that may succeed in reversing important efforts to improve the environment. It is time to abandon our efforts to make property owners supply public open space and to redirect our energies to persuading the electorate to invest in public parks.

The main obstacle is money. Public officials are no more willing to increase spending on park development today than they were a century ago. But the opposing argument, given by the Minneapolis Board of Trade in 1883, is as valid today as it was then: parkland, "when secured and located as [it] can now be at comparatively small expense, will in the near future add many millions to the real estate value of [the] city."[14]

The wisdom of this advice is illustrated by Pioneer Courthouse Square in Port-

Alexander Garvin (1979)

The city of Portland, Oregon, purchased a two-story garage in 1979 and replaced it with landscaped open space —Pioneer Courthouse Square—which was adjacent to the new light-rail line that opened during the mid-1980s. This visionary public action brought much private development, including a new Saks Fifth Avenue and Pioneer Place, a multistory atrium with shops, restaurants, and tourist-oriented retail establishments.

land, Oregon. The city's 200-foot by 200-foot blocks provide unusually ample opportunities for convenient pedestrian circulation. During the 1970s, civic leaders embarked on a program to make downtown Portland even more pedestrian-friendly. In 1977, Fifth and Sixth avenues were transformed into red-brick transit malls with flower-filled containers, bubbling fountains, and public art. Nearly all of the city's 71 bus lines run along one of these two parallel transit malls.

The city planned to open a Metropolitan Area Express (MAX) light-rail line in 1986. This light-rail line was scheduled to operate along two parallel streets that crossed the transit malls and continued 15 miles into the suburbs. The block enclosed by MAX and the transit malls was destined to become one of the most valuable locations in Portland. The city purchased the site for $3 million in 1979, just before property values escalated.

This prime block had once been occupied by McKim, Mead, and White's Portland Hotel. In 1951, the hotel had been replaced by a two-story parking garage. The city decided to replace the garage

with a public park and held a design competition for the new Pioneer Courthouse Square. Of the 162 submissions, the winning project, submitted by a team led by Martin/Soderstrom/Matteson (architects) and Douglas Macy (landscape designer), cost $4.3 million.

When Pioneer Courthouse Square opened in 1984, it became the most convenient spot in downtown Portland. Nordstrom built a new store opposite the square. The Rouse Company converted the nearby Olds & King Department Store into The Galleria, a 75-foot-high shopping atrium. Saks Fifth Avenue and Pioneer Place (a multistory shopping arcade) opened a block away. There are few better examples of public open space acquired "at comparatively small expense" that "in the near future add [so] many millions to the real estate value of [the] city."

Most public officials are not courageous enough to spend $7.3 million to transform less than an acre of prime real estate into public open space. There are too many other competing public purposes (preventing crime, educating children, moving traffic, etc.) that have larger

Boulder's dedicated sales tax provides the city with the money to add to and maintain more than 40,000 acres of park properties.

constituencies. Public officials would, however, support creation of additional public open space if they did not have to appropriate the money. Fortunately, Minneapolis, Boulder, Denver, and New York City have devised a mechanism that allows this to happen: *the dedicated tax.*

From its inception in 1883, the Minneapolis Park and Recreation Board has been allocated a portion of the city's real estate tax revenue. This guaranteed revenue stream has allowed the park board to plan for land acquisition, park development, and ongoing maintenance without worrying about competition with other more powerful city agencies or more popular public objectives.

Boulder allocates a portion of its sales tax to acquire and develop public parks. Its citizens do so because they wish to preserve the foothills of the Rocky Mountains as public land, to create a greenbelt encircling the city and protecting it from suburban sprawl, to maintain the wide range of ecosystems that characterize the area, and to provide in-town recreational facilities. In 1967, the city dedicated to park purposes a sales tax of $0.004 per

dollar. During the next 18 years, the city added 12,000 acres to its park system. The impact of these additions to public open space was that by 1977, the price of a house was higher by $4.20 for every foot that the house was nearer to the greenbelt.[15] The city was sufficiently impressed that in 1989 it voted to raise this dedicated tax to $0.0073 per dollar. Consequently, Boulder now contains more than 40,000 acres of public open space—quite impressive for a city that has not yet reached a population of 100,000.

More recently, property owners have been willing to pay additional real estate taxes to support business improvement districts (BIDs). Initially, BIDs were used as an equitable way to pay for the cost of pedestrianizing shopping streets, maintaining and patrolling the newly created public open spaces, and financing promotional activities that allowed city merchants to compete with suburban shopping centers.

The Downtown Denver Partnership, for example, operates the Sixteenth Street Mall Management District. Its work is financed by assessments on 865 property owners within the 120-block district surrounding this 13-block-long public open space. The money is spent on maintaining trees, flowers, and other plantings; sweeping pavements, removing litter, and emptying trash receptacles; providing security services; programming outdoor entertainment; and all the other services that make the Sixteenth Street Mall one of the most successful public spaces in the country.

Manhattan's Bryant Park BID is financed in a similar way. However, in 1996, real estate taxes provided less than half of its $1.8 million operating budget (see the case study on Bryant Park). The city parks department continues to pay the $250,000 it paid prior to transferring management to the Bryant Park Restoration Corporation. The rest comes from concession revenues, sales, grants, and park rentals.

The success of Denver's Sixteenth Street BID and Manhattan's Bryant Park BID is not just a matter of creating a dedicated income stream to pay for intelligently designed and well-maintained public open space. In both instances, the BID also pays for the sort of aggressive, entrepreneurial management that would be impossible within standard governmental bureaucracies.

Denver's Sixteenth Street Mall and Manhattan's Bryant Park are models for future open space development. They demonstrate the effectiveness of a dedicated tax, combined with entrepreneurial management that is directly accountable to nearby property owners and, in a more general way, to the broader public. Unfortunately, this model is usable only in situations where surrounding building occupants are willing and able to pay for facilities and services that they would not otherwise have available. Areas with

New York's Bryant Park—once a derelict, uninviting public space—has been transformed into an award-winning asset through a creative management and fundraising plan that involves the private sector and the city parks department.

Alexander Garvin (1996)

substantial numbers of low-income residents or marginal businesses are unable to generate the necessary money—which is all the more reason for citywide expenditures for public parks.

As an increasing number of communities adopt these new entrepreneurial approaches, we will be in a position to create substantial amounts of new, usable public space in both cities and suburbs. If we do so, we will be able to pick up where the park advocates of the early 20th century left off, discard the more recent attempts to create public open space on the cheap, and resume the effort to provide every American with the parks that Olmsted advocated more than a century ago—places where "vast numbers of persons [are] brought closely together, poor and rich, young and old . . . each individual adding by his mere presence to the pleasure of all others."

Notes

1. Tom Fox, *Urban Open Space—An Investment That Pays* (New York: The Neighborhood Open Space Coalition, 1990), p. 11.

2. Frederick Law Olmsted, "Public Parks and the Enlargement of Towns" (paper prepared for the American Social Science Association at the Lowell Institute, 25 February 1870); reprinted in *Civilizing American Cities*, ed. S. B. Sutton (Cambridge, Mass.: MIT Press, 1971), p. 75.

3. Olmsted and Vaux to Salem H. Wales, President of the Board of Commissioners of Central Park, New York, 11 October 1873, *The Papers of Frederick Law Olmsted*, vol. 6, Charles Capen McLaughlin, editor-in-chief (Baltimore: Johns Hopkins University Press, 1992), p. 653.

4. Ibid., p. 655.

5. Forest Park was later reduced in size to 1,293 acres.

6. Frederick Law Olmsted, letter to Howard Potter, 16 March 1883.

7. Frederick Law Olmsted, *Seventh Annual Report of the Board of Commissioners of the Department of Parks for the City of Boston for the Year 1881*.

8. Ibid.

9. Daniel Burnham and Edward Bennett, *Plan of Chicago* (Chicago: The Commercial Club, 1909), p. 53.

10. Roberto Brambilla and Gianni Longo, *For Pedestrians Only—Planning, Design, and Management of Traffic-Free Zones* (New York: Whitney Library of Design, 1977), p. 197.

11. Ibid., p. 134.

12. Formerly the New York State Urban Development Corporation.

13. *Environmental Planning and Design: Mellon Square Improvements,* Allegheny Conference on Community Development, Pittsburgh, undated.

14. Resolution of the Minneapolis Board of Trade, 29 January 1883; quoted by Theodore Wirth in *Minneapolis Park System 1883–1944* (Minneapolis Board of Park Commissioners, 1945), p. 19.

15. Mark R. Correll, Jane Lillydahl, and Larry D. Singell, "The Effects of Greenbelts on Residential Property Values," *Land Economics* 54 (1978), pp. 205–217.

Executive Summary:
Creating Better Urban Parks and Open Space

Christopher B. Leinberger and Gayle Berens

The efforts of the citizens' group Save Cedar Lake Park made it possible to turn a railyard into a much-used linear park and to preserve a natural expanse of meadows, trees, and wildflowers just a few short miles from downtown Minneapolis.

The 15 case studies presented in this book represent 15 very different efforts by the public and private sectors to bring much-needed urban parks and open space to their communities. Although this volume could not include every possible type of project, it does represent a healthy cross section of park projects and partnerships that have brought value to the cities where they are located. Many of the parks profiled here also represent efforts to ensure sustainability, so that these new parks do not meet the fate of so many other well-designed parks, falling into disrepair and becoming liabilities instead of assets.

The case studies include many lessons worth looking at closely. Ultimately, they

demonstrate that each generation, through its public and private sectors, must keep investing and reinvesting in its urban parks and open space in order to ensure that the next generation has an environment worth preserving. It's easy to forget that each generation has different open space needs. Like fashion and music, parks and park design become passé. Recreational preferences change: thirty years ago, no one used in-line roller skates, and few Americans played soccer. City, state, and federal funding priorities shift. The public sector often forgets what successful private sector entrepreneurs never do: maintaining a continuous connection to market preferences is critical to success.

How individual Americans value their parks and open space changes from generation to generation and does not always reflect public sector budgeting priorities. Our parks have never had as many visitors as they have now, and many suffer from overuse and insufficient public funding. Many of our large city parks have been allowed to deteriorate, in large part because they came to be regarded as insecure environments, and city budgets were inadequate to counter real or perceived safety issues. A 1993 study by the Trust for Public Land found that the following issues were considered the most serious in public parks and open space: inadequate maintenance (ranked severe in 17 of 23 cities); safety concerns (severe in 10 of 23 cities); difficult access due to remoteness, inadequate public transportation, physical barriers, or limited hours of operation (severe in 10 of 23 cities); deficient recreation programs (severe in 10 of 23 cities); and design that does not serve current user needs (9 of 23 cities).

But usable open space is an invaluable amenity that most people instinctively desire. Unfortunately, we have difficulty isolating and measuring the many tangible and intangible benefits that parks and open space provide. In our "bottom-line" society, only short-term benefits are usually attended to. The long-term, qualitative benefits of outdoor space defy the rigors of discounted cash flow analysis.

The emotional attachment that people have to open space (and the idea of it) is often the catalyst that drives parks to be revitalized over and over again. Central Park—arguably the most famous U.S. city park—was allowed to degenerate until some citizens with a love for the park worked to raise money and set up a plan for its revitalization. Through that private involvement, it has once again become —and can remain—the great park that Olmsted and Vaux envisioned. Through Forest Park Forever, Forest Park in St. Louis is undertaking a large-scale fundraising effort to revive its once-grand form. The creation of a greenway alongside the Los Angeles River, if successful, will be the result of a tremendous, caring effort on the part of many different parties, that could create one of the great stories of greenspace rebirth and its role as a unifying element in the resurgence of a vibrant American downtown.

San Antonio's Riverwalk is a similar story. In the 1930s, the San Antonio city fathers wanted to pave over the river but were defeated by historic preservationists. Today, the widely studied and imitated Riverwalk is the major source of vitality in downtown San Antonio—the second most important tourist attraction in the state after the Alamo—and is estimated to generate $1.2 billion for area businesses each year.

For our urban residential neighborhoods to survive and prosper, parks and open space have to be vital unifying elements working with the built environment. Walking access to parks and community gathering places is one of the few reasons for urban neighborhoods to continue to be meaningful competitive alternatives for middle-class households that have the option of moving to the suburbs. To maintain their middle-class tax

Because of the natural features that many cities were originally built around, cities are often able to offer much more dramatic spaces than suburban areas. This new pier was erected in the San Francisco Bay as part of the redevelopment of the San Francisco waterfront.

base—a necessity for remaining fiscally viable—cities must focus on things that they can do better than the suburbs: one of the most important is to provide parks and open space within walking distance of every household, reinforcing the urban neighborhood's viability in this automobile age.

Assessing Value

That the American public values parks and open space more than nearly every other land use has been confirmed by many surveys and studies.

Two 1995 surveys, conducted by American LIVES, Inc., and InterCommunications, Inc., showed that homebuyers identified natural open space and walking and biking paths as among the top four features (77 and 74 percent, respectively) that they ranked very or extremely important. Also highly ranked were gardens with native plants and walking

paths (56 percent); wilderness areas (52 percent); community/recreation centers (52 percent); and interesting little parks (50 percent).[1] Another 1995 poll measuring quality of life showed that two major elements were critical to a satisfactory quality of life: first, low crime and safe streets; and second, greenery and open space.[2]

This preference for greenspace, as several studies (although few large-scale ones) have shown, translates into dollar value for homes located near to or on the edge of parks. While not all the studies are recent, their findings are consistent. As early as 1856, when Frederick Law Olmsted began tracking the value of the real estate surrounding Central Park, he found that by 1864, when the park was only half-finished, it had begun generating a net revenue of $55,880. He also charted the average increase in property value in the three wards surrounding the park and in the city's other wards. If the

When it constructed a park and playground, the Elliott Donnelley Youth Center on Chicago's south side relied heavily on the participation of neighborhood children. By involving them early on, the center created a partnership with the children that gave them an almost immediate sense of ownership and pride in the community effort.

three wards around the park had increased in value 100 percent between 1856 and 1873, as did other wards throughout the city, in 1873 their appraised value would have been $53 million; instead, it was $236 million. Although Olmsted's analysis was simple (and there were other variables that influenced value), the difference was striking.[3]

In the early part of this century, a study in Elizabeth, New Jersey, showed that from 1922 to 1939, values for properties within 1,300 feet of Warinanco Park increased 631.7 percent at a time when the overall increase in property values in Elizabeth was 256.7 percent. It was later reported that it took only five years for incremental tax revenues to equal the $1.2 million spent to acquire and develop the park.[4]

A 1973 study in the Columbus, Ohio, neighborhood of Whetstone Park showed that over 7 percent of the selling price of a house was estimated to be related to its proximity to the park and river.[5] In a 1974 study, property values were shown

to correlate significantly with proximity to Philadelphia's 1,300-acre Pennypack Park, when allowance was made for the type of house, year of sale, and special characteristics such as a corner location. The park accounted for 33 percent of land value at 40 feet from the park, 9 percent at 1,000 feet, and 4.2 percent at a distance of 2,500 feet.[6] (This study also showed that while property owners want to be very near a park, they don't want their backyards to border one; properties bordering the park were slightly lower in value than those across the street.)

In Dayton, Ohio, a 1985 study showed that 5 percent of the average selling price of homes located near the Cox Arboretum and Park was due to their proximity to the open space.[7] A 1991 survey of Denver residential neighborhoods showed that from 1980 to 1990, the percentage of residents who said they would pay more to live in neighborhoods with greenbelts and parks rose from 16 to 48 percent.[8]

This sampling of surveys shows that residents and property owners place a strong value on proximate open space, but it does not represent the value that commercial enterprises realize through proximity to trails or other recreational amenities.

The efforts at measuring economic impacts of urban parks and open space have yielded important information for researchers and developers. But the value that most *individuals* place on parks has to do with "softer," quality-of-life issues, which are often less quantifiable: parks and open space can provide recreational amenities; make an aesthetic contribution to the neighborhood; offer educational opportunities through the study of nature or science; nurture and preserve the natural environment; create an image or identity for a city or neighborhood; and boost morale by providing something residents can point to with pride. Moreover, people's commitment to these "softer" values is often a powerful catalyst, driving the economic value that accompanies preservation or creation of public open spaces.

By illustrating both the economic and the "softer" value of parks and open space, the 15 case studies in this book confirm the important role that urban parks can play in strengthening neighborhoods, attracting development and new residents, and revitalizing cities.

Urban Parks and Suburban Development

Since World War II, the ongoing competition between older urban neighborhoods and their newer suburbs has most often resulted in the loss of urban jobs and residents. The suburbs offer larger lots for more privacy; homogeneous neighborhoods where residents feel that they

The restoration of Bryant Park in Manhattan is one of the great success stories in urban park revitalization. Through the use of a business improvement district, the Bryant Park Restoration Corporation was able to take advantage of the creativity and entrepreneurial spirit of the private sector, ridding the park of its reputation as an unsafe place and making it a welcoming spot for visitors.

Norman Mintz

Private sector creativity made it possible to bring golf to Manhattan, a small, densely populated urban island. At Chelsea Piers Sports and Entertainment Complex, golfers can take advantage of stunning Hudson River views and innovative Japanese technology to practice their swings.

can be with "their own kind"; low-density campus settings where workers are protected from urban distractions (and presumably more productive); and huge shopping complexes with plenty of free parking. Cities, with their high-density environments, have found it difficult to compete with these features. However, the suburban growth and land use patterns of the past 50 years may be suffering from too much success. Suburbanites must drive nearly everywhere for nearly everything, struggling through congested streets filled with other suburbanites doing the same thing. And social isolation is now seen as the flip side of privacy.

Hundreds of billions of privately invested dollars depend on cities' ability to compete with the suburbs. To do so, cities must emphasize the unique advantages of social integration and pedestrian access to amenities. By knitting together physical and social space, parks and open

space play a crucial role in defining and strengthening the advantages of city living. In terms of aesthetics and transportation, urban neighborhoods with access to open space may be particularly suited to compete with the suburbs. Thus, there may be solid economic reasons for increasing urban investment in parks and open space.

Most older cities made that investment in parks long ago, but many of the parks have been neglected because of budget cuts and local governments' decisions to focus on other services. When a local parks department cannot ensure a safe and enjoyable experience for all segments of the community, fewer visitors use the park, and lack of use becomes another reason not to invest more tax dollars in parks. And when occasional public enthusiasm for parks and open space does arise, the burst of capital improvements over a few years is often followed by decades of deferred maintenance and ever-lower operating budgets, as municipal priorities shift to other, apparently more pressing, needs. Left in a state of benign neglect, many urban parks are perceived to be—and may eventually become—dangerous. "Economizing" can thus begin a downward spiral in which each element reinforces the other: a run-down appearance leads to perceived and real safety concerns, which lead in turn to lack of use. Believing that government's track record has not been exceptionally good, citizens and investors have been reluctant to agree to the tax increases that would strengthen government's ability to do the job.

While such mistrust of government is not always justified, the conventional public sector approach to providing parks and open space is at times fundamentally flawed. As the case studies demonstrate, private or civic sector partners can sometimes provide better financing, marketing, and management of parks and open space. It is encouraging to see innovative joint ventures between public, private, and civic groups succeeding in cities across the country.

Trends in Open Space Development and Management

The case studies in this book illustrate the continuum of approaches to park development and highlight some emerging innovations in development and planning. The case studies can be organized into three basic management and development models—two conventional models and one newer, more resourceful model.

The first model is a purely public sector approach: under pressure from a neighborhood, an individual, the business community, or a politician, a city agrees to provide a new park or renovate an existing one. Designs are agreed upon (often with some citizen involvement), construction estimates are made, and public money is allocated. Once built, the park is put under the management of the parks department.

In the second model, the public sector maintains ownership and responsibility for the park, but coventures with the private sector for development or redevelopment through traditional fundraising programs, donations, benefactors, etc. Once complete, the park is fully under public sector purview, although the private sector may continue to be involved through special fundraisers for various programs or improvements, or through concessions or sponsorships that provide supplemental revenue.

The third approach, which could be called the market-oriented civic model, is newer and more controversial: it relies on a long-term partnership between the public and private sectors for park development and management. Using mechanisms such as a nonprofit development corporation or a business improvement district (BID), this approach brings together private sector responsiveness to market needs, dedicated taxes from surrounding property owners, private donations, better accountability to user needs, and revenue-producing functions to provide for the improvement and management of parks and open space for all. During the past 15 years, the market-oriented civic model has been successfully employed enough times to be considered proven and viable. (The advantages and disadvantages of each of these three approaches are outlined in Figure 1.)

Appropriate Use of Each Model

All three models play major roles in meeting urban park and open space needs. The public approach has been and should continue to be the main approach to the development and operation of our urban parks. Park creation is a key role for governments. However, the days when a fig-

Figure 1 • Park and Open Space Models

Model	Advantages	Disadvantages	Case Examples
Public Sector	• Broad-based funding. • Broad-based view of needs. • Obvious choice for addressing needs. • Long history of meeting the public's needs for parks. • Ability to address large-scale park needs. • Openness to citizen and business involvement in design.	• Public can be mistrustful of government's ability to manage parks. • Lack of effective management by many parks departments. • Lack of creativity and entrepreneurial ability compared to private sector. • Decisions can be influenced by special-interest groups. • Park budgets generally get cut first in times of municipal fiscal pressure. • Occasional bursts of enthusiasm for parks, resulting in capital improvements, followed by deferred maintenance and low budgets.	• Embarcadero Promenade (San Francisco) • Riverbank State Park (New York City) • Shreveport Riverfront Park (Shreveport, La.)
Public/ Private Coventure	• Attention to market needs. • User fees raise capital. • Broad-based constituency can be served with selective subsidized improvements that will be a minor part of the park (unless a major corporation underwrites it). • Openness to citizen and business involvement in funding of development and maintenance.	• May not serve a broad constituency if user fees are employed. • Few corporations are able to subsidize improvements for an extended period of time, especially given the changing business environment. • Relies on long-term, ongoing enthusiasm, commitment, and contributions from private sector.	• Downtown Park (Bellevue, Wash.) • Cedar Lake Park and Trail (Minneapolis) • Elliott Donnelley Youth Center Park (Chicago) • Flagstar Corporate Plaza and Jerome Richardson Park (Spartanburg, S.C.) • Hawthorne Park (Kansas City, Mo.) • Mill Race Park (Columbus, Ind.) • Pinellas Trail (Pinellas County, Fla.) • Turtle Park (Kansas City, Mo.)
Market-Oriented Civic Model	• Attention to market needs. • Innovative user fees and dedicated taxes provide services to a broad-based constituency. • In high-land-cost parts of city, extraordinary level of capital improvements and level of management can be provided. • In low-land-cost parts of city, the combination of inexpensive or free land and volunteer labor can provide necessary capital improvements and ongoing management. • Self-perpetuating financial and legal mechanisms and management motivation will continuously improve park and maintain high level of service.	• Support for improvements throughout the city, not just high-land-cost areas, may be diluted. • In low-land-cost neighborhoods, the volunteer management structure may be unsustainable long term. • Public sector agencies may feel challenged by strong private sector leadership and will need to be won over.	• Bryant Park (New York City) • Hudson River Park Conservancy and Chelsea Piers (New York City) • Park at Post Office Square (Boston) • Philadelphia Green (Philadelphia)

ure like Robert Moses could influence every detail of park planning and development are over. Decisions are now more often made from the bottom up, with both citizens' groups and businesses actively lobbying for improvements and with additional funding provided by "friends of the park" organizations. This political and financial clout makes parks departments far more responsive today.

The public model is also essential for large-scale park development. Riverbank State Park, built for over $100 million as part of a larger, billion-dollar sewage treatment plant, would probably never have been created by the private sector. Similarly, the Embarcadero Promenade was a rather inexpensive ($5.4 million) project that was attached to a much larger ($91 million) transportation and development project—again, a public sector investment that would probably not have been made by the private sector.

The second model, the public/private coventure, and the third model, the market-oriented civic approach, have proven particularly successful for the development or rehabilitation of small or medium-sized parks, providing valuable additions to the efforts of city parks departments.

The public/private coventure model is best employed to bring the variety and innovation of the private sector to special opportunities available within the context of a larger public purpose. The Tavern on the Green in Central Park, vendors in many parks, and special musical events add a great deal to the park experience —as well as providing much-needed revenue to the parks department. Similarly, some cities have experimented with corporate sponsorship of a city park, which gives an amenity to the public in exchange for a public relations opportunity.

Within the public/private coventure model (and the public model), local governments, usually under pressure from citizens' groups, are being forced to be more creative in their approaches to park development. At Hawthorne Park in Kansas City, the city, along with citizen and advocacy groups, redeveloped a neighborhood park to accommodate children with disabilities on all the play equipment and throughout the park. That effort took much more work and time than a quick fix-up would have, but the result has been an overwhelming success and is leading to the development of a second such park.

Boston's Park at Post Office Square came about because some of the most creative business minds in the city came up with an innovative approach to financing and developing a park that is supported by an underground parking garage.

Bill Horsman

The market-oriented civic model has much to recommend it, particularly given the limited budgets and rising social and infrastructure needs that all American cities face. Whether in downtowns, where land is expensive, or in blighted neighborhoods, where it may be far less expensive, this model can provide the best of both the public and the private approaches, with few drawbacks.

First, the costs and the benefits are intimately connected to the users and the funding sources. Whether funds come from a dedicated tax on local property owners or from user fees, volunteer efforts, or gifts, the providers of both financial and labor capital are usually the same people who benefit from the park. This connection allows the users to gain a better understanding of how the park is being improved and maintained, and by whom; it also provides a sense of ownership. Vandalism is minimal in those parks that are developed and maintained by market-oriented civic groups, not just because of adequately funded security but because users tend to enforce a standard of behavior in "their" park that discourages rowdy or destructive actions.

Second, under the market-oriented civic model, the level of capital and operational funding is generally higher than that provided by the public sector,

and is often designed to be maintained at an adequate level for many years to come, if not in perpetuity. This is because of the direct connection between users and the benefits they receive, as mentioned earlier, but it also stems from the fact that market-oriented civic managers are, by necessity, generally more creative than public sector managers. Finding multiple ways to finance the capital and operating costs of Boston's Park at Post Office Square or Manhattan's Bryant Park took some of the brightest and most sophisticated real estate and environmental professionals in those cities—talent not often found in a parks department accustomed to simply asking for an appropriation from city council. When Bryant Park was run by the New York City Parks Department, its operational budget was $250,000 per year and it was a drug-infested, crime-ridden place. Under the management of the Bryant Park Restoration Corporation, which manages Bryant Park and its revenue-earning amenities on a day-to-day basis, this oasis in midtown Manhattan now has an annual budget of over $2 million (which includes a contribution from the original parks department budget). Planning the development of a grand space and ensuring its continued greatness through self-supporting, revenue-generating mechanisms—if the space remains democratic space and open to all—may help stave off the budget "ups and downs" typical of city parks.

Third, the motivation of the market-oriented civic management team combines the best traits of the private and public sectors. On the one hand, members of the management team tend to be people who, like private developers, believe that anything can be done if only enough thought and commitment can be brought to bear on "the challenge" (as opposed to "the problem"). On the other hand, these managers, like many people who enter public service, want to make

The community has been involved every step of the way in the planning process for Manhattan's Hudson River waterfront—a project that has the potential to change a large section of Manhattan in a way that will affect generations to come.

Quennell Rothschild Associates

Mill Race Park, in Columbus, Indiana, is a lovely use of bottomlands prone to severe flooding. The design of the park was enhanced through the use of existing historic structures as well as striking new architecturally significant structures.

Michael Van Valkenburgh

a long-term difference to society. In other words, they are people who want to do well while doing good.

Fourth, once the public understands the model, a market-oriented civic project generates an extremely high level of goodwill. These projects can motivate people and companies to give money, raise taxes, donate time and services, and sell land or lend money at below-market rates. The public sector can rarely motivate this kind of behavior, and the private sector can rarely inspire gifts and tax incentives.

The need to balance public access (particularly when a user fee is charged) with private economic objectives is one important issue that arises with the market-oriented civic approach. The successful private redevelopment of New York's Chelsea Piers, which includes substantial public space, is a good example of a balanced strategy. Its success has led to plans for similar approaches to other piers and riverfront land: a combination of public funds and privately generated revenues will ultimately make it possible to reclaim all of the Hudson River waterfront.

One of the criticisms of the market-oriented civic model is that it depends on neighborhoods with high land costs

and well-to-do residents and workers, and therefore excludes the poorer sections of town and dilutes support for the city's efforts to provide public parks for all. The past decade's explosive growth of downtown BIDs, primarily in commercial neighborhoods, has prompted this complaint.

However, the case studies in this volume show that such complaints are not justified. The Park at Post Office Square, Bryant Park, and Hudson River Park—three case studies illustrating the market-oriented civic approach in urban areas with high land costs—are open to anyone, without charge. In Bryant Park, the management has actively discouraged what it deems inappropriate behavior, such as drug dealing and living in the park; but in the past, such behavior had driven away the vast majority of users to the benefit of a small minority. And the Philadelphia Green case study shows that the market-oriented civic approach works equally well in poor neighborhoods, where small-scale initiatives have been a substantial part of a larger effort to revitalize residential neighborhoods, which are not generally suited to the kinds of commercial efforts described in some of the other case studies.

Lessons Learned from the Case Studies

In addition to illustrating the three basic models of park development and management, the 15 stories in this book offer many hopeful and instructive examples of how parks can be reborn. Not surprisingly, there are many commonalities among the various kinds of park efforts. While each city, each piece of land, and each parks department is unique, and each effort must be started anew, lessons can be learned from other cities' efforts. This section lists some of the tools and practices that have helped create and rejuvenate parks. Clearly, not all the lessons are applicable to all parks and all cities, nor are they intended to be in order of importance, but they are worth considering by all future planners and participants in the park designing process.

Lesson 1: Involve the Neighborhood

Encourage—and do not bureaucratically resist—the active participation of neighborhood groups in planning, funding, and maintaining parks. In virtually every case study, residents provided input and oftentimes resistance that ultimately made the park a better place. Cedar Lake Park and Trail would not have been built if not for a group of tenacious Minneapolis citizens who were willing and able to put all their resources—intellectual, networking, financial—into creating what is now a cherished and much-used greenspace. At Chicago's Elliott Donnelley Youth Center Park, a design charrette was held in which the children who would be the park's ultimate users dressed up as pieces of playground equipment and situated themselves in various places on the future playground. Involving the children in decisions about where each piece would finally be set up helped ensure their ongoing commitment to the park and its maintenance.

In Philadelphia, Norris Square Park and the surrounding neighborhoods were reclaimed from brazen drug dealers only because of the perseverance and commitment of the community. Working in cooperation with the city and later with the Philadelphia Green program, residents were able to obtain a much-improved park and to undertake more than 70 community greening projects, which have provided a new sense of hope and involvement for the neighborhood.

In Kansas City, the Hawthorne Park planning committee was composed of people living in the neighborhood, corporate groups located in the neighborhood, and a variety of health professionals who provided expert advice on play and safety issues related to children with disabilities. In Shreveport, Louisiana, the Riverfront Development Committee, comprising representatives from the city council, the Downtown Development Authority, the metropolitan planning commission, the tourism bureau, and the Red River Revel Arts Festival, along with more than two dozen citizens, debated and planned the future of the riverfront.

Mill Race Park, in Columbus, Indiana, involved a four-month master-planning process, during which the landscape architect met with community leaders, interested citizens, and groups such as the River Rats, and even made presentations to elementary schools. The landscape architect said that the process not only allowed people to feel involved in the development of the park, but also aided him in creating a vision for the park.

Downtown Park, in Bellevue, Washington, came about because of the involvement of the private sector and the value it placed on such a park. The park's importance was reflected in the fact that the community took responsibility for financing and building the first phase with the city's oversight.

While some park developers—be they private or public sector—may privately complain that neighborhood involvement holds up the development process,

Parks are often an appropriate use for unused, underused, or unusual spaces. Harlem's Riverbank State Park, on the roof of a wastewater treatment plant, provides the neighborhood with much-needed recreational space—from swimming pools to skating rinks to an athletic building, as well as numerous outdoor courts.

Stanley Greenberg

residents ultimately feel more of a sense of ownership when they have been active participants in park development. And that translates into cleaner, safer spaces that are actively used instead of being avoided or abandoned.

Public participation also helps generate local support for use of the park and for protection from vandals. And active community involvement helps win political support for public funding of parks in general, which can be matched with private funds.

Lesson 2: Design with a Vision

Don't underestimate the power of imaginative design. Park design is more than a matter of recreating the soft, pastoral, "Olmstedian" spaces beloved in many American cities. Visionary design can affect a park's safety, viability, and usability—and most certainly affects its long-term success.

Whether the dangers are perceived or real, safety concerns are among the biggest contributors to the downfall of urban parks. But even in neighborhoods where safety has been a long-standing concern, changes in design, landscaping, and use patterns can make parks viable

once again. All of the park designers in these case studies have considered safety and security issues and taken innovative approaches to dealing with them.

Bryant Park's 1930s design, while lovely in its heyday, was no longer workable in today's urban environment. The park had been intended to provide seclusion and quiet spaces for users; instead, the closed environment encouraged crime, and the park's nickname—"Needle Park"—was deserved. Designers of the new Bryant Park kept many of the basic elements of the park, but pried open the space by removing shrubbery and by providing more and larger entrances and better lighting. The design has been a major contributing factor in the increased safety of the park.

Many other parks have simply kept plantings low and therefore hard to hide behind. At Shreveport Riverfront Park, where crime was not much of a problem to begin with, the redesign incorporated crime prevention design elements such as open sight lines and low plantings. The original design of Bellevue's Downtown Park had small enclosures on its periphery, which were removed at the advice of the police department.

Safety and security are just one element of park design. Using art as a fundamental feature of a park can provide a special quality that will endure over time. In Turtle Park in St. Louis, a rather small space (300 by 100 feet) was transformed into a vibrant neighborhood amenity through the use of art objects—sculptures—that are also play equipment. The whimsical sculptures are so appealing that children come from beyond the neighborhood to play on them. The Ribbon in San Francisco's Embarcadero Promenade is an art piece that not only serves as an identifying image for the project but is a functional element as well, providing seating and tables in various sizes and combinations. At the Elliott Donnelley Youth Center Park, where art was the driving force behind the restoration, local artists and neighborhood children created unique environments that are grounded in the locale and that residents point to with pride.

Incorporating old uses and structures into the design of a park can also add

character and provide an inexpensive link to the past. Building on the history of a site can provide an unusual and visually interesting theme and may be less expensive than clearing the site and creating a theme from scratch. The designers of Mill Race Park incorporated existing structures, added other historical structures, and designed a set of striking new structures for the park. Cedar Lake Park and Trail's effort to reintroduce and sustain indigenous prairie grasses has set it apart from the many other lovely parks in Minneapolis and given the community a focal point for future efforts.

Lesson 3: Revive Underused or Unused Space

Underused, unused, or unusual space—such as underground parking garages, piers, air rights, and floodplains—can be successfully transformed into viable parks and open space. In Harlem, the state of New York provided much-needed recreational facilities by building Riverbank State Park atop a wastewater treat-

ment plant. Careful planning of load capacities and the use of lightweight materials did not upset the integrity of the park's design. In Boston, the Park at Post Office Square rests on top of a seven-level underground parking garage. Park users sit in peace, barely aware of entrance and exit ramps for the many vehicles that use the garage daily, and the revenues from the garage support upkeep of the park. Chelsea Piers in Manhattan, a large-scale private recreational facility, took advantage of the enormous spaces created by once-decrepit piers that jut into the Hudson River and created completely modern facilities that provide New Yorkers with a dramatic venue for recreation. Even in Bryant Park, the redesign took advantage of the unused space beneath the great lawn and provided room for much-needed book stacks for the New York Public Library; by accommodating the needs of the library, the thoughtful redesign of the park made it possible for that vital institution to remain next to the park.

As illustrated by the Mill Race Park and Shreveport Riverfront Park case studies, formerly underused or abandoned floodplains—particularly when they are adjacent to expensive downtown real estate—can be transformed into parks and open space that recover easily after flooding. Instead of fighting Mother Nature, it is wise to consider accommodating the low-cost, flood-prone land that may be adjacent to some of the highest-priced land in the region. Mill Race Park, for example, was successfully reclaimed through a design that allowed all elements to withstand annual flooding; among other features, the park has an automatic shutoff for electric power that goes into effect when the water reaches a certain height, and rest room walls that begin eight inches from the ground to allow easy drainage. While flood cleanup may be time consuming and add costs that would not be associated with a park that is not in a flood-

plain, the cost of cleaning or rehabilitating flood-damaged open space is almost too small to measure when compared with the cost of rebuilding flood-damaged residential or commercial neighborhoods.

Lesson 4: Program Parks

Make a concerted effort to program activities in the park, insofar as programming is manageable and appropriate for the type of park and open space. Steady use has been shown to enhance revenues —and, as Page Gifford in the Mill Race Park case study put it, "A high level of activity is the cheapest security there is." At the redesigned Shreveport Riverfront Park, increased usage coincided with an increase in programmed events, eventually causing debate about the primary focus of the park: passive versus programmed use. At Mill Race Park, steady use is greatly enhanced by programmed events, typically around the amphitheater, and nearly every weekend is programmed from June through September. Bryant Park's programmed events are calculated to provide a benefit to the participants, the sponsors, and the revenue-generating mechanisms within the park.

The use of Flagstar Corporate Plaza and Jerome Richardson Park, in Spartanburg, South Carolina, for civic programmed events has given the city a new focal point and brought people downtown. Using specific programmed events to draw people to a park increases potential users' awareness of and interest in the park, increases overall use of the park, and can help to create the kind of community gathering places that can have other social ramifications in building stronger neighborhoods.

Lesson 5: Remember that Cleanliness Equals Respectfulness

Keep public open spaces clean and well maintained. This lesson is backed up by each of the case studies. Several factors can influence the cost and relative ease of maintaining a park: first, the availability of adequate operating funds, whether from public, private, or civic sources; second, strategic use of maintenance staff; and third, a design that is not only attractive but also inherently low maintenance.

Users tend to respond to a pleasant, well-designed space with pleasant, orderly behavior. As the Bryant Park case study demonstrates, park users can be trusted —in this instance, trusted not to make off with movable chairs. However, to encourage appropriate behavior, it is essential that the park be well maintained: high standards of maintenance are a sign of respect to users—which will, in turn, elicit respectful treatment of park property.

Lesson 6: Be Creative in Funding Parks

By "pushing the envelope" of possibilities, resourceful public and private sector groups have been very successful at finding money to develop and maintain parks. They have, for example, taken advantage of federal programs that may not be intended for parkland per se. For example, the Intermodal Surface Transportation Efficiency Act (ISTEA), due for reauthorization and probable modification in 1997, has been an important source of funds for rail-to-trail conversions. Linear park development can be a particular boon to a region because it not only adds recreational space but also adds to the transportation network of a region or community. While obtaining such funds may involve cumbersome bureaucratic processes, a certain percentage of ISTEA money spent in every metropolitan area must be spent on nonhighway, transportation-related projects.

In addition, groups like the National Endowment for the Arts have various public arts program funds that can be applied to parks and open space, as was the case in the Embarcadero Promenade. At the time of the redevelopment of the Shreveport Riverfront Park, a special program of the Small Business Administration —an unlikely resource for park development—provided the city with a $9,000 grant to plant trees.

The sale of shares at the Park at Post Office Square was an innovative entrepreneurial approach to funding that jump-started that project and provided purchasers with a real benefit: access to parking in a dense city center. Private sector donations for a successful first phase may spark increased public support for subsequent phases (see the case studies on Downtown Park, Hawthorne Park, and Flagstar Corporate Plaza).

Lesson 7: Consider Using Parks as Organizing Elements

An urban park can create a sense of place, a landmark, and a community focal point, which may in turn increase property values and create incentive for new development. Since few great downtowns have evolved without a sense of connection to nature, an urban park should be an important component of any successful city redevelopment.

Bellevue's Downtown Park was a critical element of a vision to create a livable downtown for a rapidly growing suburban area with no center. The Pinellas Trail connected seven communities that had previously had little to do with one another. Philadelphia Green, through its network of community gardens and greening projects, weaves connections between different sections of a neighborhood.

And two large-scale waterfront projects —the Hudson River Park Conservancy effort and the Embarcadero Promenade —have the potential to reshape substantial portions of two major cities. The revival of large, underused spaces will put a new focus on an underdeveloped resource.

Lesson 8: Parks Departments Must Play a Leadership Role

While many of the case studies focus on private sector involvement and leadership, one small park stands out and provides a valuable lesson for other cities. Hawthorne Park, thought to be the nation's first fully accessible park, came about because of a parks department that had vision and leadership. Using the talent already available on the parks department staff and drawing in equally talented private sector participants, the parks department exemplified an entrepreneurial approach to park development that produced an innovative, precedent-setting park facility. The creativity and perseverance of park planners and designers transformed Hawthorne Park from a somewhat run-down, nondescript neighborhood park into a model park and play area that is 100 percent accessible to able-bodied children and children with disabilities, setting a new standard that is receiving nationwide attention. Most other parks departments in the country have the capability, but for many reasons may lack the motivation and leadership to play a strong role.

In some cases, like Minneapolis, segregating the tax base to support the parks department can make it easier to take the kinds of risks that were required to build Cedar Lake Park and Trail. A guaranteed budget, not subject to political whims, ensures basic park maintenance, leaving room for the vision and leadership that have helped give Minneapolis perhaps the finest park system in the country.

Sometimes leadership must come first from elected officials. The city councilwoman—and later mayor—in Bellevue who had a vision of a grand city park was able to lead her colleagues to take the risk that will forever shape Bellevue's downtown. But regardless of whether the impetus comes from an elected official or a city department, the public sector needs to reclaim its leadership role in protecting some of our cities' most valuable assets.

Conclusion

For relatively little money in comparison to the private capital and public improvements invested in our cities, the character and civility of our cities can be vastly improved through the development and adequate maintenance and operation of our parks. Moreover, parks and open space can significantly increase the value of the private capital base. The leverage

Bellevue's Downtown Park was designed to provide a center for the burgeoning suburb. The vision of a grand central park was realized through the efforts of many public and private entities.

The parks department in Kansas City, Missouri, showed some private-sector entrepreneurship in transforming a nondescript, somewhat run-down neighborhood park into an innovative park and play area that is 100 percent accessible to able-bodied children and children with disabilities.

in value gained through properly developed and maintained parks is one of the great unexploited opportunities in our cities today.

An urban park can create a sense of place, a landmark, and a community focal point, which may in turn increase property values and create incentive for nearby development. Yet it takes effort to create a space that works and provides value. Most often, that effort is best made by taking advantage of the skills and initiative of the public, private, and civic sectors. Relying on the public sector alone risks limiting the resources and creativity that can be brought to bear on urban parks and open space and the sense of ownership and interest that communities feel toward their greenspace.

Notes

1. Brooke Warrick and Toni Alexander, "Looking for Hometown America," *Urban Land*, February 1997, pp. 27–29, 51–53.

2. The poll was conducted by the Regional Plan Association and Quinnipac College Polling Institute in Hamden, Connecticut. Some 1,500 residents in 31 counties in New York, New Jersey, and Connecticut, and 400 people living in Los Angeles/Riverside/Orange County, Dallas/Fort Worth, Atlanta, and Seattle/Tacoma/Bremerton were polled. See the summary of results in "Avenues for Social Programming," *Urban Land*, February 1997, pp. 30–31.

3. Tom Fox, *Urban Open Space: An Investment That Pays* (New York: Neighborhood Open Space Coalition, 1990).

4. Charles Little, *Challenge of the Land* (New York: Pergamon Press, 1969), p. 87; cited in Fox, *Urban Open Space.*

5. John C. Weicher and Robert H. Zerbst, "The Externalities of Neighborhood Parks: An Empirical Investigation," *Land Economics* 49, no. 1 (1973), pp. 99–105.

6. Thomas R. Hammer, Robert E. Coughlin, and Edward T. Horn IV, "Research Report: the Effect of a Large Park on Real Estate Value," *Journal of the American Institute of Planners* (July 1974), pp. 274–277.

7. Margaret M. Kimmel, "Parks and Property Values: An Empirical Study in Dayton and Columbus, Ohio" (thesis, Miami University, 1985).

8. Rocky Mountain Research Institute study, 1991, referenced in *Economic Impacts of Protecting Rivers, Trails, and Greenway Corridors,* 4th ed. (Washington, D.C.: U.S. Department of the Interior, National Park Service, 1995).

Case Studies

Bryant Park
New York City

Gayle Berens

The New York Public Library has graced Fifth Avenue since it was built in 1911, serving as a beacon of civility to users and passersby. Directly behind the grand beaux-arts structure is Bryant Park, which by 1980 had become a haven for drug dealers ("Needle Park") and an area studiously avoided by others. Everything about the design of Bryant Park made it easy for criminals to conduct their business there. Raised above sidewalk level, the park had protective shrubs and a tall iron fence surrounding the outer rim, and could be entered only through a few narrow gateways. Furthermore, the park was subdivided by more shrubs, bushes, and culs-de-sac, creating what should have been intimate, secluded spots for visitors in search of calm. Instead, drug dealers were delighted at the ease with which they could conduct their business.

But in 1980, a neighborhood and city effort began transforming the park through an innovative private management and financing program and the establishment of a business improvement district (BID). Bryant Park, formerly a dangerous eyesore, eventually became the anchor for a larger effort to revitalize midtown Manhattan, and a model for park management and restoration around the country. Drug dealers and muggers have been replaced by workers from nearby buildings who enjoy lunch in the sun while sipping latté, listening to music, and moving their chairs from time to time to catch the most rays. Located between Fifth and Sixth Avenues and West 42nd and West 40th Streets, this award-winning park is now the venue for outdoor movies, jazz performances, fashion shows, a complex and wonderful urban garden, and restaurants and concessions that help keep Bryant Park the glistening but friendly showcase of Midtown.

The Rise, Fall, and Long Rebirth of a Park

First laid out as a potter's field in 1823, the site that is now Bryant Park was developed as a park in 1847, when it was named Reservoir Square—after the city reservoir that was constructed on the site now occupied by the public library. With the construction of the large reservoir in Central Park, the Bryant Park reservoir became obsolete and was drained in 1899 to make room for construction of the library. In between, from 1853 to 1858, the Crystal Palace stood on the park site. Built for the World's Fair, the palace remained as exhibition space until it burned to the ground in 1858. A new park was then erected in the style of an English square. In the meantime, by 1911, the New York Public Library, designed by Carrère and Hastings, had been built on the east end of the park.

In 1884 Bryant Park was named after poet William Cullen Bryant (1794–1878), who was a proponent of parks. As editor of the *New York Post* for 50 years, Bryant pushed hard for the city to create a large urban park, which later became Central Park.

Bryant Park remained as it was until 1934, when Robert Moses took over as head of the parks department in New York City and made the refurbishment of Bryant Park one of his first big efforts.

Before the restoration, Bryant Park was poorly maintained, and shrubs grew up against the iron fence surrounding the park, making it relatively easy to hide "Needle Park's" flourishing drug trade.

Moses held a design competition and chose the design submitted by Lusby Simpson, an out-of-work draftsman. The parks department built the project using labor from one of its make-work programs. Gilmore Clark, the architect of record, did the final construction documents and ultimately won an award from the American Society of Landscape Architects for the six-acre park.

Until the 1930s redesign, the park was on grade with the sidewalk, but Moses took material from the construction of the Sixth Avenue subway and used it for fill, raising the level of the park. Some would argue that the raised level of the park was the first element that contributed to the park's decline.

Problems with the park began as early as the 1930s, but the park began its dramatic decline in the late 1960s, and for the next 20 years, Bryant Park was relatively ignored by leisure-time users, even though efforts were made to bring music and other activities into the park to encourage lunchtime visitors.

The park might have continued to decline, and concerned citizens and park officials might have continued to wring their hands indefinitely, had it not been for a comparable decline in the structure that housed the library. Years of deferred maintenance had left their mark, and in the late seventies, when the Rockefeller Brothers Fund began to consider contributing money to renovate the library, the fund concluded that the library renovations should proceed only if the park's problems and derelict condition were dealt with.

The Rockefeller Brothers Fund turned to William "Holly" Whyte, the eminent author of *The Organization Man* and several books on urban life. Whyte's observation of people's behavior in cities had led him to conclude that "success or failure of open space depends on its relationship to the street. In other words, welcome the street, bring it in. We had done exactly the opposite in Bryant Park by raising it and sticking a rail around it."

Whyte, with the Project for Public Spaces (PPS), wrote a report outlining his observations about the park and his recommendations for its improvement. Ultimately, many of those suggestions were followed in the restoration process, but Whyte's main point was that the problem with Bryant Park was not the drug dealers per se; it was underuse. "Access is the nub of the matter," he wrote. "Psychologically, as well as physically, Bryant Park is a hidden place. . . . The best way to meet the problem is to promote the widest possible use and enjoyment by people."

Whyte suggested that if you wanted to apply the principal findings of research in reverse and create a park that few people used, you would do exactly what had been done in Bryant Park—elevate it above street level, put a wall around it, put a spiked iron fence atop the wall, and line the fence with thick shrubbery. Even Frederick Law Olmsted in the 1800s had warned against that type of design.

One of Whyte's theses regarding park use is that a park's success can be measured in part by the percentage of female users. When women feel safe in a space, they are likely to use it more frequently. The 1979 PPS report noted that use by females had fallen from 42 percent in the early seventies to 29 percent. By 1995, after its successful renovation, Bryant Park reported an average of 43 percent female users.

In addition, the average number of people using the park at lunchtime in the late 1970s was 1,000, with occasional peaks of 1,400. According to Whyte's work, the bottom end of the scale for little-used places was about five people per 1,000 square feet—which, in Bryant Park's 237,000 square feet, would be about

1,000 people a day. He estimated that during peak hours on summer days Bryant Park should have at least 2,500 people.

When everyone involved agreed that Bryant Park could and should be saved, a young MBA named Dan Biederman was hired, and in January 1980, Biederman and Andrew Heiskell—chairman of the board of the public library and a New Yorker of substantial cultural and political clout—formed the Bryant Park Restoration Corporation (BPRC), which was charged with developing a plan for the park. As Biederman described it, he sat alone in an office in an abandoned building, trying to come up with a viable method for restoring and maintaining the park, to prevent yet another expensive restoration from falling quickly into disrepair.

Biederman's approach was to interview as many experts as he could—from managers of vest-pocket parks, to managers of Rouse festival marketplace facilities, to people at Rockefeller Center, another model of effective open-space management. He talked to crime-control experts, library staff, and former parks commissioners, and he spent time with Holly Whyte, talking with him about people's behavior in urban spaces.

About the time that Biederman was beginning his effort to come up with a plan for the park, the architecture firm of Davis Brody was beginning work on the interior restoration of the library, and the firm brought in landscape architect Laurie Olin, then of Hanna/Olin, to resuscitate the front terrace of the library. Sealed off by privet hedges in front of unused floodlights, half of the upper terrace lay unused, a dark and functionless space. Even on Fifth Avenue, drug deals were taking

place on the front terrace, people were getting mugged, and homeless people had set up encampments. So Olin began the process of "opening the space," making it more inviting both to passersby and to library users.

While Biederman was looking at ways of generating revenue for the park, several things were happening that influenced the final shape of the park and its financial structure. For one, Biederman and the nonprofit Parks Council had been experimenting with efforts to bring people back into the park—refreshment kiosks, bookstalls, etc.—with a fair amount of success.

At about the same time, in recognition of its centennial, the New York–based Architectural League sponsored an artist/architect collaboration. The league was originally founded in 1881 with the aim of encouraging architects to work closely with sculptors and painters. To revisit that concept, the league invited 11 prominent architects to team up with artists and create proposals for projects that were to be visionary yet remotely possible. Architect Hugh Hardy, of Hardy, Holzman, Pfeiffer & Associates, joined with artists Jack Beal and Sondra Freckleton and proposed the creation of two pavilions designed for dining. And the site they chose was Bryant Park because, according to Hardy, this prominent Midtown site had become "a disgrace and a degrading experience and it was time to try something new." Their fanciful design was never to be built, but it succeeded in spurring interest in the idea of having a noteworthy restaurant in the park. Their design called for the pavilions to be built around Lowell Fountain, but when the idea of a restaurant was looked at seriously, the terrace along the back wall of the library was designated as

With Bryant Park's successful renovation, women felt comfortable enough in the park to bring children—one indication of the public's perception that Bryant Park had become a safe place.

the likely location. Considered by many to be the most dangerous part of the park, that section was most in need of restoration. Biederman himself was mugged there in 1980.

When the BPRC issued a request for proposals, four of the best-known restaurateurs in New York responded. The restaurateur chosen developed a grand plan for a 1,000-seat, two-story, steel-and-glass restaurant, designed by Hugh Hardy, to run the entire length of the back wall of the library. His showy vision also involved changes to the park, including the addition of flowers and a fountain. Plans included moving the beloved statue of William Cullen Bryant housed on the terrace. The team working on the restaurant decided a landscape architect was needed, and Laurie Olin also began work on the park.

Of course, objections came from many sources when it was announced that a two-story restaurant running the length of the library was going to be erected in Bryant Park. Besides being outraged at the scale, preservationists objected to obscuring the library's back wall, which the New York City Landmarks Preservation Commission had designated a landmark.

The original plans were overreaching, and it was inevitable that the restaurant would be scaled back. Knowing that, the original restaurateur withdrew from the project, but the idea of a restaurant didn't die. Because it would be a fairly large source of revenue for park maintenance and would also be a key source of off-peak activity, the restaurant was critical to the overall park plan. When it became unclear when and how much income a restaurant would contribute to the park's upkeep and management, BPRC formed a business improvement district, which generates about $.16 per square foot from commercial property owners and now totals $1.2 million annually for Bryant Park (see feature box).

In the meantime, work had to continue on the restoration of the park. In New York, citizens and the public sector take the built environment very seriously and are known for their vociferous objections to most plans. Not surprisingly, the first plan that Olin proposed for the park was very different from the final design. For example, Olin originally proposed taking down the iron fence (which Holly Whyte had also recommended) and building steps all around the park to render it accessible at

Business Improvement Districts

Business improvement districts (BIDs) are a relatively new form of partnership designed to help the private sector supplement services typically offered by the public sector. BIDs are popping up in cities all over America; some estimates put over 1,000 BIDs in existence. Essentially, BIDs are self-financed legal entities that allow local property owners and business leaders in downtowns and other commercial areas to provide common services beyond those that the city can provide. The designated city blocks form a partnership financed by a tax on the property owners (and sometimes tenants) located within the district. The money from the tax is used to augment specific elements of municipal services within the area. Typically, the services include sanitation, maintenance, and security, and may also include street improvements, sidewalks, signage, lighting, trash receptacles, and landscaping. Some BIDs undertake nongovernmental services such as planning and executing marketing and other programs aimed to improve business retention or to attract businesses, residents, and tourists into the district. In addition, the money supports a BID staff and overhead.

While the initiative for a BID comes from a group of property and business owners seeking common services, the city (on the basis of state enabling legislation) must approve the BID's boundaries, the annual budget and financing strategy, and the services to be provided by the BID. Generally, for the plan to be approved by the city, a prospective BID must demonstrate the support of a majority of the property owners in the district.

Establishing a BID in New York City involves approval from the city council as well as from the majority of the property owners or owners of taxable real estate in the designated BID area. Assessments are levied by formula and type of property.

While BIDs like the Bryant Park Restoration Corporation have effected noticeable changes, their emergence as a leading force in cities like New York has opened them up to criticism—notably, that they are not accountable to voters or to the public at large. In addition, because they are dependent on residents who can afford an additional tax burden, they are less likely to be found in the poorest districts of cities, which may need additional services the most.

In New York City, BIDs provide a range of services, including daily street sweeping, daily security patrols, the removal of graffiti and bills from street furniture, and improved signage.

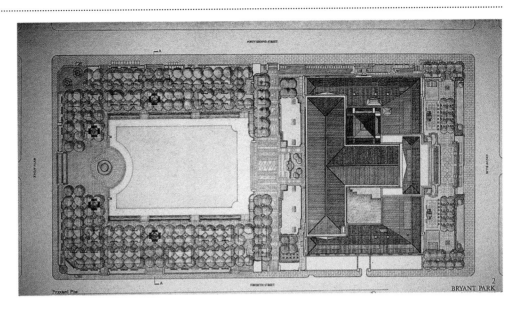

Bryant Park before the most recent renovation had fewer and narrower access points. The designers kept all the access points, widened some of them, and added four new entrances. In addition, the removal of the shrubbery from around the fence increased the feeling of openness and connected the park to the street.

any point. The goal was to pry open the park, letting it spill into the street, and thereby make it more attractive and less forbidding to potential users. The plan also called for adding basins of water around the sides, ripping out shrubs, cutting a main cross-axis through the park, and moving the fountain.

When the designer and the development team went public with the plans, various groups immediately stepped in to block certain elements of the proposal. The Friends of Cast Iron Architecture objected to taking down the iron fence, which dated from 1934 and was of historic value. A council member insisted that the water feature should not be built because of liability issues.

Two-and-a-half years of hearings with citizens, community boards, and public officials brought suggestions, objections, and ultimately many changes. "Our original plan was too ambitious. We were changing too much," said Olin. "Instead it became a fine editing process. We took things that were there and renegotiated them so that they physically and optically looked different. For example, I took several flights of stairs and pulled them out like a chest of drawers and added landings to make a gentler entry. We cut new big openings in midblock. Since we were forced to keep the iron fence, I ripped out the shrubs around the fence to give it an openness."

In addition to many design elements that enhanced the safety and appearance of the park, Biederman came up with several revenue–generating mechanisms that would be used to sustain a high level of maintenance and security, including concession stands, two restaurants, and rental of the park for special events; smaller revenue-generating ideas, such as sponsorship opportunities, were also added.

While the end result has been a successful park, getting approvals was, according to Biederman, "nine years

of frustration." Among the government reviewers were the landmarks group, the arts commission, the community board, the city planning department, and the department of transportation (which provided some lights); in addition, an environmental impact review had to be undertaken for the restaurant.

To facilitate the cumbersome review process, Arthur Rosenblatt was brought in as associate director of BPRC. Rosenblatt's knowledge of New York and his range of professional experience—fellow of The American Institute of Architects, former first deputy commissioner of the New York City Parks Department, former director of capital projects for the New York Public Library, former vice president of architecture and planning for the Metropolitan Museum of Art—made him an invaluable asset for completing the park in a reasonable amount of time.

One of the primary objections, which is still of concern to some, was the idea of raising money from several private sources to pay for what should be a public function: maintenance of city parks. The city was accused of abdicating its responsibility. Others feared that if the city became dependent on private involvement, it would not be able to sustain parks in neighborhoods where there are fewer financial resources or less leadership capacity. Biederman claims that in the 1980s, some critics pointed to him as the person who would bring an end to parks in New York City because he was bringing the private sector into the park business. It became clear, however, that unless much private money was involved in the process, the park was not going to have the kind of overall restoration it needed to survive.

In the end, the approvals were granted, and the city agreed to contract with the Bryant Park Restoration Corporation to manage the park. As part of the agree-

Although the flower gardens require full-time attention, they are among the most popular and beloved elements of the park. The perennial gardens are designed to bloom from April through October.

ment, the city turned over to BPRC the $250,000 allocated annually for park maintenance. Those funds, in addition to funds BPRC had accumulated through revenues and grants, were to be applied to park management and maintenance expenses.

The entire process took well over ten years, and there were fits and starts and many surprises along the way, but none matched the bomb that the library dropped about midway through the project. When all the sign-offs had finally been obtained but construction had not yet started, the library board announced at a meeting that the building on Fifth Avenue was no longer adequate for the library's needs. The stacks were full, and as the main reference library for the whole system, the building had to be large enough to house the collection.

The library board did not want to leave the building, but it had considered every possibility for staying and could not find a solution. The board had seen how difficult it was for the BPRC to get permission to put a restaurant on the back of the building, so the board members knew that adding on to it would be well nigh impossible. They had considered building under the terrace, but the building's foundation made that impossible. They had considered a satellite location but couldn't make it work financially or practically.

Laurie Olin said he sat at that meeting stunned. Unless this problem could be solved, all their work in Bryant Park might be lost. But then Marshall Rose, chair of the library's building committee, came up with the idea of constructing a tunnel under the terrace leading to the area under the great lawn and building the stacks there. Everyone agreed in principle that it was a good solution and left it to the architects and engineers to decide if it were possible. Olin's one stipulation was that there be

no vertical expression of the stacks in the lawn itself—which proved to be a challenge when it came to constructing emergency exits and smoke purges.

The stacks needed two emergency exits. After several iterations, the plan called for one emergency exit to go back into the library and for the other to lead to the opposite end of the park. The only evidence of the outdoor exit is in the lawn, at the west end of the park, where a pop-up lid for the exit has been disguised as a plaque for park restoration donors. The smoke purges were located in the flower beds.

And the library was able to add two floors of underground stacks housing 84 miles of library shelves. The addition of the underground stacks added some construction time. The park restoration effort took some three-and-a-half years and cost approximately $18 million. The city funded two-thirds of the effort, the private sector the remaining third. Currently, maintaining and operating the park costs about $2 million a year. The money comes from the city's contribution of $250,000; the BID money; donations; and revenues generated by the coffeehouse, the kiosks, the restaurants, and special events rentals and programming.

Design and Construction: A Touch of the Tuileries

In discussing the design of Bryant Park, Dan Biederman, Laurie Olin, and others involved in the redevelopment always refer to the standards set by the great parks of Paris—Monceau, the Luxembourg Gardens, and in particular the Jardin des Tuileries, the half-mile-long series of neoclassically inspired gardens between the Louvre and the Plâce de la Concorde. Their love of those gardens is evident in the care they took to create a feeling of Paris in the park. The space is at once understandable and defined, yet inviting and elegant. Underlying the discernible order of Parisian parks is an undeniable feeling of comfort and safety, also evident in Bryant Park.

All the elements of the park revolve around the great lawn, which takes up 18 percent of the total six acres. While the great lawn existed in the park's earlier form, it was completely excavated during the renovation in order to build the underground library shelves and is now slightly crowned to encourage better drainage. Running the length of the great lawn are side promenades of London plane trees planted in 1934. Tightly packed gravel paths line the lawn. The carefully restored cast-iron fence encloses the park, and a limestone balustrade surrounds the lawn.

The 1930s park design had beds of clipped shrubs with long-neglected annuals. Although everything else included in the 1990s restoration was designed for a relatively simple maintenance program—trees, gravel, ivy, and grass—the designers decided to revive a variation of the flower beds, which require an intensive maintenance program and commitment.

As it turns out, the gardens, designed to be interesting and active year round, are among the most popular and beloved elements of the park. Garden designer Lynden B. Miller, who was well known for restoring the Conservatory Gardens in Central Park, was brought in to work with the landscape architect to create the gardens, which consist of six beds, including two mixed herbaceous borders paralleling the lawn. Year round, the 300-foot borders have several thousand plants— some 360 shrubs (evergreen and deciduous) and 2,500 perennials, which bloom continuously from April to October. In the summer, about 1,000 annuals add bright colors, and 5,000 bulbs herald the arrival of spring. The beds are backed by tall, dark green yew trees. Because the north border is mainly sunny and the south border is in the shade of the nearby office towers, the borders have different characters.

The gardens require a full-time gardener and several part-time assistants, but Miller said, "Bryant Park Restoration Corporation has a great commitment to the horticulture in the park because we all know that's one of the things that separates this park from other spaces." The designers placed benches right within the lush beds, and users are very respectful of the plantings (the biggest problem is people placing briefcases on plantings). Pigeons and English sparrows, also a problem, require the use of netting in the spring. "My gardener used to say working in Bryant Park was like being in a receiv-

ing line in a wedding because everyone always has something nice to say," laughed Miller. "The horticultural aspect makes it very alive and personal. People can relate to it and stand around and discuss it."

Another very important element of the restoration, and one that gets much attention, was the introduction of movable chairs. "One of the most important features of the park that I recommended was to give people a place to sit," said Whyte. "The movable chairs were very hard to sell. I can't tell you how many people snickered and said they'd all be stolen. But we've proven them wrong."

The idea for the movable chairs came from the experience at the Metropolitan Museum of Art. In 1969, Arthur Rosenblatt put out some 200 chairs in front of the museum. Despite everyone's skepticism, the chairs proved to be an immediate success, enlivening an area that had much less foot traffic than Bryant Park. Although the chairs at the Met were eventually replaced by benches, Whyte, Olin, and Biederman were encouraged by the way users had responded at the Met and felt that movable chairs would be a critical addition to the new Bryant Park.

According to Whyte, "The folding chairs are very important for several reasons. They make the user of the park sort of a planner because the user has to decide where to sit. It's interesting to see the way people move the chairs. Most of the time they don't move them more than a few feet, but somehow it's a declaration of independence."

The green chairs are metal and wood and come from France. In the early stages of the park, BPRC ex-

The green metal and wood chairs give the park a comfortable, at-home feeling and are an easy, flexible means of increasing the capacity of the park.

Jake Wyman

The goal at Bryant Park is to pick up paper almost as soon as it hits the ground.

perimented with different types of chairs. They tried plastic chairs, which were functional but not the right look. Eventually they settled on the European café chairs, which are inexpensive, relatively durable, and light enough for people of all sizes and strengths to move.

Many people assumed that the chairs would quickly end up in New Yorkers' apartments or in homeless dwellings, but in fact, few of them have been lost to theft. Most are removed because they need repair from overuse. BPRC initially brought in some 1,200 chairs and has since purchased additional chairs annually, bringing the seasonal total up to 2,000. With 2,000 people on the chairs, 1,000 people in the restaurant and on the café terraces, and some 2,000 people on benches and on the lawn, the park can easily hold 5,000 at lunchtime on any given day. The chairs provide an easy, flexible way to increase the capacity of the park.

Safety and security issues were a critical element of the planning process. Besides the fact that in 1979, an average of 150 robberies per year occurred in Bryant Park, the public's perception was that it was an unsafe environment and should be avoided. Biederman's goal was to get the incidence of robbery down to zero. "We've had one robbery in the park since 1991 and it was in the middle of the night against one of our employees," said Biederman. "Now people are thrilled to be there because of attractive plants, events, chairs, monuments, clean rest rooms. They feel safe there and when they feel safe, thousands of them come in. It's harder to commit a crime because criminals feel conspicuous. Even though we have our own security force, which is unarmed, a lot of our security is what I would call 'self-enforcing.'"

BPRC has two to three security officers on patrol during park operating hours and two after hours. In addition, the New York City Police Department initially assigned a complement of four police officers to the park and its neighborhood. Those officers proved unnecessary over time and were moved elsewhere in Midtown.

To open up the park and increase the sense of safety, the designer removed the shrubbery around the fence and added four new entrances, making a total of 11. Some of the existing entrances were also widened, in particular the one at 42nd Street, where the subway entrance is located.

In addition, lighting was carefully planned. The park has four different types of lighting. Lining the promenades are standard light fixtures restored and recast, respecting the original beaux-arts style from the 1934 park redesign. Framing the entrances to the park are ornate pedestals and globes in the style of those of the public library, some 20 of which were added with money from Enid Haupt, a private donor. In addition, the park's sidewalks have modified "teardrop" fixtures with double-headed luminaires. The lighting designers urged the BPRC to use metal halide lighting, which casts a white light that is more pleasant to the eye than the yellow-orange light cast by the standard, high-pressure sodium lighting typically found in urban areas. However, more metal halide lights are needed to achieve the same effect as the high-pressure sodium lighting. In addition to the lighting around the park, 11 1,000-watt floodlights have been placed atop the New York Telephone building and aimed at the park, casting a soft, moonlightlike glow.

The park also has several monuments of note—in particular, two monuments to women. Eighty years after it was built and after years of disuse, the Josephine Shaw Lowell fountain is once again functioning. A second sculpture, a 1923 bust of Gertrude Stein, was contributed to the park.

Fresh flower displays and baby-changing stations are found in the women's and men's rest rooms. One employee is assigned exclusively to keeping the rest room facilities clean and safe. The rest rooms are open to the public whenever the park is open.

In addition, the bust of Goethe has been restored, as have the bronzes of William Earl Dodge and José Bonifacio de Andrada e Silva. The William Cullen Bryant sculpture, which is housed in a niche on the terrace at the east end of the park, has been carefully restored with $369,000 of public and private funds.

Cleanliness Equals Respectfulness

Dan Biederman is executive director and president of the Bryant Park Restoration Corporation and the Bryant Park Management Corporation, the two groups that manage the park in cooperation with the city. A coordinating supervisor is in the park daily. Because Biederman also runs two other private downtown redevelopment efforts (the Grand Central Partnership, Inc., and the 34th Street Partnership, Inc.), he can combine some functions; for example, one head of security serves all three partnerships. In Bryant Park, at its summer peak, there are some 55 employees working in security, sanitation, gardening, and special events. Except for the few occasions when some work is outsourced to the private sector, all park employees work for the private nonprofit corporations that manage the park.

Biederman says his goal is to pick up paper almost as soon as it hits the ground. Although most of the users are very respectful of the space, heavy use inevitably creates litter: when 5,000 people are eating lunch, napkins are dropped or blown away by the wind. The park remains generally clean, however, because of high staffing at lunchtime hours.

Clean, safe, and free public rest rooms are almost nonexistent in New York City, so the accessible, well-maintained rest rooms at Bryant Park are a welcome anomaly. Originally the park contained two separate comfort stations, one for men and one for women. This time around, only one of the 1911 landmark structures, located at the 42nd Street park entrance, was refurbished as a rest room. The structure, serving both men and women, was renovated at a cost of about $160,000. (The other rest room, located at the 40th Street entrance, was converted to park office space.) Bryant Park's rest rooms are open whenever the park is open and available to all—with some rules of conduct, however. For example, no bathing is allowed in the rest rooms. One employee is assigned only to the rest rooms, so they are cleaned every few minutes and consistently attended. Fresh flower displays can be found in both rest rooms, and the women's has full-length mirrors as a result of feedback BPRC got from users. Both of the well-lit, remarkably clean rest rooms include baby-changing stations.

Not only the rest rooms have strict rules about use. Throughout the park, clearly posted rules for behavior

The Monday night movies shown in the summer are among the most popular events at the park. The movies are projected from a 4,000-watt projector in the back of a trailer onto a 20-by-40-foot screen that is set up in front of the fountain.

indicate that alcohol and drugs are prohibited, as are dogs on the lawn; pigeon-feeding; panhandling; organized ball games; and loud, amplified music. Smoking is limited to identified smoking sections. Although the park has defined opening and closing hours, there are no gates to shut off access. Instead, BPRC simply puts up chains or blocks entrances with stanchions (known as Belgian Barriers), neither of which would physically keep people out of the park at night. However, because the rules are clearly posted, the security force can ask late users to leave.

Even though approvals were received before the Americans with Disabilities Act was in place, the park is accessible to handicapped users. The first effort was to put in a handicapped-accessible ramp to the library on 42nd Street, at a cost of about $900,000. Then Olin designed a ramp for the 40th Street park entrance, which also allows access to the restaurant. The gravel walkways that line the great lawn are not ideal for wheelchairs, but their compacted crushed stone is usable. Only one retrofitting was undertaken after the park was completed: two sloped openings were cut out in the east side to allow access to the lawn from the walkway.

The Value of the Park

Since Bryant Park reopened in 1992, media coverage has been relentlessly positive. One event in particular that drew crowds, including paparazzi, was Bryant Park's successful bid to lure the fashion industry. Beginning in October 1993, the Council of Fashion Designers of America erected enormous white tents in the park for runway shows showcasing almost the entire New York fashion establishment. Previously, designers had shown

Over 80 years after the fountain was first built and after years of not being usable, the Josephine Shaw Lowell fountain is once again functioning. The restoration included the addition of underwater lighting and a testimonial to Lowell, a Civil War abolitionist, set in the fountain plaza.

Jake Wyman

their new lines at less-than-ideal venues—lofts, hotel ballrooms, nightclubs, and auditoriums—scattered throughout the city. For several years, parts of "7th on Sixth," as the fashion show is known, took place twice yearly at Bryant Park. As time went on, the fashion show in the park was scaled down, and in 1997 it moved to another location, in part because the fashion industry depends on exciting new ideas to keep people's interest. But Bryant Park benefited from the show's early presence and the amount of positive attention it brought.

Musical events are now planned regularly at Bryant Park. The annual JVC Jazz Festival, for example, offers some free concerts in Bryant Park. Performers from the Juilliard School give free concerts periodically during lunch hour, when the park is full of brown-baggers and passersby who stop to enjoy the lively scene.

The success of Bryant Park has brought other activities to the park. Among the most popular events are the Monday night movies, which were started by Michael Fuchs, then chief executive of HBO and later chairman of BPRC. Monday night is traditionally a slow night in restaurants and cafés, and during the summer months, the movies succeed in drawing people into the park to use the concessions. The movies are projected from a 4,000-watt projector on the back of a trailer onto a 20-by-40-foot screen that is set up in front of the fountain. The movable chairs are ideal for these events, but thousands of people watch from blankets placed all over the lawn.

After 14 years of effort, the Bryant Park Grill opened in May 1995. The restaurant was originally proposed in 1981 as a source of revenue and activity for the park. When the original restaurateur left the project, BPRC

ultimately decided to build the restaurant first and get the restaurateur later. Eventually, Michael Weinstein, a well-known and successful restaurateur with projects in several cities, took over all the concessions in the park, including the first of the proposed restaurants. The BPRC got a $4.2 million loan to build the restaurant and paid for $750,000 worth of tenant improvements.

The grill building was one of two restaurant pavilions designed by Hugh Hardy to complement the glory of the public library building. Instead of the two-story, steel-and-glass structure originally proposed, the restaurant is a pavilionlike structure with walls of windows framed by green steel, wooden trellises, and ivy. Diners look out on a vista of color—the great lawn, the trees, and the flowers. "We wanted to make the pavilions an extension of the landscape instead of something that is an imposition to the landscape. You don't feel as if you are entering a room; you feel as if you are entering a place in the park," said Hardy. The interior of the restaurant, designed by Cary Tamarkin and Nancy Mah, feels open and airy, with decor that includes an 86-foot-long mural of birds painted by Hunt Slonem, a New York artist. Bryant Park Grill recorded an $8.6 million gross in the first operating year and paid a large percentage rent toward amortization of the mortgage. Within the next five to seven years, Biederman expects to pay off the debt and provide the park with an operating endowment that will eliminate any reliance on city funding.

The Bryant Park Café, also run by Weinstein, which opened in 1995 on the deck next to the library, quickly became the place to go on Thursday, Friday, and Saturday nights in the summer months. This open-air café, featuring casual food and drinks, was started with a modest amount of money (entirely out of Weinstein's pocket) and little fanfare; it became such a popular after-work spot for young professionals that lines to get into the café became a problem. Simon Sips, Inc., a gourmet coffee stand, the first kiosk concessionaire in the park, was followed by kiosks selling Italian- and French-style sandwiches and salads.

The overall success of the park feeds the success of the neighborhood. Seven million square feet of office and retail space border Bryant Park. Twenty-four months after the newly refurbished park opened, leasing activity on Sixth Avenue had increased 60 percent in the first eight months of 1994, compared with 1993. Leasing agents have reported that the park, which used to be a deterrent to leasing space, is now a marketing tool. Some brokers have referred to the park as the "deal-clincher."

Bryant Park's biggest problems are now those of success. BPRC has had to turn down proposals for special events that may be good for the promoter, but bad for the park. While special events may be excellent at gen-

The green of the great lawn comes from aerating, feeding, mulching, weeding, and trimming on a regular schedule. Rents for offices around Bryant Park have gone up as much as 40 percent since the renovation.

erating revenue and publicity, everyday public use is the priority, and BPRC aims to protect that. According to Biederman, promoters tend to care about events first and venues second, and are often less respectful of the park than its regular users.

Everyone who has worked on the park is proud of the final result and the way that people have embraced the park. Laurie Olin says he gets puffed up with pride every time he sees it.

William Whyte declared that one of the reasons the park has been so successful is that "the park is a statement of faith in the city. It's a celebration of the city. People enjoy watching other people enjoy the city. By and large, Bryant Park is weatherproof in a way. People

The outdoor café was popular as soon as it opened. Café-goers enjoy looking at the great lawn and the beautiful flowers that line it. People-watching is also a popular side dish.

Bryant Park Restoration Corporation

use it all year round. I'm very very happy at how it's worked out."

Garden designer Lynden Miller said, "We sent an important message in treating this open space—we have fixed this space up for you and you're worth it—so people rise to the occasion and they love it. This kind of effort doesn't come cheap, but the value of restored parks is beyond measure to a city. It must be the cheapest way a city can fix itself up. What it does for the morale of the city is immeasurable." Architect Hugh Hardy believes that even though the park itself "feels splendid, the best thing about it is the diversity of people who use it."

Now Bryant Park is looked upon as a model by park designers around the world. Its beauty and success are of great interest at a time when safety and security are primary on people's minds. Some critics say that the park has no sense of intimacy and does not allow people the seclusion and peace that other designs do, but Laurie Olin believes that intimate spaces at this point in history, in the middle of Manhattan, "would be difficult and imprudent." He says he's been attacked by academics for the design: they've claimed it's exclusionary; it's "yuppification"; it's no longer democratic space because it is designed against one of the original user groups of the park—homeless people. But Olin points out that "there are still homeless people there, but they're so much a minority that they behave in a different way than if there weren't so many middle-class, scrubbed working people around. If you have a successful space that looks healthy, people go into it. It's like the stock market. It's kind of a confidence game. We create a kind of self-fulfilling prophecy in how we treat our environment."

Project Data • Bryant Park

Development Schedule

Initial site acquired	Remains New York City park
Planning started	January 1980
Design competition conducted	NA[1]
Master plan approved	1980
Construction started	1988
Construction completed	1991
Park opened	In phases–1991, 40%; 1992, 50%; 1995, 10%
Project completed	May 1995

Construction Financing Information

Source	Amount (in millions)
Private	
Grants and donations	$3.2
Bank loans	4.2
Business improvement district assessments	1.0
Private venture capital	4.0
State	
Environmental quality bonds	.125
Local	
NYC capital funds	5.7
Total construction financing	$18.225

Development Cost Information

Site acquisition costs	None; lease for "negative rent" from New York City Parks Department

Construction Costs

Basic park rehabilitation	
Excavation/demolition	$320,000
Foundation/slab/stairs/walls	573,000
Entrances/ramps	1,470,000
Paving/curbs/cobbles	1,324,000
Utilities	278,000
Irrigation	83,000
Electrical	170,000
Lawn	152,000
Planting	216,000
Maintenance of existing plants	55,000
Site furnishings	172,000
Monuments	83,000
Miscellaneous	350,000
General conditions	702,000
Total rehabilitation costs	$5,948,000

Concessions, monuments, horticulture	
Restaurant—core and shell	$2,405,000
Restaurant interiors—tenant allowance	750,000
Restaurant interiors—investment by tenant	2,500,000
Café installation—investment by tenant	1,000,000
Upper terrace restoration	316,000
Upper terrace electrical	98,000
Fountain restoration	160,000
Park houses restoration	230,000
Gatehouse/in-park kiosks	465,000
W.C. Bryant monument	369,000
Miscellaneous monuments	23,000
Fence restoration	150,000
Perennial gardens	225,000
Signage/graphics	75,000
Lighting (ornamental, moon, street)	996,000
Total costs for concessions, monuments, and horticulture	$9,762,000
Total construction costs	$15,710,000

Soft Costs/Fees

Contractor	$193,000
Landscape architects	691,000
Surveyor/engineering	100,000
Building/restoration architects	405,000
Lighting consultant	50,000
Permits	6,000
Financing fees	24,000
Legal fees	147,400
Construction interest	365,100
Total soft costs/fees	$1,981,500
Total hard and soft construction costs	$17,691,500

Note

1. Not applicable.

Bryant Park Restoration Corporation, Current Cash Flow Report and Budgets for Fiscal 1998

General Fund	FY 97 Budget	FY 98 Budget
Square feet	7,528,917	7,528,917
Rate/square foot	12.617950 cents/ square foot = $949,995 total assessment	16.104574 cents/ square foot = $1,212,500 total assessment
Rate increase/square foot		3.486624 cents/ square foot (27% increase)

Revenues

	FY 97 Budget	FY 98 Budget
Business improvement district	$950,000	$1,212,500
Earned income (rentals and concessions)	395,000	442,500
NYC expense payment (parks department)	200,000	200,000
Grants	117,500	125,000
Interest	2,500	10,000
Café receipts (net of sinking fund)	140,000	0[1]
Other (miscellaneous location fees)	2,000	2,000
Reserve for uncollected assessments	0	0
Total revenues	$1,807,000	$1,992,000

Expenses

Personnel costs	FY 97 Budget	FY 98 Budget
Executive staff	$155,000	$156,000
Accounting	40,000	53,500
Clerical staff (shared with GPC)	50,000	57,500
Benefits (health)	27,500	42,000
Payroll taxes	30,000	25,000
Total personnel costs	$302,500	$334,000
Administrative costs		
Rent	$47,000	$36,000
Office services/supplies	4,000	6,500
Telephone	5,500	8,500
Auditing fees	19,000	20,000
Travel and entertainment	3,000	2,000
Postage	6,000	6,000
Conferences, meetings, lectures	1,000	1,000
Memberships, periodicals	2,750	1,200
Equipment	4,000	6,500
Banking fees/miscellaneous/ internal expenses	5,000	6,500
Total administrative costs	$97,250	$94,200

General Fund	FY 97 Budget	FY 98 Budget
Operations		
Coordinating supervisor	$38,000	$37,500
Maintenance and cleaning	450,000	450,000
Extermination	3,000	3,100
Capital maintenance (Schedule A)	56,200	51,000
Security	450,000	465,000
Horticulture	95,000	106,000
Insurance	26,800	25,700
Total operations costs	$1,119,000	$1,138,300
Park programs		
Capital enhancements (Schedule B)	$90,500	$190,500
Music/Entertainment	65,000	60,000
Legal	5,000	0
Promotion		20,000
Social services	10,000	10,000
Streetscapes/debt service (estimate)		75,000
Interest and Repayment- Loan (NYPL)	70,000	70,000
Total program costs	$240,500	$425,500
Total operating and program costs	$1,759,250	$1,992,000
Contribution to reduction of operating deficit	$47,750	$0

Schedule A: Capital maintenance	FY 97 Budget	FY 98 Budget
NYNEX lighting maintenance		$3,000
Lighting maintenance		12,000
Cobblestones/drains		36,000
Total capital maintenance costs		$51,000

Schedule B: Capital enhancements	FY 97 Budget	FY 98 Budget
Stone path work	$87,500	$87,500
Fifth Avenue kiosks	3,000	20,000
Park lighting		25,000
Park entrance barrier		38,000
Police kiosk		10,000
Shoeshine		10,000
Total capital enhancement costs	$90,500	$190,500

Note

1. Revenue pledged to refinancing of restaurant.

Cedar Lake Park and Trail
Minneapolis

Peter Harnik

Robert Engstrom

Minneapolis, the city that already has perhaps the nation's finest urban park network, has just made it a bit better through Cedar Lake Park and Trail—a paragon of public/private cooperation that is transforming derelict acreage into an urban asset.

Both the bikeway and the nature preserve are built on old railroad tracks, but Cedar Lake is not a traditional rail-trail: it is a trail-*with*-rail, a sanctuary of greenery pressed against the rumble of continued commercial vitality. Although most of a former Burlington Northern railyard was purchased, dismantled, and landscaped, busy freight trains roll along the one remaining track, carrying grain, coal, building materials, and containers to and from the coalfields of the Dakotas and the ports of the Pacific Northwest.

Cedar Lake Park and Trail's conception was so unusual and its creation so unlikely that the story has an "only-in-Minneapolis" feel. Few communities have the level of trust, the tolerance for discussion, the history of public/private cooperation, the openness and responsiveness of government, and the willingness to spend money on a public purpose that Minneapolis does.

But the money has been well invested. According to David Fisher, superintendent of the Minneapolis Park and Recreation Board (MPRB), "Downtown Minneapolis Central Riverfront is coming back, and it's parkland that's helping to make it happen. The $40 million we've spent on parkland acquisition and development in the central river area is leveraging nearly ten times that amount in private expenditures for housing, office space, and commercial development. People are now realizing that downtown is where they want to be."

The successful outcome of this experiment will profoundly influence other communities searching for innovative approaches to urban park, trail, and transportation projects in the 21st century.

The Site

Depending on one's point of view, Cedar Lake Park is either a recreational trail with a wide spot in the middle or a nature preserve with long, thin panhandles. Located on the west side of the city, the park originally extended 3.5 miles, from the suburb of St. Louis Park to Seventh Street at the edge of downtown. The trail was then extended another mile to the Mississippi, connecting with the existing park-and-trail system along the river. Totaling 48 acres, the park ranges in width from about 1,600 feet to about 20 feet. Where there is space, it includes three parallel asphalt treadways —two one-way lanes for bicyclists and in-line skaters and a third treadway for walkers and runners. Where the trail is constricted, the lanes narrow and merge.

Although the long, thin site is extraordinarily beautiful in places and home to marvelous wildflowers, birds and mammals (even foxes), marshes, forests, and a picture-perfect lake, elsewhere it is challenged by modern urbanity—freeways, relay towers, train tracks, a pavement recycling yard, eutrophic streams, parking lots, chain-link fences, and occasionally a homeless person or two.

Like most former rail corridors, the trail corridor had, over time, become a collecting point for less than desirable uses. Ironically, just up the embankment, a stone's throw from the tracks, are two upscale neighborhoods, Kenwood and Bryn Mawr, home to a good number of well-to-do Minneapolitans. They reside there, in part, because of Cedar Lake and the Chain of Lakes flowing north and south from it. These lakes are but one important component of the extraordinary, 6,000-acre park system often credited with keeping Minneapolis near the top of the yearly "most livable city" surveys.[1]

The Park Effort Begins

It takes an ardent visionary to imagine creating a park on a railyard, even after the tracks and ties have been removed. Fortunately, Cedar Lake Park and Trail had at least two visionaries. Doris Peterson, a retired preschool teacher, walked her three dogs down by the tracks and found the ghostly quiet area "wonderfully nice." When Burlington Northern started taking out the tracks in 1986, she was concerned enough to call the railroad and begin talking to her neighborhood association, in fear that the land would be used for development.

On the other side of the ravine, Dan Dailey, a self-employed writer and strategic consultant, also began walking through the abandoned area and developed a special relationship with it. Dailey's preference was that

Cedar Lake Trail was intended to be a viable, uninterrupted biking and skating commuter path to downtown Minneapolis as well as a recreational trail. Unlike most rail-to-trail projects, this one has an active railroad track that runs alongside the trail. The park and trail are host to a mix of urban elements—train tracks and relay towers—as well as marshes, wildflowers, and other reminders of nature's wonders.

Cedar Lake Park stands out among the city's parks as a less manicured and more natural expanse of meadows, trees, and wildflowers. The Cedar Lake Park Association has won several awards for its efforts, including the Federal Highway Administration's Environmental Excellence Award; it is the only citizens' group to be given the honor.

it be left exactly as it was—untamed, undefined, unpublicized, a place where nature truly reigned. But when he read one day that a young woman had been abducted and raped in the corridor, he realized wild spaces in urban areas need special consideration. "I felt I had to do something, so I began collecting trash and putting it in large, visible piles," he said. "I wanted people to think there was some kind of organized effort going on there."

Dailey didn't have a definite plan, but he did have a deep, abiding reverence for nature, ecosystems, and Native American customs, and he envisioned converting the whole area into a combination prairie and anonymous graveyard, similar to the prehistoric Indian burial mounds in Ohio and elsewhere.

About then, reality intervened. Surveyor's stakes and signs went up advertising the 28 acres' availability for development, and one builder announced plans to lay out roads and construct houses. Alarmed, Peterson and a neighbor, Brian Willette, called a community meeting attended by Dailey and over 60 others. Although the entire shoreline of Cedar Lake was surrounded by a narrow band of parkland, there had never been a formal plan to create a park alongside Cedar Lake.

In short order, the group devised its goal of preserving the land as a nature sanctuary, named the parcel Cedar Lake Park, organized itself into Save Cedar Lake Park, and met with Glacier Park Company, Burlington Northern's real estate division, to learn that the asking price was $1.7 million. They also met with David Fisher, superintendent of the Minneapolis Park and Recreation Board, from whom they learned that the city had such a large

backlog of park acquisition and improvement expenses that a normal public purchase of Cedar Lake Park would entail many years' delay—much longer than the railroad would consider.

Without an extraordinary effort by the community, the park would never come to life.

A Partnership Evolves

Cedar Lake Park would probably not have been created without the involvement of two exceptional organizations. Save Cedar Lake Park, later renamed the Cedar Lake Park Association, Inc. (CLPA), is the kind of citizens' group that most activists only dream of. The group had talent—speakers, writers, photographers, lobbyists, botanists, engineers, visionaries, politicians—all held together by the inclusionary style of president Brian Willette. (One woman, Laurie Lundy, signed on as a volunteer only two weeks after she moved into the neighborhood and worked so diligently that she was hired as a full-time staff member a few years later.) It had people of significant financial means and people who weren't shy about asking. Perhaps most important, it had members who were deeply committed to their community and who were able—emotionally and financially—to devote endless hours to meetings.

The other partner was the Minneapolis Park and Recreation Board, an exceptional public agency. Although Superintendent Fisher was bluntly honest when he informed the members of the Cedar Lake Park Association that he couldn't create their park for them, he was astute enough to hold open the possibility of working together.

"The first time I met Dan Dailey and he told me of his idea to create a cemetery without headstones, I knew I was dealing with a special project," Fisher said afterward. "This park was not even in the top 20 projects on our list, but we decided to stick with it and encourage the neighborhood residents. We were dealing with a neighborhood that didn't really trust the government but did have a powerful vision of what it wanted."

The Minneapolis Park and Recreation Board is perhaps the nation's preeminent city park agency, largely because the board is elected rather than appointed and because two-thirds of its budget stems from an automatic payment from property taxes. While closely linked to the mayor's office, the park board is able to budget and spend money with much greater freedom and certainty than sister agencies in other cities, where parks are frequently near the bottom of the list of City Hall's concerns. Partly as a result of these special circumstances, Minneapolis has 17 acres of parkland per 1,000 residents, more than any other large city in the country.

And Fisher is unabashedly pro-park. "A park is not just a place," he said. "It's a philosophy. It's a gathering place—the commons of the neighborhood. As go the parks, so go the neighborhoods. The parks are the oases of our neighborhoods, the salvation of the city. That's why we have a policy—which we have achieved—of providing a park within six walking blocks of every residence in the city."

The leafy areas near Cedar Lake didn't lack parks; needier people around Minneapolis already enviously referred to the neighborhood as "Kenwood by the Lakes." Yet through the strength of the vision, the concern about what else might be developed in the ravine, and the extraordinary skills and connections of the participants, the project took on a vibrant life of its own. Dailey's group reached an unwritten agreement with Fisher that if private dollars could be raised to cover one-third of the cost, public funds would be sought for the rest.

In less than 18 months, the park board and the Parks and Open Space Commission of the area's Metropolitan Council had completed and approved a rough plan for a nature park with connecting foot and bicycle trails; state legislators had made a commitment to try and appropriate some state funds for the acquisition; and $435,000 in private money had been committed, the largest chunk from Ellen Sturgis, a member of Minneapolis's prominent and philanthropic Dayton family. Enthusiasm for the effort was so great that members of the Minnesota Orchestra staged a benefit concert, and the local Audubon chapter donated its entire $15,000 Sanctuary Fund, money that had been accumulated over a 30-year period to buy a bird habitat in the city.

The Vision Expands

In 1990, Glacier Park Company jolted Save Cedar Lake Park's leadership by demanding that the association purchase 48 acres, not the original 28 on the table. The extra acreage was of a profoundly different character—straight, long and thin, not really amenable to the plans

Minnesota, "Land of 10,000 Lakes," is also the home of one of the best park systems in the country. The Minneapolis park system consists of over 1,400 acres of water surface along with some 4,600 acres of land.

for contemplative woods, groves, and meadows. To some, the additional land meant the demise of a pastoral park; others found the possibilities exciting and suited to the needs of bicycle- and skate-crazy Minneapolis.

The addition of the long western segment, which actually extended the preserve into the neighboring suburban jurisdiction of St. Louis Park, greatly improved the political climate for receiving public funding. For one thing, it added a number of pro-park legislative districts. It also suddenly gave advocates the ability to talk about Cedar Lake Park in terms of regional benefits. "Hennepin County already has a great trail system," explained Fisher. "I was able to go to my board and say, 'If we can get a little three-mile connection, it will open up 30 or more miles of the county's trail system to all our users.'"

In late winter 1991, the full political strength of the fledgling coalition was mustered. Project coordinator Laurie Lundy "lived in the capitol" for three months, while numerous volunteers walked the halls, packed meetings, made phone calls, distributed fact sheets, and lobbied representatives. Finally, minutes before the legislature adjourned, a park bond measure with $1.1 million for Cedar Lake Park was passed. Eight months later, with $487,000 of private money plus a $46,000 loan from the James Ford Bell Foundation, the land was bought for $1.6 million from Glacier Park and deeded to the Minneapolis Park and Recreation Board.

An Uneasy Coalition

Now money needed to be found to create the trail—and that breakthrough occurred 1,000 miles away, in Washington, D.C. Less than a month after the land was acquired, President George Bush signed the Intermodal Surface Transportation Efficiency Act (ISTEA), a radical transformation of the nation's highway law that mandated, for the first time, major expenditure of road monies on nonautomobile projects, including trails, bikeways, and the restoration of historic transportation facilities.

Even before ISTEA, bicycling was a big item in the North Star State: Minnesota already had 502 miles of rail-trails, an active state bicycle coordinator within the state department of transportation, and even an annual mass bicycle ride led by the lieutenant governor. Minneapolis itself was rated among the most bicycle-friendly of the nation's large cities, with on-street bike lanes; a continuous, 42-mile, off-road trail system through the parks; and thousands of cycling commuters to the University of Minnesota. Nevertheless, as in every other state, bike projects were severely backlogged by a dearth of funds.

After a long effort to get funding for the trail, participants in the groundbreaking ceremony are exuberant. The park development occurred only because of residents' strong involvement. Even today, the park department's efforts are supplemented by those of volunteers, who plant flowers, remove debris, pick up garbage, and remove graffiti.

The opportunity provided by ISTEA was electrifying, and no one grasped the potential more quickly than George Puzak, a Kenwood realtor and bicycling devotee who had been an early participant in the Cedar Lake Park effort. Puzak and his bicycle allies may not have been wealthy philanthropists, but through ISTEA, they were the entrée to hundreds of thousands of dollars of public money that the Cedar Lake group could not otherwise have obtained.

Like every marriage of convenience, this one had its rocky moments. "All of us were rooted in ecology," said Puzak, "but we were coming from different places. They would say, 'Speeding bikes will scare the wildlife and ruin the environment.' We would say, 'Driving to a refuge pollutes the air and ruins the environment.' It was a question of who exactly was the environmentalist. Fortunately, we kept talking and realized that this park could be a winner if everyone gave a little bit."

The issue that almost fractured the coalition's unity was the surfacing material of the park's trails. The nature faction insisted on gravel, the cyclists on asphalt. Asphalt was ultimately chosen, largely because of political pressure from the in-line skating community and administrative pressure from the Minnesota Department of Transportation (DOT), which claimed that the Americans with Disabilities Act required the use of a wheelchair-friendly surface. However, several concessions were made to the advocates of a "softer" look. The trails were designed to include graceful, curving meanders. The walking and cycling treadways were separated to the maximum extent possible. And a soft shoulder for runners, made of recycled, crushed city curbing, was added to the walking treadway.

A New Vision for the Future

Seldom is there an opportunity to reclaim a large tract of land in the center of a major metropolitan area, create a nature preserve, and develop a compatible trail system for nonmotorized transportation. When the opportunity occurs, it must be seized and made a reality.

To meet such a challenge, it is vital for individuals, business, government, institutions, and organizations to work together at unprecedented levels of service, commitment, and cooperation. When these partnerships unite in efforts to improve the quality of life and the liveability of our communities, we see the world as it can truly be.

Cedar Lake Park with its connecting trails is a unique opportunity to transform our urban landscape and the way a city functions. To create a nature park with a variety of ecological communities and trails in the heart of the city provides real hope for a new vision for the future. With a significant land base now secured, the challenge of Cedar Lake Park and Trail must be met through a sensitive and creative design.

—From the *Statement of Philosophy*, Cedar Lake Park and Trail Citizens' Advisory Committee

Eight Objectives

The following are the objectives recommended by the Cedar Lake Park and Trail Citizens' Advisory Committee:

PROTECT and improve the water resources and soils.

RECONSTITUTE a wide variety of native plant communities which reflect lake, wetland, prairie, savannah, woodland, and forest ecosystems.

MANAGE the plant and animal communities for their long-term integrity, stability, and beauty.

CONNECT ecosystems, green corridors, and trail systems.

MINIMIZE human artifacts and amenities within the conservancy area.

INTEGRATE the surrounding land and land uses to complement and enhance the park.

FACILITATE experiences in whch people learn about nature and gain greater appreciation for humanity's role in the web of life.

CELEBRATE people living in harmony with nature and each other.

The Grand Partnership

Keeping the park effort going took a year's worth of weekly meetings—hundreds of hours of talking by a committed group of residents who knew they had to put their mouths where their money already was. The process was smoothed by the unflagging support of the park board's Fisher and also by what is called "Minnesota nice"—the Scandinavian commitment to civility even in the face of disharmony.

A 54-member citizens' advisory committee, working in an unprecedented partnership with both the park board and the city's department of public works, developed a statement of philosophy and design principles to guide the development of the park (see feature boxes). On the basis of this statement, two landscape design teams were contracted with: Jones & Jones/ Richard Haag Associates, of Seattle, to work primarily on the trail portion; and later, Balmori Associates, of New Haven, to help design sites within the park.

The effort soon developed astonishing power. In short order, more than $1.8 million was brought in for trail design and construction from the Minnesota DOT, the Minnesota legislature, the Metropolitan Council, the city, and the private Hedberg Family Foundation. Never before had a parcel of land gone from being "off the chart" to becoming a park in such a short time. Completed during the summer of 1995, Cedar Lake Trail was offically dedicated on September 9 of that year.

The Park's Design

Acre for acre, no park development in Minneapolis has received as much time and attention as Cedar Lake Park. Because of the intense involvement of the surrounding community—and the neighbors' ability to back up their interest with time and money—the park board invested unusual amounts of staff time and consultants' time in the process (so much so, in fact, that other communities are now asking for equal treatment).

Some issues were easy. Most of the trail corridor was to be planted with native grasses and wildflowers. When the park board realized in 1995 that regular mowing of its huge holdings was costing too much, it proposed reducing its grass-cutting operations and allowing some of its lands to develop a "meadow" look. A cry of outrage arose from much of the populace, but not from Cedar

Lake Park: the "no-mow" concept fit in exactly with the "nurture nature" approach and was heartily endorsed.

Other issues were tougher. The dispute over asphalting the treadways was deeply divisive, as was the question of trail width. Similarly, the purists of the group didn't want any lighting along the trail, while some cyclists wanted a fully lit facility for wintertime evening commuting. As a compromise, the trail was left unlit except in a few potentially dangerous locations, such as under freeway bridges.

Thanks to the design process and to the luxurious width (which stemmed from the fact that the abandoned site was a railyard rather than a single track), Cedar Lake Trail is without question the most serpentine rail-trail in the nation. Freed from the horizon-to-horizon linearity characteristic of midwestern rail-trails, the designers created a panoply of low prairie ridges and swales with shallow pools of standing water that make cycling and skating a sensuous, memorable experience. And they did so with a good understanding of a bike's speed and dynamics. All the undulations are easily negotiable at the 20-mile-per-hour design speed, and sight distances are appropriate everywhere.

Meanwhile, for those who are intimidated or annoyed by fast-moving wheeled users, the primary walking trail has been separated from the bicycle trail both by distance and by a combination of topography and vegetation; there are places along the trail where cyclists and walkers cannot see or hear each other. In addition, a subsidiary walking-trail system, perhaps of a softer material such as crushed stone or wood chips, is contemplated for the heart of the natural conservancy area of the park.

Another major project in the works is the Cedar Grove, a collaborative effort between the CLPA and the MPRB to memorialize loved ones as well as to re-create the native plant communities that existed in the area before European settlement. Thanks to intense community interest plus an outpouring of financial support that made possible the purchase of many red cedar and other trees, it will be much more than a typical grove. According to Cedar Lake Park Association member Keith Prussing, the grove will be laid out as a "great two-armed spiral that has been oriented toward the eight directions" found in Native American lore. Moreover, a Native American spiritual leader officiated at the preconstruction dedication ceremony, and future planting ceremonies will be planned to take place at special times, such as the equinox.

"Working with Cedar Lake Park Association was a real treat for us," said Steve Durrant, senior associate with Jones & Jones, the Seattle-based design firm selected, through a competition, to plan the park. "Our philosophy is to learn from the land itself. We tried to answer the question, 'What kind of park does this land want to be?' The citizens understood this approach. In their deliberations with us they discussed matters from the cosmos down to individual strands of DNA and everything in between. We tried to design a park that would give as much as possible back to the city and to the earth—be it oxygen, tranquility, or poetry."

Further east, close to downtown, Cedar Lake Trail becomes engulfed in urbanity and loses its natural character. Initially, the CLPA attempted to deindustrialize the corridor by asking the city to convert a pavement-

Where there is space, the Cedar Lake Trail includes three parallel asphalt treadways—two one-way lanes for bicyclists and in-line skaters and a third treadway for walkers and runners. Elsewhere, the lanes narrow and merge. Here, an early-morning biker is about to pass under I-394.

The Cedar Lake Park Association and its many volunteers track birds and other wildlife throughout the year. For the first time since the 1950s, bluebirds (sialiasialis) have returned to Minneapolis. Nesting boxes placed in the park have signs encouraging people to observe the bluebirds from a distance.

recycling facility to parkland, but the association was roundly rebuffed. ("Not only does Minneapolis save a huge amount of money by recycling and relaying old pavement," explained department of public works [DPW] engineer Rhonda Rae, "but we are on the cutting edge of this pro-environmental technology—without it we'd be strip-mining a lot of gravel from some pristine area.") The association now intends to plant vines along the fence to soften the view—and also to mount educational boards informing trail users about the public works department's environmental programs.

As is the case with many rail-trails, the railroad heritage of the area has been emphasized by the Cedar Lake Park Association. Through serendipitous timing and quick collaboration, a charming visual memento has been created. CellularOne company needed to erect a small utility building alongside the communication tower it proposed to erect near the trail. Instead of constructing a standard square cinderblock building, the firm agreed to spend $25,000 modifying the design to "19th-century cute rail depot." Although not open to the public (it merely houses communication equipment), the depot has been christened Linden Yards, and its walls will support storyboards about railroading and the United Transportation Union.

Park Use and Management

Once the new land was acquired and the park established, the recreation constituency and the naturalist constituency began to pursue their separate interests.

Fortunately, with enough room in most portions of the park, those interests rarely impinge on each other.

Of the two, the recreationists had the easier task; they simply began bicycling, skating, and skiing on the two smooth, ten-foot-wide meandering treadways—some for pleasure and fitness, others for commuting and purposeful travel. There is a third, semi-parallel path for running and walking—six feet wide, part asphalt and part gravel. In places where the corridor narrows, the two bike trails are combined to a 14-foot width, or all three trails are merged to a 20-foot width. Even at its narrowest, Cedar Lake Trail is wider than 99 percent of all trails in the nation.

When the city did bicycle counts in the summer of 1996, it found an average of 700 weekday users, about three-quarters of them commuting to work; the record so far was 1,461 trail users on Sunday, July 14, 1996, although that number is certain to be eclipsed as more Minnesotans discover the facility. (Interestingly, the trail has already proven itself during a local emergency. Early in 1996, during a transit strike, the number of rush-hour cyclists on the trail doubled to 181 every 60 minutes.)

The naturalists, as usual, set themselves more challenging goals. Led by Dailey and Willette, they are seeking to re-create and restore native plant communities not commonly found in Minneapolis—dry and mesic prairies, climax lakeside maple and basswood forests, oak savannahs. They are encouraging and nurturing all kinds of experiments—reintroducing ospreys and bluebirds, propogating wildflowers, and using ecological principles to manage the park. Indeed, the first of several planned wetlands has been constructed near Cedar

Lake to remove nutrients from stormwater and improve the water quality of the lakes. "We're figuring it out as we go," said Dailey. "Our relationship with the park board is undefined and challenging because there's no roadmap, but what we want is the recognition of parks as sacred spaces."

While other Minneapolis neighborhoods may agree that their greenspaces too are sacred, the difference is that the residents around Cedar Lake Park have the time and resources to invest in creating a sacrosanct park and keeping it that way. All told, the Cedar Lake Park Association has raised nearly $1.2 million of private money, and its 3,000 members have devoted untold thousands of volunteer hours, both in meetings and out in the field.

Most residents believe that this park is being treated differently from the others, and some fear that a precedent is being set for other people with money and power to work on their own neighborhood parks. Minneapolis does have a citywide People for Parks organization that buys trees and donates money and services for all the city's parks, which alleviates some of the concerns about favoritism. But people fear that poor neighborhoods could be left behind because of lack of private money and resources.

The park board's David Fisher recognizes the potential for inequality and has visions of trying to combat it. "There's another abandoned railroad track in Minneapolis that is a potential linear park," he said. "It's the 29th Street corridor, what we're calling the Midtown Greenway. It runs through a lower-income neighborhood and could be a great amenity. But inner-city people are so busy making a living, they don't have the time to go to all these meetings. We're trying to see if there isn't some way that the park board—the government—can't make it easier for these working people to participate in the park development process."

Bicycling and the City

Minneapolis has a solid commitment to bicycling; of the nation's big cities, it has perhaps the second most comprehensive program, after Seattle's. Cedar Lake Trail is amplifying that commitment.

"When our mayor, Sharon Sayles Belton, first came to office, she announced eight goals for her tenure, and goal 2(d) was to make Minneapolis bicycle-friendly," said the DPW's Rhonda Rae, the city's personable and enthusiastic bike coordinator. "In 1990, 1 percent of our mode share into the central business district was coming in by bike. Six years later it was over 2 percent. The University of Minnesota, with 60,000 students and staff, has a bicycle-mode share target of 20 percent and is

already up to 5 percent. Our transportation department has an exchange program with the transportation agency in Finland specifically to deal with cycling issues affected by a cold climate. Even in the winter, we get 2,000 cyclists a day entering the business district, which eliminates enough cars to fill our single largest municipal parking garage. Our next goal is to increase the bike share to 10 percent while reducing the number of accidents by 10 percent. Cedar Lake will be a key part of that effort on both counts."

The power of Cedar Lake Park and Trail stems from the linkages it fosters. The route itself serves a relatively narrow slice of the city—and, as some critics have pointedly noted, none of the lower-income neighborhoods to the north, which are currently denied access to the trail by the active Burlington Northern track on the north edge of the park—but its very existence is driving new interest in additional trail connections. With the park board and the city's public works department diligently working on both the Kenilworth connection

This bridge carries trail users over the lagoon between Brownie Lake and Cedar Lake.

(from the south) and the Bassett's Creek Trail (from the north, with a bridge over the tracks), and with the city of St. Louis Park studying an extension of the trail to the city of Hopkins, Cedar Lake Trail could become the commuting and recreational link for a large segment of the city's west side. Moreover, the success of Cedar Lake Park and Trail has given impetus to the effort to create the Midtown Greenway on the corridor of the abandoned Milwaukee Railroad, where tracks once went all the way to the Pacific. The portion of these tracks to be used for the greenway extends nearly the entire width of the city, connecting the Chain of Lakes with the Mississippi River.

The final trail segment to the Mississippi River is even more exciting. Not only is there an existing (and growing) park and trail system along both sides of the river in the downtown area and on Nicollet Island, but the city also converted the famous Stone Arch Bridge into a dramatic walkway/bikeway/skateway. The striking bridge, which was built in 1883 by railroad magnate James J. Hill to take the Great Northern Railroad westward to Seattle, not only serves as a quiet, car-free transportation route but is also a stunning tourist expe-

rience, offering views of a working barge lock on the river and of working and abandoned flour mills on both shores.

The Verdict

Cedar Lake Park's birth was not an easy one; there were several midwives, all with differing philosophies and experiences. Many participants were burned out by the process, and some were emotionally drained from the cross fire. The result is something unique among modern urban parks—a piece of public space that is designed, managed, and overseen with as much care as if it were private.

"I've never devoted as much staff time to a project as I have to Cedar Lake Park," said the park board's Fisher. "There is so much mistrust of government. It's much worse than it was ten years ago. That's why you need so much vision-building and consensus-building. What else would explain the size of the advisory committee and the amount of work performed by the group? But this worked out great. Neither we nor the citizens abdicated anything; we magnified each other's respon-

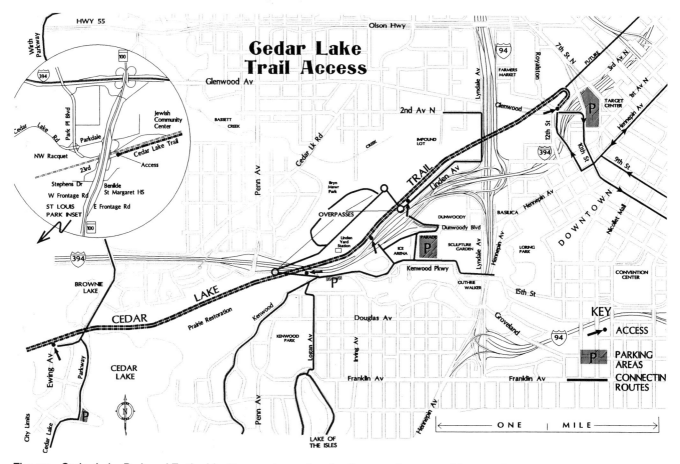

The new Cedar Lake Park and Trail adds 48 acres to an already vibrant park system. Minneapolis boasts 17 acres of parkland per 1,000 residents—more than any other large city in the country.

Project Data • Cedar Lake Park and Trail

Development Schedule

Initial site acquired	1991
Planning started	1991
Design competition conducted	1993
Master plan approved	1994
Construction started	February 1995
Construction completed	1997
Park opened	September 1995
Project completed	1997

Development Costs (in thousands)

Acquisition	$1,600
Park and trail planning	87
Park and trail construction	1,789
Total development costs	$3,476

Revenue Sources (in thousands)

Acquisition	
State of Minnesota	$1,067
Cedar Lake Park Association	533
Total	$1,600
The trail	
Minnesota DOT (ISTEA)	$641
Legislative Committee for Minnesota Resources (park construction funds)	610
Metropolitan Council/Minnesota Department of Natural Resources	354
City of Minneapolis	71
Hedberg Family Foundation	200
Total	$1,876

sibilities and powers. In this case it was one plus one equals three."

Whether the experience can be duplicated in a less economically and culturally homogeneous neighborhood in a more diverse city—perhaps in a part of the country lacking what landscape designer Diana Balmori calls "the great midwestern sense of citizenship"—is not clear. But Minneapolitans seem thrilled with their new park and trailway.

Note

1. Approximately 4,600 acres of land and more than 1,400 acres of water surface.

Downtown Park
Bellevue, Washington

Terry Jill Lassar

Once the butt of Seattle cocktail-party jokes, downtown Bellevue—known as Car City, and strewn with gas stations, strip malls, sprawling office buildings, asphalt parking lots, and other hallmarks of suburbia—has been working for nearly 20 years to transform itself from a suburban bedroom community into a regional urban center. Located ten miles east of Seattle across Lake Washington, Bellevue offers spectacular views of Mount Rainier, Lake Washington, and the Seattle skyline. With a population of 103,000, the city is the finance, business, and retailing center of the "greater Eastside" suburban expansion.

Work on a new downtown plan started in 1978, and in the early 1980s, Bellevue passed a radically revised land use code to achieve an intense, compact commercial core. The downtown was totally redefined as a 144-block area where development was to be directed. The edges of the central business district (CBD) were redefined so that high-quality residential neighborhoods could coexist alongside high-density development.[1] The comprehensive plan also contained a strong statement about the need for a 24-hour downtown and a mixed-use urban core where people could live, work, and enjoy cultural and recreational activities.

Today, with 5 million square feet of office space, 4 million square feet of retail/mixed-use development, and some 1,000 housing units, Bellevue is closer to its goal of becoming a true regional center. However, creating a sense of place has proven to be a challenge. The city's street system of large superblocks limits the creation of a pedestrian orientation. In addition, downtown development was scattered and too far from existing development to create the concentration of uses that makes for a dynamic environment.

In response, the city has undertaken a series of planning and development projects to enhance the pedestrian environment and instill a sense of place in the CBD. It also embarked on an ambitious public building program, including a regional library and a convention/performing arts center. But one of the critical elements of the plan was the addition of new downtown parks, urban plazas, and open spaces. In particular, Downtown Park, the "Central Park" of the city's open space network, was envisioned as a pastoral retreat and an organizing element surrounded largely by residential towers. And because of the value the private sector placed on such a park, it took responsibility for financing and building the first phase with the city's oversight.

Seizing the Opportunity

In the early 1980s, the Bellevue School District offered to give the city of Bellevue five acres of land for park development. In exchange, the school district wanted the city to rezone the remaining 12.5 acres, which it envisioned turning into commercial development as a long-term investment. The site, occupied by abandoned school administration buildings and a former junior high school, had been declared surplus property.

Rather than accept the gift of five acres, then-mayor Cary Bozeman pressed to purchase the entire 17.5-acre parcel. According to Bozeman, urban parks, such as Vancouver's Stanley Park and the Boston Common, are key "image setters and are critical to shaping the quality of urban living. Cities have a responsibility as they grow denser to provide open spaces as a way to sustain the quality of urban living."

In 1983, the city purchased the initial 17.5-acre site for $14.3 million—the largest sum paid for a municipal park site in the state's history. The purchase was financed through councilmanic bonds backed by a 0.2 percent increase in the local option sales tax.

Controversy surrounded the park acquisition from the start. Citing the high price paid for the land, critics claimed that the city was catering to its business and development interests at the general public's expense. Some thought that such a large expenditure should have been put to a public vote. Others questioned whether the site, on the western fringe of the CBD, was the best location for a "central" park, even though the former site of the junior high school had been noted as a "special-opportunity site" in the city's 1979 downtown plan, and open space had been identified as one of the options for that site.

Despite criticism, Bozeman wanted to seize the opportunity to create an ambitious central park for the city. "Every once in a while," said Bozeman, "as an elected official, you have an opportunity to do one of these visionary things where you're not sure you have the public support, but you know in your heart it's the right thing to do."

Although Bozeman envisioned a dense residential neighborhood growing up around the edges of the park, downtown Bellevue in 1983 was mainly an office core that was deserted after five p.m. "The park," said Bozeman, "would not realize its full potential to serve the public for another 15 or 20 years. But if you waited until then, when you had those densities, it would be too expensive to acquire the land."

Designing a Suburban Central Park

Downtown Park, a two-block area of 20 acres, is located several blocks west of the office core and immediately south of Bellevue Square, a 50-year-old regional shopping mall that is probably the city's best-known landmark. Today, the now-20-acre Downtown Park is the crown jewel in the emerald necklace of the city's park system. The park's bold circle-within-a-square design includes a large, grassy meadow encircled by a canal and a tree-lined walkway. The canal is about 1,200 feet long; water spills over a series of small waterfalls and cascades into a shallow, one-acre pond in the park's southwest quadrant. The 20-foot-wide promenade is lined with London plane trees that will reach a height of 80 feet. Light standards in the classic shape of obelisks also line the promenade; designed to demarcate the circular area, the lights create an immediate sense of place.

The park's bold circle-within-a-square design includes a large grassy meadow encircled by a canal and tree-lined walkway.

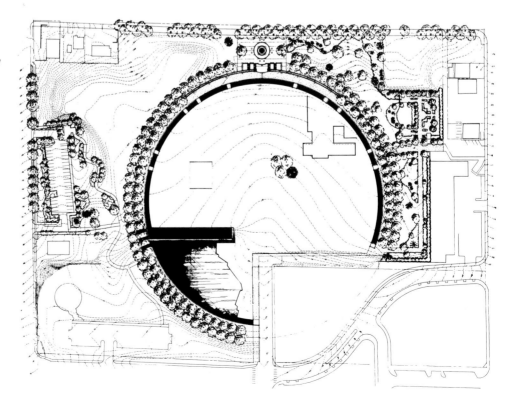

In contrast to most of Bellevue's more naturalistic recreational parks, Downtown Park looks to French 17th-century landscape designs where open spaces were arranged in a more formal, geometric composition and where hard surfaces and objects were used to frame space. At the north entryway to the park, a belvedere—a raised platform that can be used as a performance stage—affords dramatic vistas of the entire park.

Adrienne Teleki

At the northern entrance to the park, a belvedere—a raised platform—provides visitors with a dramatic vista of the entire park. The east entrance leads from a busy street toward a grove of elms that serves as a memorial to three local soldiers who died in World War I. Low walls mark the foundations of original buildings on the site and provide seating for picnickers and concert-goers.

The city set ambitious goals for the park. Like New York's Central Park, Downtown Park was conceived as a haven, a place where people who live and work in the CBD can take respite from an intensely urban environment. The city also envisioned the park as a natural destination to which people would walk to attend concerts, outdoor theater, and community events.

City staff viewed the park as a way to improve the city's pedestrian circulation system—thus supporting the city's land use code, which was revised in the early 1980s to encourage a more pedestrian-friendly downtown environment. The park was also intended to provide a transition between adjacent retail areas, multifamily housing, and high-rise commercial office towers. Finally, city officials and planners aspired to create a signature park that would help forge a new identity for the downtown as a distinctly urban place. Up to this time, Bellevue was best known as the home of the Bellevue Square regional shopping mall.

The Design Competition

To muster political and financial support and provide direction for the park's development, Bozeman created

the 28-member Downtown Park Citizens Committee, which represented a broad spectrum of civic and business interests. One of the committee's first recommendations was that the city hold an international design competition to generate enthusiasm for the project.

The program for the competition was based on the results of a survey asking 55,000 households and businesses what they wanted to see in a downtown central park. Most of the 5,000 respondents asked for a passive, open greenspace where they could sit and read, eat lunch, or just people-watch.

The park committee raised $140,000 from businesses and private sources to fund most of the competition. The city elected to finance the $30,000 required to conduct the survey and to acquire professional assistance to set up the competition process. The cost of $170,000 for the survey and competition represented about 3.5 percent of the total cost of designing and constructing the first phase of the park.

A total of 67 participants, each of whom paid $100 to enter the competition, submitted entries to be judged by a jury of design professionals and lay people. At the recommendation of competition consultant Edward Wundram, Vincent Scully, then Sterling Professor of Art and Architecture History at Yale University, served as jury adviser.

The first stage of the competition limited the contestants to a proposal for the city's 17.5 acres. The three winners of the first stage were then asked to make recommendations for a master plan. In December 1984, the jury recommended the concept submitted by Beckley/

The wide promenade is lined with London plane trees that will reach a height of 80 feet. Light standards in the classic shape of obelisks line the promenade. The hardscape that is used throughout the park holds up better under heavy use than softer lawn surfaces. The crushed granite paths do not rut as much as some other materials and are thus easier for handicapped people to use.

Michael I. Shopeun

Myers, a Milwaukee-based architecture firm that had worked largely in urban locations. After city staff completed an environmental impact statement on the three final designs, the city council voted in April 1985 to accept the jury's recommendation.

Although there was surprise that the winning team was an out-of-town architecture firm rather than a local landscape architecture firm, the simple, bold form of the winning design lived up to Bellevue's hope of creating a park that would serve as a strong identifying image for the city.[2] Beckley/Myers teamed with a local landscape architecture firm, MacLeod Reckord, for input on some technical design issues, such as selection of vegetation and construction materials.

The design competition was an important element of the entire development process. It helped Bellevue's image by showing that the city had come of age as an urban center. (Indeed, the covers of Eastside telephone books now feature Downtown Park instead of the Bellevue Square shopping center.) It helped the city and the public visualize in precise physical terms their long-term aspirations for park development. All entries were displayed at public places throughout the city, and citizens were encouraged to comment by filling out cards. And to some extent, the competition protected the design selection process from political compromise.

The Beckley/Myers design draws from a landscape tradition rarely seen in the Northwest. For the most part, Seattle-area parks are influenced by English country garden design, which emphasizes a natural, informal look. By contrast, Downtown Park looks to the work of André Le Notre and other 17th-century French landscape designers, who arranged open spaces in more formal, geometric compositions and used objects and hard surfaces to frame space. In the Beckley/Myers design, it was the powerful geometry and sheer simplicity of the circle as the main unifying form that ultimately won over the jury.

Today at the park, the circular canal drops down a few inches at regular intervals to match the slope of the land. The canal is ringed by a wide path of crushed granite (like that used in Parisian parks), which is in turn ringed by a circle of plane trees that alternate with obelisk-shaped light fixtures. Within this series of concentric circles lies an open meadow with a slightly off-center cluster of trees. Sherrill Myers, who worked in Europe for many years, also looked to the works of the French Impressionists to imbue this urban oasis with a spirit of tranquility and calm.

As is the case with most urban parks, safety was a concern. Myers initially wanted to strengthen the edges of the park by creating a series of small enclosures on the periphery, an approach that was abandoned on the advice of the police department. To encourage extensive use by women and children, the spaces needed to be open, relatively free of shrubs, and with unobstructed horizontal sight lines.

Easy-to-maintain vegetation and materials help to control maintenance costs in the park. For example, the hardscape used throughout the park holds up better under heavy traffic than do softer lawn surfaces. Crushed granite does not rut as much as some other materials and thus provides a stable surface for wheelchairs. In addition, granite is relatively porous, minimizing the need for detention facilities for runoff. London plane trees were selected for their durability: if they are vandalized, their exfoliating bark grows back. Also, because the leaves are large and tend not to decay in water, they do not easily clog the water features of the park.

Private Contributions for the Public Good

The Bellevue Downtown Park project was financed and developed through a public/private partnership approach that involved close cooperation among city government, business leaders, and elected officials. The estimated cost for developing the park was $4 million. The city had purchased the site with councilmanic bonds, but in late 1984, a $2 million general-obligation bond issue for park development lost by a 0.4 percent margin. A coalition of Bellevue's civic and business leaders then formed a nonprofit organization to lease the site from the city for $1 per year. The nonprofit group launched a fundraising drive to raise $1.8 million for development of the park's first phase—about one-third of the project (mainly the eastern section), including construction of two-thirds of the belvedere and nearly half the canal. Once Phase I was completed, the improved site was returned to the city for maintenance and operation. At that point, citizens voted to use public bonds to fund the second development phase.

Part of the success of the fundraising drive was attributed to the strategy of creating a private entity to develop and construct the first development phase. Many private contributors, particularly in the city's corporate and business segments, believed that their dollars would be better spent and more efficiently managed by a private entity than by a public one. This arrangement helped dispel the belief that the public sector ought to be financing this public project.

The fundraising drive, led by John Ellis, then president of a Bellevue-based utility company, set a target of $1.8 million in private contributions. A main strategy was to solicit contributions of $30,000 to $125,000 from major corporations including Boeing, Pac Car, Rainier Bank, and Puget Sound Power and Light Company. A second major funding source was smaller businesses and corporations located in Bellevue, whose contributions ranged from $1,000 to $30,000. Major individual donors contributed between $1,000 and $50,000 apiece, and some 2,000 individual donors contributed anywhere from $5 to $1,000 (see Figure 1).

While more than 2,000 businesses and individuals contributed to the campaign, the major corporate donors provided the lion's share; their generosity was fueled, in part, by awareness that the park would provide an important amenity for Bellevue's rapidly burgeoning CBD. The announcement of several significant donations from large corporations jump-started the campaign. After the largest corporations had established a contribution ceiling, a subcommittee of influential business people systematically canvassed the business community. Once the bank with the largest asset base had contributed, say, $100,000, other banks were approached to contribute an amount proportional to their share of the market.

An additional fundraising tactic was to inscribe the names of all donors contributing $100 or more on a granite monument located in the belvedere at the north entry to the park. The monument was the main "hook" in a direct mail brochure and in newspaper solicitations.

A public-relations firm created a series of radio, television, and newspaper advertisements and televised public service announcements. An advantage of these media bursts—apart from the money they generated—was that they represented a level of sophistication and credibility not generally associated with public sector marketing programs. According to Lee Springgate, director of Bellevue Parks and Community Services Department, "There is no question in our minds that a private public-relations firm is in a much better position to churn out professional, state-of-the-art products. Public agencies are all too frequently constrained by low budgets, limited expertise, and the realities of political life."[3]

Additional marketing endeavors included a five-minute video, feature stories, direct mailings, special events, displays, promotional breakfasts, service-club appeals, and associated merchandising. Because of these efforts, Downtown Park received much greater exposure and recognition than any of the city's other parks.

Development and Construction

For the first phase of development, a public oversight committee—which included the city manager, the park director, a park board member, the mayor pro tem, and representatives of the private nonprofit group—was created to hire the architect, review and approve drawings and specifications, and monitor construction. The private corporation complied with all applicable federal, state, and local laws; secured insurance coverage; and obtained the required permits. It was also bound by the terms of the lease to construct the park according to the master plan approved by the city council. The lease terms required the corporation to submit monthly status reports

Michael I. Shopeun

Water spills over a series of small waterfalls and cascades into a shallow pond in the park's southwest quadrant.

to the city, which had the right to suspend work that did not meet with approved plans and specifications.

Fundraising was on an almost parallel track with construction. This pay-as-you-go approach was politically expedient in that beginning work immediately demonstrated visible progress and assured the community that the park would become a reality. This strategy also lent a sense of urgency to fundraising efforts and left no doubt in contributors' minds about how the money would be spent. However, it also raised some concerns: mainly, that the city might inherit a partially finished site and would then have to use public funds to protect it from deteriorating.

A disadvantage of the pay-as-you-go approach was that some construction had to be delayed to enable the fundraisers to keep pace, thus extending the construction schedule from nine to 18 months. Delay also created a number of construction glitches, making it difficult to purchase supplies ahead of time and to coordinate the work of subcontractors.

Unlike Phase I, which was built by the private sector, Phase II was paid for exclusively with public funds. Public satisfaction with Phase I paved the way for 70 percent approval of a 1988 park bond, which included $3 million for the second phase of development for the park. Phase II included completion of the western half of the canal, meadow, and promenade; construction of the waterfall and pond; and completion of the belvedere. Phase I was completed in the fall of 1987, and Phase II in September 1990.

The city had far greater control over the development and construction of Phase II. The lease agreement under Phase I, specifying roles, responsibilities, and consequences for both the public and private partici-

pants, substantially curtailed the administrative control of the Bellevue Parks and Community Services Department and removed its authority over certain construction decisions. Richard VanDeMark, who managed the park development for the city, noted that jurisdictions considering using a similar public/private approach for park development should be prepared to deal with the delicate situations that may arise when the public partner does not control the purse strings.

Downtown Park Spurs Additional Park Development

When public interest generated by Downtown Park translated into an unprecedented level of financial and political support for other park projects, no one was more surprised than Lee Springgate, who had anticipated that the downtown park would be a "zero sum game where investment in the downtown park meant less money for parks elsewhere in the city." Between 1984 and 1990, $84 million was authorized for acquisition, development, and renovation of other parks.

The public/private partnering approach, which was first used for Downtown Park, is now de rigueur for park development in Bellevue. For example, in the case of the 100-acre Wilburton Park, home to the Bellevue Botanical Garden, Springgate forged a financial partnership with the Bellevue Botanical Garden Society to raise private contributions for park development and maintenance. He has also worked with the city's historical society to help raise funds to renovate a home in the Mercer Slough, an area that is now preserved as wetlands and a large green open space. Springgate believes that when public entities team up with private partners, they need to be willing to alter routine decision making and implementation processes. "When you have a partner and you ask them to help achieve a goal," said Springgate, "you have to give them some authority. That's part of the deal. You can't ask people to give financial and political support and then expect it to be done exactly the way you want. Not everything with Downtown Park went exactly the way we planned. But without our private partners, the park would not have been built."

Completing Downtown Park

Since 1990, the city has gradually acquired additional parcels of the 600-square-foot superblock to add to the park site, which now totals some 20 acres, including several parcels on the southeast corner of the park that were necessary to complete the original circle design. Against the staff's advice, the city council originally resisted spending more money on the park, but when

Figure 1 • Sources of Funds

	Amount	Percentage
Private contributions for Phase I	$1,700,000	6.0%
General CIP revenue		
Councilmanic bonds	14,388,000	48.0
Debt service	7,108,000	24.0
Other	1,460,000	5.0
1988 bond issue	3,450,000	11.0
Land purchase revolving fund	600,000	2.0
Rental revenue	423,000	1.0
1984 bond interest earnings	360,000	1.0
Forward thrust bond interest	170,000	0.5
Private contributions	145,000	0.5
Miscellaneous revenue sources	42,000	1.0
Total revenue sources	$29,846,000	100.0%

a developer secured an option in 1995 to purchase one of the parcels to build a residential project, political pressure mounted for the city to buy out the option, and it ultimately did.

Skyrocketing land values have been the principal challenge to additional land acquisitions. Since the park site was purchased in 1983, costs in the immediate vicinity have about doubled.

Parking and Other Issues

Downtown Park has about 100 dedicated parking spaces, and parking has been controversial from the start. Although the intention was that the primary users—downtown residents and workers—would walk to the park, the reality is that many people drive to the park, and additional parking is needed. Because Downtown Park is adjacent to Bellevue Square, which provides acres of free parking for shoppers, the management of the shopping center has been concerned that park users would occupy parking spaces intended for shopping center patrons.

One proposal to increase available parking is to build a municipal garage beneath the park, which might be shared by the Bellevue Art Museum, currently tucked away on the top floor of Bellevue Square. The museum is considering the park as one of three potential sites for its future home. Retailers located on Bellevue's Main Street, a block south of the park, would also welcome additional parking for their customers. Because it has a major grade difference, which could lessen excavation costs, the southwest corner of the park may be a good location for a garage. However, this spot is now occupied by an intensively used temporary children's playground, which would need to be moved elsewhere in the park.

Downtown Park was always envisioned as a city park designed for passive recreational uses, not as a regional facility. Programming is deliberately low key; public events include the Fourth of July celebration, Shakespeare in the Grass, and a series of children's concerts. (One reason for downplaying public events that would draw large crowds was to assure Bellevue Square owner Kemper Freeman that mall parking spaces would not be usurped by park patrons.)

Whether or not to include active recreational activities at the park is still being debated. Although the original citizen survey showed a strong preference for a passive "green oasis" to offset Bellevue's increasingly urban

The city of Bellevue wanted to create a tranquil green oasis like New York's Central Park, where people who live and work in the CBD can take respite from an intensely urban environment.

The city's land use code required developers to build a through-block pedestrian connection to strengthen links between Main Street, in "Old Bellevue," and the park.

• Freezing the pond for ice skating during the winter months;
• Setting permanent park boundaries and clearly delineating future parcels for public acquisition (to give more security to owners of adjacent property);
• Completing the original circle design;
• Improving the design of entryways from the south and northeast corners.

Using the Park to Spur Residential Development

The strategy of developing parks and open spaces in downtown Bellevue was part of the city's overall effort to create a more lively pedestrian environment, which would in turn enhance the market for multifamily development and draw a residential population to the city. The strategy is slowly working: the two principal residential neighborhoods now developing in downtown Bellevue are both adjacent to parks or urban open spaces. To capitalize on the cachet of a park address, several developers have incorporated the word *park* into the names of their developments—Parkridge and Parkside, for example.

"I strongly believe that the development of Downtown Park was a catalyst for the residential development around it," said Matthew Terry, director of the Bellevue Department of Community Development. Developers confirmed this view. One property owner said that the close proximity of Downtown Park to his parcel was critical to his decision to buy the land. When Levin Lynch bought his parcel in 1980, he thought he was lucky to be close to a major regional shopping mall. Then when Downtown Park was developed next to his site, "that was like winning a lotto ticket," said Lynch. "It's a blue-ribbon location to be next to a regional mall and a park."

Many of the residents in Bellevue's recent urban developments are empty nesters. Instead of doing yard work, these people want to exercise by jogging in the park or walking their dogs there. Robert Wallace, managing partner of Wallace Properties Group, says that it is the pastoral character of Downtown Park that makes it a valuable amenity. The park's value in relation to residential development would diminish, according to Wallace, if ball fields and more active uses were introduced.

character, some residents believe that converting the space to more active uses, such as ball fields and tennis courts, would make the best use of the public's investment. In the view of city park staff, many other parks in the system provide active recreational opportunities, and Downtown Park should provide unique opportunities instead of duplicating those already available at other locations.

Downtown Park was designed to serve office workers in the CBD and residents in the high-density housing planned nearby. Although some new multifamily housing has been built adjacent to the park, the neighborhood is still in the embryonic stage. Since most future park users—neighborhood residents—have not yet arrived, a conundrum emerges: how does the city simultaneously plan and design a park for the future and maximize public investment to meet present needs?

To address these and other park development issues, a task force was organized to make recommendations to the city council regarding the update of the master plan for Downtown Park. Some of the issues being considered by the task force include the following:

• Identifying a location for a permanent children's play area;
• Developing an amphitheater, as originally planned, which would bring a new dimension of entertainment to the park—dance, opera, classical music performances, and live theater;

Housing in Bellevue's CBD

In 1994, when a 24-story, mixed-use residential development opened, it was the first high-rise condominium built in the city's CBD. That same year, a 97-unit condominium development opened on the south edge of Downtown Park. Several apartments and condominium projects were also built next to the new multistory regional library. But the market for urban housing in Bellevue is a recent phenomenon. Until the early 1990s, there had been no residential growth in the downtown for some 20 years. As Matthew Terry noted, the demand for urban housing was untested, so lending institutions viewed the downtown as a risky investment. Moreover, during the mid-1980s, overwhelming pressure for office and retail development virtually squeezed out opportunities for residential growth. Finally, said Terry, "there was a lack of amenities that would create the kind of character to make residential development successful."

To make up for this lack, the city invested in a host of public improvements and amenities in the downtown, specifically with an eye toward residential development— parks, open spaces, cultural facilities, and pedestrian improvements. These include the 400-seat Meydenbauer Convention Center, new parks and public plazas, the Metro Transit Center, and the Bellevue Regional Library. The private sector has also invested in amenities that support residential growth, including a 100,000-volume bookstore, a doll museum, a major hardware store, a supermarket, drugstores, banks, and boutiques, not to mention a spate of restaurants with international cuisine. However, amenities such as movie theaters, which generate nighttime activity, are still lacking, although mall owner Kemper Freeman is seeking permits to construct a multiplex theater northwest of Bellevue Square.

The first new housing development, the McKee/Parkside, which borders the south edge of Downtown Park, opened in March 1994 and sold out almost immediately. The mostly two-bedroom luxury homes face Main Street in "Old Bellevue," with views of Meydenbauer Bay on Lake Washington to the west. Parkside, the second phase of the project, faces NE 1st Street and looks directly onto Downtown Park. Units in this second phase are larger and significantly more expensive. The five-story, wood-frame structure, with two levels of below-grade parking, contains 97 units at a density of about 80 units to the acre.

Intracorp's McKee/Parkside development represents the urbane, high-quality development that city planners had always envisioned for the park's edge. Local developers are encouraged by the quick sellout of the Intracorp project. Intracorp's strategy was to persuade potential buyers that the concentration of nearby urban amenities justified a major change in lifestyle. Many of the residents had left large, single-family homes in the Eastside suburbs. Downtown Park, an old-fashioned Main Street, as well as restaurants, specialty boutiques, and a regional shopping mall—all within walking distance

—were some of the urban amenities that Intracorp actively marketed.

The other main residential neighborhood in the CBD is located in the northeast quadrant, in the vicinity of the Bellevue Regional Library and Ashwood Park. The city persuaded the library district to jointly purchase the ten-acre site, part of which would be used for the new regional library; the remaining four acres—Ashwood Park—have not yet been developed and are now used mainly as a soccer and baseball field.

The regional library has acted as a magnet for residential development. Su Development Corporation built Park Place, a six-story luxury condominium project, across from the library. The ground floor retail space, occupied by a deli and a hair salon, sold out almost immediately. The development attracted mostly older residents, between 55 and 70 years old. The same developer is building another for-sale project two blocks away and is considering developing a rental project one block south of Ashwood Park. President John Su notes that the library and park are highly desirable amenities for his developments. Many prospective buyers tell him that the attractive appearance and high-quality design of the library building also drew them to this location.

The city recently completed construction of Ashwood Plaza, which features several major art pieces and serves as a public gathering space at the southeast entry to the library. Bellevue's insistence on high-caliber design

The park has become a popular spot for walkers and joggers.

The park was a catalyst for residential development such as the McKee/Parkside on the south edge of the park. The five-story, wood-frame building above a podium garage is becoming the model for residential development in the area.

for its public places has helped raise the design threshold for private development.

SECO Development is also building several residential projects in the same area. Parkridge apartments, located next to Park Place, is targeted to a broad range of renters. President Michael Christ is proceeding with several additional mixed-use developments nearby, including two projects that will cater to seniors. Christ notes that seniors already living in the area enjoy walking to Ashwood Park and watching the baseball or soccer games. This park, along with the nearby community and cultural facilities—the library, the doll museum, and the performing arts center—is an important part of the nexus of activity that is drawing seniors to this part of town.

To better connect these different facilities, the city invested in a variety of pedestrian improvements, including sidewalks and street trees. The city also created a local improvement district (LID) for NE 10th that runs on the south side of the library and park. The LID paid for landscaping improvements, wider sidewalks, and a midblock pedestrian connection. Michael Christ emphasized that "good pedestrian streets, where traffic is slowed to no more than 25 to 30 miles an hour, are essential to the success" of his residential developments. The older residents he is targeting for his current projects want an environment where they can walk safely and cross the streets comfortably.

Linkages to Other City Parks

Downtown Park is a focal point for the city's Olmsted-inspired park system, which includes 2,000 acres of parks and open space connected by the Lake-to-Lake

Trail and Greenway, which extends from Lake Washington to Lake Sammamish. Fifty years after Frederick Law Olmsted designed New York City's Central Park, the city of Seattle commissioned his son and stepson to design a network of open spaces. The Olmsteds envisioned a system of parks, greenbelts, and boulevards wrapping east all the way around Lake Washington. They likened the greenway to a string of jewels in an emerald necklace, where parks and open spaces would be visually and functionally interconnected.

Eight decades later, a number of Eastside parks and open spaces carry out the Olmsteds' vision. Much of the greenway has been completed in Bellevue with uniform directional signage and pedestrian amenities. Meydenbauer Beach Park, to the west, connects to Downtown Park via a street and walkway system. Downtown Park will also connect with the nearby marina, which the city purchased in 1985.

Notes

1. See Terry Jill Lassar, *Carrots & Sticks: New Zoning Downtown* (Washington, D.C.: ULI–the Urban Land Institute, 1989), 124–127, 148–152, for discussions of the Bellevue downtown plan and land use program.

2. The Beckley/Meyers proposal was also the only one to call for the acquisition of three additional acres to complete the two-block area containing the 17.5 acres.

3. A primary source of information and commentary for this report was Lee Springgate, "Public/Private Park Development: A Case Study" (paper presented to the National Recreation and Park Association, New Orleans, September 1987).

Bellevue Regional Library has been a popular amenity for residents. Ashwood Plaza, at the southeast entry, was one of several public improvements made by the city to enhance the pedestrian environment and provide public gathering spaces.

Project Data • Downtown Park

Development Schedule

Initial site acquired	December 1983
Planning started	August 1983
Design competition conducted	July 1984
Master plan approved	April 1985
Construction started (Phase I)	August 1986
Construction completed (Phase I)	September 1987
Construction started (Phase II)	September 1989
Construction completed (Phase II)	September 1990
Park opened (Phase II)	September 1990
Project completed	Ongoing

Financing Information

Funding Source	Amount	Percentage of Total
Private	$1,766,000	6%
Local	28,234,000	94
Total	$30,000,000	100%

Development Cost Information

Site acquisition cost	$23,618,000
Site improvement costs	
Excavation/demolition	$942,000
Grading	1,092,000
Utilities	1,013,721
Paving	90,000
Curbs/sidewalks	124,700
Landscaping	251,650
Fees/general conditions	211,300
Concrete	1,114,700
Other	462,662
Total site improvement costs	$5,302,733
Construction costs (buildings)	
Structure	$300,000
Heating, ventilation, and air conditioning (HVAC)	5,000
Electrical	75,000
Plumbing/sprinklers	5,600
Fees	NA[1]
Total construction costs	$385,600
Soft costs	
Architecture	$17,500
Landscape architecture	241,798
Engineering	76,810
Project management	284,777
Marketing	NA
Other (taxes)	441,360
Total soft costs	$1,062,245
Total site acquisition and development costs	$30,368,578

Construction and Operating Costs

Amenity	Construction Cost	Operating Cost
Streetscapes	$160,000	$15,000
Parking lot landscaping	43,000	8,000
Parking	180,000	10,000
Signage	5,000	500
Plantings		
(foundation, specimens, gardens)	208,650	108,000
Water features	1,013,721	100,000
Entrances	490,000	16,000
Land engineering (e.g.,contouring)	1,092,000	NA
Furniture	58,000	4,000
Plazas		12,000
Hardscape features	500,000	13,000
Environmental features	35,000	NA
Lighting (decorative/safety)	48,000	2,200
Special plantings (annual flowers)	0	4,300
Other park amenities	1,169,362	50,000
Rest rooms	300,000	12,000
Total	$5,302,733	$355,000

Operating Information

Annual operating expenses	
Taxes	NA
Insurance	NA
Repair and maintenance	$250,000
Management	10,000
Utilities	100,000
Total operating expenses	$360,000
Annual gross revenues	
Special event rentals	($5,000)
Total	$355,000

Note

1. Not applicable.

Elliott Donnelley Youth Center Park
Chicago

David Mulvihill

The Elliott Donnelley Youth Center (EDYC) sits on South Michigan Avenue on Chicago's south side in an area known as Bronzeville. In the 1930s and 1940s, Bronzeville was Chicago's answer to Harlem, the hub of African-American culture in that city. The neighborhood makes claim to such notable figures as Nat King Cole, Sarah Vaughn, and Jimmy Williams, all of whom performed at the blues and jazz clubs that once lined the streets. Other famous names to spring from the neighborhood include Redd Foxx, Joe Louis, Marla Gibbs, and heavyweight boxer Oliver McCall. Author Richard Wright and poet Gwendolyn Brooks have also called the area home.

Unfortunately, like many other once-great inner-city neighborhoods, this section of Chicago is more likely to be featured on the evening news than in an entertainment guide. Now it is best known as the site of the world's largest public housing complex, the infamous Robert Taylor Homes. Often referred to as one of the most crime-ridden and impoverished communities in the country, the complex was named for the former chairman of the Chicago Housing Authority—who was, ironically, a strong advocate of low-density, scattered-site housing.

The Elliott Donnelley Youth Center, a former Boys Club built in 1924, is one of eight Chicago Youth Centers (CYCs) serving low-income communities throughout the city. Founded in 1956, the CYCs provide educational and recreational programs for young people, working with local corporations, cultural institutions, and educational institutions to develop programs that range from computer labs to video production. Besides being safe places for local kids to hang out, CYCs offer youth and adults courses in swimming, literacy development, GED (general equivalency diploma) preparation, graphic arts, and use of the Internet. Funding for the CYCs comes from the United Way, Community Development Block Grants, and private donations. CYC programs serve more than 10,000 young people each year. About 200 to 250 young people use the Elliott Donnelley Youth Center daily, and about 2,000 annually participate in the center's educational programs.

Across the street from the entrance to the EDYC is a dilapidated, multistory brick building that once housed an ice cream factory. Adjacent to the center on both sides of the building were vacant lots where a grand hotel and retail store once stood. For many years, the lots next to the center stood vacant, littered with rubble and debris. Today, through the efforts of center staff and youth, the Openlands Project, local artists, and a host of sponsors and volunteers, two of the lots have been transformed into a colorful playground, sculpture park, and community garden. Development of the park evolved over a period of more than two years and was a genuine community effort that involved scores of local residents, particularly children, and more than a dozen sponsors.

A Trip to England and Two Bags of Dirt

In 1992, Mr. and Mrs. Laurin Healy, longtime supporters of Chicago Youth Centers and the Openlands Project, made a trip to England. The Healys admired the beautiful gardens they found in England and wondered why such beauty couldn't be replicated in America,

Before: On the site of a once-grand hotel, an empty, litter-filled lot adjacent to the youth center provided the space for the sculpture park and community garden. The lot was donated to the EDYC by the city of Chicago.

particularly in the inner cities, where it is most lacking. After returning to the United States, the Healys shared their thoughts with Jerry Adelmann, executive director of the Openlands Project, a Chicago-based, not-for-profit organization dedicated to improving life in northeastern Illinois by increasing and enhancing open space. Adelmann, in turn, contacted Delbert Arsenault, executive director of Chicago Youth Centers, to set up a meeting.

Even before the Healys' trip, Marrice Coverson, director of the EDYC, had had a similar notion. Coverson purchased a couple of bags of topsoil and some seeds, and with the help of the kids at the EDYC began a modest community garden in one of the vacant lots adjacent to the center. The project was an instant hit with the kids, and Coverson began thinking about how to expand the idea.

Arsenault was aware of Coverson's efforts at community gardening and thought the EDYC was the ideal place for the Healys' idea to take form, especially given the large (90-by-160-foot) vacant lot that sat on the south side of the center. In late 1992, the Healys and staff from the Openlands Project and the EDYC met over lunch to discuss the possibilities. During the meeting, the Healys offered $50,000 in seed money to get the project started, and the outline of the plan was arranged. Karen Hobbs, of the Openlands Project, was assigned to work with the youth center to facilitate a community-based approach to developing the project. The vision for the project quickly moved beyond the creation of a community garden, expanding to include a recreational component for the children. Although the youth center houses a gymnasium and swimming pool, residents of the neighborhood had long bemoaned the lack of other recreational activities for local children.

Shortly after the meeting with the Healys, Jerry Adelmann visited the site, and the scope of the project was further expanded. Mr. Imagination (a.k.a. Gregory Warmack), a local, self-taught artist whose work is part of the Smithsonian Institution's permanent collection and who is a friend of Adelmann, had told Adelmann of his desire to construct a grotto in Chicago.

After visiting the site with Adelmann, Mr. Imagination —best known for his bottlecap thrones and clothing items, paintbrush people, and reliefs carved in sandstone material reclaimed from a local foundry—decided that he would like to build his grotto at the EDYC, using recycled materials and found objects from the neighborhood. He also recruited the talents of Kevin Orth and David Philpot, two other local, self-taught artists, both of whom also work with recycled and found objects. Orth and Philpot, who have been represented in galleries in Chicago, Michigan, and New York City, were enthusiastic about participating in the project. It had a particularly special meaning to Philpot, who was from the neighborhood and had learned to swim at the EDYC in his youth. Philpot thought his involvement in the project was an ideal way to give something back to the EDYC, which had given him a place to go in his youth. He also felt that "it was a great opportunity for the children to observe a living artist in their own community," as opposed to watching "sports heroes on television that the children never see in their community." Other local artists also eventually became involved.

A Sense of Ownership

The staff of the EDYC and officials from the Openlands Project agreed from the beginning that for the project to

Children from the EDYC were intimately involved in the park's construction. Here, children work with a local artist constructing planters for the center's entrance.

be successful and remain viable, the community would need to be intimately involved in all aspects. Said Coverson, "We wanted to instill in the children and residents a sense of community ownership." Karen Hobbs, of the Openlands Project, was given the task of sparking local interest and involvement by going into the community to explain what the project was and how the residents could help.

In January 1993, meetings began with community residents, children, and parents from the EDYC to discuss development of the playground and gardens and to set priorities. At this time the EDYC board, made up of local school representatives and residents, was put in charge of project oversight. The board took charge of publicizing the project and seeking donations of money, talent, and labor. Because the project relied heavily on donations and sponsorships, planning did not proceed in a typically linear fashion. Project funding and the availability of talent and labor were sporadic, so the park's planners were forced to continually rethink their plans in light of available resources.

To create a vision for the park, a design charrette for children was organized over several Saturdays. The staff at the EDYC was aware of studies showing that children's perceptions of parks can differ markedly from those of adults, so about 20 randomly chosen children aged five to 13 were asked to draw what they felt the park should look like. Landscape architect Daryl Garrison was hired to participate in the charrette and was charged with formulating a design for the park by synthesizing the ideas depicted in the drawings. The children's sketches were also used to determine the criteria for selecting playground equipment, and the children took part in the final selection of equipment. A field trip was organized in which some of the children visited existing playgrounds —and even playground equipment manufacturers—to explore further options.

To accurately envision where and how the equipment should be placed, children from the EDYC participated in a mock development of the site, dressing as different pieces of playground equipment and situating themselves in various positions on the site. According to Karen Hobbs, "The kids had a lot of fun with this exercise and it worked to reinforce the notion that they were the decision makers for the park."

Local residents and children were also closely involved in the planning and development of the landscaping portion of the park. It was decided early on that the park would include a community garden and landscaping component, both to fulfill the Healys' original idea and to expand on Coverson's activities. Grading of a portion of the site for planting began in May 1993. After working in the charrettes to determine the placement of the

Landscaping and gardening are an integral part of the park. Installation of the plantings and garden was a community-wide effort involving more than 150 local residents.

plants, more than 150 local residents and youth came together to plant many of the trees, shrubs, and flowers that now fill the park. Artist Kevin Orth worked at the same time with the children to design two planters at the entrance to the center. The planting was supervised by two staff members, program coordinator Leslie Clark and facilities manager Jerome Washington, both of whom had obtained certification as master gardeners in order to ensure the proper installation and maintenance of the gardens and landscaping.

Completion of the site grading was delayed by an unforeseen problem: the site's sewer system had deteriorated over the years, and the resulting drainage problems had begun to cause serious damage to the building. Before work on the park could continue, a new drainage system had to be installed, and the building's south wall had to be extensively repaired. Finally, in May of 1994, site grading for the entire park was completed, and center staff, youth, and local residents once again worked side by side, this time to plant the community garden. The garden is located on a smaller lot separated from the playground and sculpture park by a narrow alley.

Found Artists and Their Art

In the fall of 1993, the restoration of an existing mural on one of the south sidewalls of the center became the first piece of art in the park. The mural, which honors the past prominence of the area as a center of African-American culture, is entitled *Another Time's Voice Remembers My Passion's Humanity*. Originally painted in 1979 by Calvin Jones and Mitchell Caton, the mural

Totems representing traditional African carvings serve as the entranceway to the park, while murals on either side of the building offer depictions of black culture in America.

was restored to its original condition by Bernand Williams and Paige Hinson, with the assistance of the Chicago Public Art Group.

Shortly after the restoration of the mural, a chain-link fence was erected around the site of the playground sculpture park to discourage vandalism and to protect the children using the playground.

Beginning in early 1994, enough funding had been raised to allow artists Mr. Imagination, Kevin Orth, and David Philpot to begin working on the project. The artists agreed that the children would be an integral part of the process. Said Philpot, "The project was a great opportunity to see how art affects kids who don't normally have a chance to be involved in artistic creations." Toward that end, the three artists began to hold workshops with the children. In these workshops, the artists discussed the media they worked with and planned with the children what form their various pieces would take. Because the artists worked with recycled and found objects, the children were able to collect many of the elements for the sculptures. While the artists were paid for their participation, Hobbs points out that "given the huge amount of time they contributed working with the children it probably worked out to earning about $2 an hour."

David Philpot had done much of his previous work in small, elegant wood carvings. For this project, he and another artist, Milton Mizenburg, chose to create "totems" carved from the trunks of large ailanthus trees, weed-like plants that grow wild on vacant land throughout Chicago. The six sculptures, which serve as entrance arches to the park, range in height from eight to 15 feet and resemble ceremonial African figure carvings. The children actively participated in stripping, sanding, carv-

ing, and applying stains and other finishes to the totems. To show what the trees looked like before being carved and to allow visitors to the park to leave their mark, the artists left one of the trunks uncarved. The totems were finished and installed in September 1994.

In August 1994, Kevin Orth began constructing his contribution to the sculpture park. Orth's *Circus Shrine* is a 14-foot-high, bright yellow, conical sculpture that resembles a clown hat. The piece is constructed of reinforced concrete, and its rough exterior is covered with a variety of objects donated by local residents, including hubcaps, bottlecaps, and costume jewelry. Red "smiley faces" on the exterior of the piece are meant to represent the children who come to the center. Children from the center helped select bricks from a nearby demolition site to be used to form the base of the shrine. A time capsule, containing items such as letters and photos from the children, is suspended from the top of the piece.

In the summer of 1994, planning began for a second mural to complement the existing mural. Artist Marcus Akinlana was hired, and community residents began to discuss the theme of the mural. The theme ultimately chosen was the great migration, African Americans' historic movement from the rural South to the industrial Northeast and Midwest in search of a better life. The site chosen for the painting was another southern wall of the center, separated from the first mural by a small courtyard. The mural, which was begun in September 1994, illustrates various occupations held by migrants upon their arrival in the North.

A fourth local artist, Phil Schuster, began working with the children in September 1994. In this instance, youth from the center actively recruited Schuster and obtained funding to work with him. Coverson explains that by this point in the process, the youth were inspired to "give something back" to the center. To do so, they wrote a successful proposal for $5,000 in funding from Youth As Resources. Schuster began workshops with the children to construct benches for the park. The concrete benches feature a mosaic exterior formed from donations of costume jewelry and from objects found in the neighborhood. Each bench features a different theme, including a leaf motif, "woman," and an aquarian scene.

One of the most ambitious pieces in the park is the meditation grotto constructed by Mr. Imagination. The cylindrical, cavelike structure has four arched entrances. Inspired by the stone structures of the European Catholic tradition, the grotto stands more than 12 feet high and has a diameter of about five feet. The frame of the sculpture is made from welded scrap metal, with a densely textured cement overlay. Atop the structure, a sculpted concrete angel overlooks the playground. Glass and terra cotta brick remnants collected from the rubble of the hotel that once stood on the lot—along with bottle caps and other found objects—were mixed into the cement, creating a glittering, mosaiclike finish both inside and outside the grotto. Children's handprints decorate the cement floor of the grotto. A dedication on one of the inside walls is in remembrance of two of the center's children: one was shot accidentally in a local drive-by shooting; the other drowned at the EDYC swimming pool. Under the floor of the grotto is another time capsule filled with letters, photographs of the children, and various other objects. In the center of the grotto is a concrete stool fished from the rubble of the hotel.

By the spring of 1995, all of the sculptures for the park had been completed, and decisions regarding the selection and placement of playground equipment had been made. With a generous contribution from the Monsanto Corporation, the EDYC was able to purchase the playground equipment, which volunteers from the company spent two full days helping to install. The equipment includes a slide; a unique, spring-loaded, multiple-rider seesaw; a diamond-shaped sandbox with a fort; and other climbing equipment.

With installation of the playground equipment complete, the final landscaping was undertaken. The ground surrounding the equipment is covered with soft wood chips, and different sections of the playground are defined by large wooden timbers donated by the city of Chicago. A brick sidewalk leads from the center to the park's entrance. The sidewalk is still being completed. Each patron who purchases a brick can have his or her name engraved on it. From the park entrance, a cement sidewalk winds through the playground to each of the sculptures and benches.

Funding and Faith

The development and construction of the playground sculpture park resulted from a concerted effort on the part of many dedicated individuals and organizations. Karen Hobbs, of the Openlands Project, points out that "the project differed from most in that it progressed in fits and starts based on the availability of funds." Balanced against this uncertainty in funding was the need to keep the process going to sustain the commun-

Originally painted in 1979, the mural *Another Time's Voice Remembers My Passion's Humanity* was restored when construction of the park began.

Artist Kevin Orth created this 14-foot-high sculpture, constructed from reinforced concrete. Its rough exterior is covered with objects donated by residents. The "smiley faces" are meant to represent the children who come to the center; a time capsule, with items donated by the children, is suspended from the top of the piece.

ity's faith in the project. The Healys' $25,000 contribution eventually blossomed into nearly $250,000 in contributions from a variety of sources. But the project's planners encountered delay and uncertainty along the way. The enthusiasm the project generated among the children helped to keep the community focused on the project's ultimate completion.

Besides the Healys, some major contributors to the project included the Joyce Foundation, the Lurie Foundation, and the Monsanto Corporation. The city of Chicago also assisted by donating the vacant lots to the center and supplying the abandoned tree trunks for the totem sculptures. The Terra Museum of Art and the Marwen Foundation served the project in an art education capa-

city. Other sponsors included the Garden Guild of Winnetka, Youth As Resources, the Chicago Community Trust Urbs in Horto Fund, the First National Bank of Chicago, Ameritech, Drexel National Bank, the Illinois Institute of Technology, and various anonymous donors.

Keeping It Green

The development of the EDYC park increased local pride in art and gardening projects and has fostered broader interest in Bronzeville and at other Chicago Youth Center locations. Coverson, her staff, and the EDYC children have been important leaders and supporters in development of a new park at the nearby Stateway Gardens public housing development; at Mayo Elementary School, where Coverson is a school council member; and at Woodson South Elementary School. The important lesson children have learned from these efforts, Coverson said, "is that they can have control over their environment. They don't see these parks as something simply built *for* them but *by* them as well."

The Elliott Donnelley Youth Center project was also the direct inspiration for a new woodland garden and sculpture park built at another Chicago Youth Center site, the ABC Youth Center on Chicago's west side, in partnership once again with the Openlands Project and the Marwen Foundation.

The lesson in community ownership has carried over into the maintenance of the park. Divided into groups of seven or eight, the children take turns maintaining different parts of the center, including the park. Once each week the children are responsible for weeding the landscaping, cleaning the litter, and sweeping the sidewalk. "The park is special because everyone can help clean up when it gets dirty, and we can plant more plants. It's fun to do all of that," said 11-year-old Ruby Houston. Seven-year-old Alston Taylor added, "I like to help them plant the garden 'cause it's fun." While not all of the children may be as cheerful about the park's maintenance, they all perform it diligently. The park has been in place for more than a year and remains in the same condition as the day it opened.

The EDYC's efforts at urban beautification have not stopped with the playground. The park serves as a model for other CYC chapters and other local organizations interested in reclaiming vacant urban land. The EDYC staff is currently looking into acquiring other vacant lots surrounding the center. Because of the success of their first project, funding for further development has already been lined up.

Project Data • Elliott Donnelley Youth Center Park

Development Schedule

Planning started	November 1992
Construction started	May 1993
First art project started	Fall 1993
Project completed	August 1995

Funding Information

Joyce Foundation	$60,000
Mr. and Mrs. Laurin Healy	50,000
Monsanto Corporation	50,000
Community Trust	25,000
Lurie Foundation	15,000
Community Development Block Grant	
Neighborhood Greening Program	18,000
Garden Guild of Winnetka	10,000
Youth As Resources	5,000
Chicago Community Trust Urbs in Horto Fund	4,000
First National Bank of Chicago	1,000
Ameritech	500
Anonymous donors	500
Drexel National Bank	500
Illinois Institute of Technology	500
Total	$240,000

Development Cost Information

Site acquisition cost	$0
Site improvement costs	
Grading (soil)	$3,400
Paving (drainage)	25,000
Curbs/sidewalks	500
Concrete	300
Watering	2,500
Playground equipment	50,000
Miscellaneous	20,000
Other (fencing)	11,220
Total site improvement costs	$112,920
Soft costs	
Landscape architecture	$2,000
Project management	15,000
Marketing	2,000
Professional services (administrative)	40,500
Miscellaneous	30,000
Other (materials)	20,000
Total soft costs	$109,500
Total site acquisition and development costs	$222,420

Foreground: The twelve-foot-high grotto is one of the park's most ambitious pieces of sculpture. All sculptures in the park are the work of local artists who used concrete and found or recycled objects. Background: Selection and placement of the playground equipment were determined by children from the youth center.

Embarcadero Promenade
San Francisco

Steven Fader

Following a tradition that dates back to the Gold Rush days, the city of San Francisco is expanding its waterfront along San Francisco Bay. Not in the literal sense, by scuttling sailing ships to make landfill, as the forty-niners did, but in an urban sense, by reclaiming for public use a semi-abandoned, two-and-a-half-mile stretch of the Embarcadero that had been blighted by an elevated freeway.

Before the Promenade was constructed, much of the Embarcadero was a gritty no-man's-land with long-abandoned freight-rail lines and half-empty warehouses. The elevated freeway had severed the connection—both visually and functionally—between the city and the bay, casting a long shadow over the water's edge.

Demolition of the freeway in 1991, and construction of the Promenade in the years since, has "given the city a whole new space," noted Jill Manton of the San Francisco Art Commission, a key participant in the project; it has also opened up breathtaking views of San Francisco Bay for residents and tourists alike.

A Ribbon of Light

Officially designated Herb Caen Way, in honor of the icon of San Francisco journalism, the Embarcadero Promenade is a 25-foot-wide (minimum) pedestrian zone, paved in dark gray concrete, that runs along the water's edge from North Point Street on the north to Pier 40 on the south. The Promenade is part of the larger Waterfront Transportation Project, which includes a light-rail line and revamped Embarcadero roadway, replacing the elevated freeway that was torn down following the Loma Prieta earthquake.

Snaking its way along the 2.5-mile length of the Promenade is an environmental art piece—dubbed "the Ribbon"—designed by architect Stanley Saitowitz and artists Barbara Stauffacher Solomon and Vito Acconci. The Ribbon is a continuous line of white concrete, five feet wide, with an eight-inch strip of sandblasted glass block running down the center. Where vehicles or pedestrians must pass, the Ribbon lies flush to the ground like a threshold, but in pedestrian zones or where opportunities to view the bay occur, the Ribbon rises, morphing into cubic bollards and linear benches.

A series of black-and-white porcelain pylons along the Promenade contrast sharply with the horizontal continuity of the Ribbon. Designed by artist Michael Manwaring with assistance from historian Nancy Leigh Olmsted, the pylons serve as historical markers and interpretive signs, relating in text, drawings, and photos the history of particular places and themes associated with the waterfront. A third art piece, located at the south end of the Promenade, is *Sea-Change,* a colossal, 65-foot, red-and-silver sculpture by artist Mark diSuvero.

The South Embarcadero and North Embarcadero sections of the Promenade were completed in 1994 and 1995, respectively. Construction of the central section, centered on the historic Ferry

Construction of the Waterfront Transportation Project is being funded by the Federal Highway Administration, state "congestion relief funds," and local sales tax revenue. The Promenade portion of the project cost approximately $3.6 million, exclusive of the Ribbon and the interpretive signage. The Ribbon portion, which cost approximately $1.2 million, and the interpretative signage, which cost approximately $510,000, were funded in large part by grants under the federal Intermodal Surface Transportation Efficiency Act (ISTEA).

While the design of the Ribbon has had several incarnations, the designers always knew, according to

The Ribbon is punctuated by 15 porcelain-enamel pylons designed by Michael Manwaring. Each pylon is surrounded at sidewalk level by a square ribbon of cast bronze on which a poetic statement appears, relevant to the historical drawings, words, and photographs that appear on the pylon. The designer chose the form of a pylon to reflect funnels on ships, in keeping with the nautical nature of the entire project.

Barbara Stauffacher Solomon, that it would be "two-and-a-half miles of *something*." Their intention was to define and celebrate what they called in their proposal "the tenuous edge,"—the "end of the city . . . and the beginning of the bay"—which has progressively changed over the past 150 years. At the same time, their intention was to maintain the sense of a working waterfront; the Ribbon was to be "like a hunk of concrete that could be there for a real purpose," said Solomon.

In fact, the Ribbon does serve a real purpose in addition to its artistic purpose. Noted Saitowitz, "We took fragmented pieces that usually are considered elements of urban design, such as benches and bollards, and accumulated them into one piece." According to Jill Manton of the art commission, the design of the Ribbon so effectively satisfied the need for benches and bollards that the city eventually eliminated its defined "furniture zone," saving the project approximately $700,000.

In the evenings, another aspect of the Ribbon is revealed: the glass blocks that run along the centerline of the Ribbon are lit from within, emitting a cool greenish glow that highlights the linearity of the Ribbon and the water's edge. The lighting apparatus consists of fiber-optic cable laid just below the glass blocks in a cavity in the concrete structure.

The character of the waterfront project is further defined by two elements: trees and lighting. On the landside sidewalk, London plane trees were planted at 25-foot intervals, giving the "city" edge a strong definition. In the center of the roadway, 30-year-old Canary Island date palms were planted on each side of the Muni tracks, at 80- to 100-foot intervals. The paired palm trees, whose trunks clear 20 feet before the palm leaves begin (which keeps the leaves from conflicting with the overhead Muni wiring), provide the dominant image in the landscape of the waterfront project. To maintain vistas of the water and to retain the "working waterfront" character, trees were not planted on the Promenade side of the project.

The choice of trees was among the most controversial aspects of the entire project, according to project landscape architect Martha Ketterer of the San Francisco Department of Public Works (DPW). DPW had a horticulturist develop a list of trees that would be appropriate to the Embarcadero's wind and salt air, questionable soil conditions, and urban environment. The horticulturist proposed 15 candidates, which DPW then ranked according to a list of criteria that included scale (in relation to the Muni wires), aesthetics, and survivability (which was double counted). The top three trees were palms.

Given that San Franciscans consider palms to be a Los Angeles tree—and that the worst fear of San Fran-

The site plan shows the many piers that the designers had to contend with when planning the Promenade. The Ribbon, designed to connect all the elements of the waterfront, is configured in many different variations, including (from left to right on plan) flat ribbon, raised bench, seat and table, two-sided bench, two-sided seat, bridge seat, and single-sided bench.

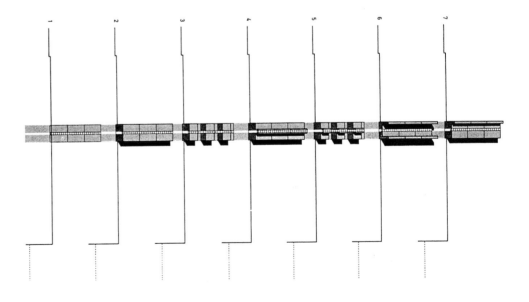

For many San Franciscans, the part of the project that caused the most outrage was the choice of Canary Island palms (*Phoenix canariensis*) for the transit median. Residents feared that they might be accused of imitating Los Angeles. But the attractiveness of the trees and the overall success of the project have laid aside any fears. Rents have been steadily increasing along the waterfront. One 85,000-square-foot office building, completed in 1995, reports virtually 100 percent occupancy and rents as high as $30 to $32 a square foot.

ciscans, according to Ketterer, is the "Los Angelization of San Francisco"—the DPW landscape architect knew that the recommendation would generate heat. In the end, endorsements by the Tree Advisory Board and the San Francisco League of Urban Gardeners (SLUG) and a carefully orchestrated media blitz by the DPW won the day.

To ensure the survival of the 250 palms planned for the site, which cost $7,000 each, specially designed planting trenches were constructed and filled with imported soil. The trenches and soil were a response to two issues: first, tests had shown that the existing soil was mostly landfill, rock, and rubble from the 19th century used to fill in the shoreline; second, compacting any new soil to 95 percent, which is the standard requirement for supporting adjacent concrete sidewalks, would be contrary to the optimal growing conditions for the palms. Instead, the imported fill was compacted to only 80 to 85 percent, then covered with "bridging" concrete slabs specially reinforced to compensate for the less dense soil underneath.

Street lighting on the landside and on the Promenade consists of antique acorn globes on closely spaced poles (50-foot intervals), which provide a strong rhythm and pedestrian scale. Lighting on the Muni medians consists of double teardrop globes on poles spaced at 80- to 100-foot intervals. These poles also serve as cable stays for the overhead Muni wires.

Routine maintenance for the waterfront facilities consists primarily of tree care. The city retains a full-time gardener to maintain the waterfront plantings, and a tree pruning crew is brought in twice a year. The Ribbon and other paving elements are not on a fixed cleaning and maintenance routine but are steam cleaned on an occasional basis.

The Use and Value of the Promenade

Once used as a location for filming the "seedy underbelly of the city," the Promenade is now actively used by strollers and joggers. In highly urbanized San Francisco, the Promenade represents a precious new resource: a place to exercise, to view the beauty of the bay and the city, or just to relax in the fresh air. Increasingly, the Promenade offers a place to dine outdoors and to view events—the Blue Angels' aerial acrobatics, for example. The Promenade is heavily used by nearby residents and by San Franciscans generally, but is also becoming a tourist destination referred to in guides to the city.

The Promenade is a truly democratic open space—treated essentially as a public way, and without restrictions on hours or use. There are no fences or other security restrictions, nor is there any monitoring of activity beyond that given to any city street. As a result, there are some "unintended users" of the Ribbon, notes architect Saitowitz—most noticeably, skateboarders.

Somewhat to the chagrin of the Promenade's planners and designers, the Ribbon has become extremely popular as a skateboarding venue. The skateboarders, who refer to the Ribbon as "the Bay Blocks" and "the New Spot," hop on and off the raised portions of the Ribbon. The popularity is ironic, given the efforts of the Ribbon's designers to discourage skateboarding by eliminating ramped surfaces. "I'm glad they love it," said codesigner Solomon. A more detached perspective is offered by fellow-designer Saitowitz, who professes to be "amazed at the scientific and serious way the skateboarders use the Ribbon."

There is real concern, however, that the skateboarders are crowding out other Promenade users. Comments Saitowitz, "The elderly don't go [to the Promenade] because they are frightened of the skateboarders." Also, the Ribbon continues to suffer damage from the skateboards. Pieces of concrete tend to spall off at the edges, glass blocks are occasionally broken or dislodged, and the paint and wheel grease of the skateboards leave black streaks in the concrete.

Roma Design Group

Pier 7, located just north of the Ferry Building, was the first pier to be built in San Francisco since the 1940s. Extending 845 feet into San Francisco Bay, the recreation and fishing pier (designed by Roma Design Group) is lined with traditionally inspired streetlights, park benches, and overlooks for sightseers, and has no tourist-oriented commercial facilities.

Various fixes have been tested to repair the concrete and to try to prevent further damage. An epoxy resin is being considered as a protective coating, and metal angles are being tested as corner guards. No attempt is being made at the moment, however, to prevent skateboarding. As Jill Manton of the art commission sees it, a tentative peace prevails with the skateboarders. They do not appear to be maliciously damaging the Ribbon or the Promenade, and so, in tolerant San Francisco, they are tolerated.

Despite the skateboarders, the Promenade and the Waterfront Transportation Project appear to be encouraging and reinforcing the revitalization of the surrounding area. On the landside, the Waterfront Transportation Project has helped to promote ongoing development in SoMa (South-of-Market). Several condominium and

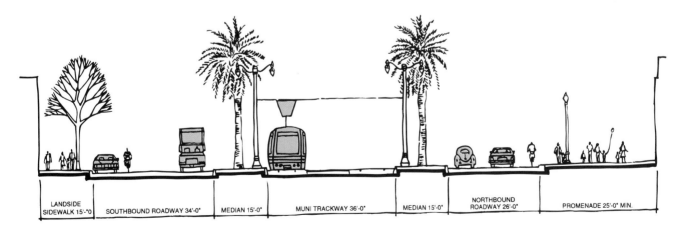

| LANDSIDE SIDEWALK 15'-"0 | SOUTHBOUND ROADWAY 34'-0" | MEDIAN 15'-0" | MUNI TRACKWAY 36'-0" | MEDIAN 15'-0" | NORTHBOUND ROADWAY 26'-0" | PROMENADE 25'-0" MIN. |

The landside edge and the waterfront edge are separated by some 126 feet of roadway and Muni rail. The extension of the Muni Metro was paid for with federal transportation funds.

Built in 1896, the 250,000-square-foot Ferry Building dominated the city skyline for more than 50 years as a transportation hub and an architecturally significant building. In the early 1900s, ferries were the only way to cross San Francisco Bay from Oakland and Marin County. Now the missing piece in the waterfront is being restored and will be ready by 1999.

apartment projects (including assisted housing) have been developed adjacent to the transportation project improvements in recent years. Interspersed among these projects are new restaurants, shops, and miniparks.

On the waterside, the Promenade now serves as the front door to the existing piers, providing encouragement for the renovation and adaptive use of the piers. Several of these piers were renovated in the mid-1990s for use as restaurants and professional offices. In addition, a marina and two parks sponsored by the redevel-

opment agency have been constructed adjacent to the Promenade.

In a city where every inch of open space counts, the Embarcadero Promenade represents a bold effort to reclaim lost territory. The three-masted schooners of the Gold Rush era may be gone, but the development of the Promenade has revived the memory of the city's waterfront heritage and provided a new place in which to contemplate it.

Project Data • Embarcadero Promenade

Development Schedule

Initial site acquired	NA[1]
Planning started	May 1985
Master plan approved	August 1989
Construction started	June 1992
Construction completed	
Phase I	June 1994
Phase II	June 1995
Phase III	February 1997
Phase IV	November 1999
Park opened	June 1994
Project completed	November 1999

Financing Information: North, South, and King Street Segments of the Embarcadero Roadway

Funding sources	Amount	Percentage of Total
Private		
Catellus Development Corp. (King Street)	$880,000	0.97%
Local		
Half-cent sales tax	$20,292,385	22.26
Miscellaneous (water department, sewer, port, general fund, Muni)	3,253,090	3.57
Total local sources	$23,545,475	25.83
State		
Flexible Congestion Relief Funds	$1,532,773	1.68
Federal (Highway Administration)		
Transfer Concept Program	$62,636,879	68.70
Surface Transportation Program	1,851,010	2.03
Transportation Enhancement Activities	735,000	0.81
Total federal sources	$65,222,889	71.54
Total funding	$91,181,137	100.00%

Development Cost Information, Waterfront Transportation Project (in millions)[2]

Site acquisition cost	$5.00
Site improvements costs	
Excavation/demolition	$5.52
Utilities	25.00
Paving	3.50
Curbs/sidewalks	7.90
Landscaping	4.40
Fees/general conditions	2.25
Concrete	2.25
Roadway sewer work	21.82
Total site improvement costs	$72.64

Soft costs	
Landscape architecture	$.55
Engineering	6.00
Project management	3.50
Professional services	2.00
Other	1.50
Total soft costs	13.55
Total site acquisition and development costs	$91.19

Development Cost Information, Embarcadero Promenade

Paving (exclusive of the Ribbon)	$600,000
Curb and gutter	250,000
Driveways	350,000
Lighting	1,750,000
Other	375,000
Ribbon (art piece)	1,200,000
Interpretive signage	510,000
Total development costs	$5,035,000

Operating Information

Annual operating expenses	
Taxes	NA
Insurance	NA
Repair and maintenance (approximately)	$600,000
Management	NA
Professional services	NA
Total operating expenses	$600,000
Annual gross revenues	
Half-cent sales tax	$600,000
Total gross revenues	$600,000

Notes

1. Not applicable.

2. For three phases completed or under construction; does not include final, mid-Embarcadero section, estimated at $100+ million total.

Flagstar Corporate Plaza and Jerome Richardson Park

Spartanburg, South Carolina

David Mulvihill

Located along Interstate 85 between Charlotte, North Carolina, and Atlanta, Georgia, the historic city of Spartanburg, South Carolina, was once a thriving textile manufacturing town. But like many blue-collar cities, Spartanburg saw its economic base steadily decline through the late 1970s and 1980s, as many of its mills closed or fled to the suburbs in search of cheaper and more abundant land. Along with the mills, much of the collateral retail, residential, and office development moved to the suburbs as well.

The area came into national prominence in 1992, when German automobile manufacturer BMW selected Spartanburg County as the site for its first U.S. manufacturing plant. Since then, the county has seen a tremendous influx of both foreign and domestic investment dollars and has rejuvenated its economic base. But very little of that development found its way into the city of Spartanburg. A locally based company, Spartan Food Systems (now Flagstar Corporation)—parent company to six restaurant chains including Hardees, Denny's, and Quincy's Steakhouse—sought to change that pattern with a bold downtown development featuring a modern, high-rise office tower; a richly designed private corporate plaza; and a traditional Southern public park. The development has helped to reinvigorate the downtown—and perhaps more important, has brought renewed attention to downtown Spartanburg as the center of civic life.

Building on the momentum generated by the Flagstar corporate development, local officials announced in late 1996 a $100 million redevelopment proposal for downtown that includes a four-star hotel; a conference center; an exhibit hall; a golf course; and new office, retail, and residential development. And right in the middle, as the centerpiece of the new activity, are the two parks that Flagstar President Jerry Richardson insisted be part of the downtown development package.

Coming Back Downtown

In many ways, the story of the Flagstar building's development mirrors the recent history of Spartanburg's downtown. The company that would become Flagstar came into being in downtown Spartanburg, later moving to the suburbs like so many other firms. Jerome "Jerry" Richardson, later president of Spartan Foods, attended Wofford College in Spartanburg in the late 1950s. After a brief stint with the Baltimore Colts, Richardson returned to Spartanburg to open the first Hardees restaurant on Kennedy Street, just a few blocks from the current Flagstar building. The franchise flourished, eventually becoming Spartan Food Systems. Until the late 1960s, Spartan Food Systems remained headquartered on Kennedy Street, but by 1969, the company had outgrown its headquarters and began to search for a larger site.

In 1970, Spartan relocated outside of town in a semi-pastoral site along I-85. The development plan called for a five-phase corporate campus. By 1985, the still-growing company had completed all five phases of the development. Ironically, Spartan found itself once again land restricted and quietly began searching for a new suburban site. Spartanburg officials learned that Spartan was looking for a new site, and in 1988 Mayor E. Lewis Miller approached Spartan about considering a downtown location. According to Olin Thomson, vice president of construction for Spartan, "within ten minutes Richardson made the decision to focus on downtown Spartanburg."

Having attended the local college and founded his corporation in the city, Jerry Richardson felt a strong attachment to Spartanburg. He chose to locate downtown because "the town has been tremendously loyal to us. It lent us money, educated our kids, bought our products, and generally took care of us. We wanted to give something back." Another factor was that many of Spartan's employees lived in or near the city and disliked the commute to the countryside.

While Richardson felt a strong desire to help turn around a declining downtown Spartanburg, he knew that simply to locate a building there would not be enough. Richardson wanted the new site to contain the open space and lush landscaping that made suburban development appealing. He was also aware that locating downtown involved issues that would not be as much of a consideration in a suburban location. For one, land assembly on a downtown site would be con-siderably more complicated than in a suburban area where large, less expensive parcels are usually available. Parking was also an issue. As a condition to locating downtown, Richardson required that the city construct a multilevel parking garage to serve both the building and future development, and city officials quickly agreed. In January 1988, after selecting a one-block site in a section of the city considered to be one of the most deteriorated, Richardson gave the city a deadline of October 1 to have the land assembled and ready for construction.

To meet the imposed deadline, the city had to work quickly and concertedly. A task force comprising the public works, community development, and planning departments, along with a representative from Spartan, met weekly throughout the planning and development process. The city adopted a two-pronged strategy that used Community Development Block Grants (CDBGs) to acquire the land and tax increment financing (TIF) to construct the parking garage. To begin the TIF process, the city first adopted a redevelopment plan for the area. The plan included development of the Spartan building; a 763-space, multilevel parking garage; and a 58,000-square-foot retail and office center across the street from the Flagstar building.

Although the development site was in a seriously declining area, a couple of small businesses operating at the location still had to be moved. More troublesome was the presence of the historic but long-abandoned Franklin Hotel. Before it would release CDBG money for acquisition of the land and buildings for redevelopment, the

Rising 19 stories into the air, the vertical orientation of the Flagstar building accomplished Richardson's goal of creating a landmark in downtown Spartanburg while also leaving land available to develop the corporate plaza and the public park. Much of the area around the project was in serious decline before Flagstar moved its headquarters downtown.

Peter Lindsay Schaudt

Inside the 150-foot-long pergola are rows of single-stem crape myrtles and a row of peach trees, selected because of their long blooming season—three to four months—and in honor of Spartanburg's reputation as the "fresh peach capital of the world." The pergola was designed with columns to help bring a sense of scale to the tower's relationship with surrounding streets, which feature mainly two- and three-story buildings.

Peter Lindsay Schaudt

Department of Housing and Urban Development (HUD) required a thorough environmental and historic review. According to Tim Kuether, director of community development for Spartanburg, "it took some doing" to convince HUD that the hotel was no longer a viable property and that its demolition was necessary to bring new development to the area. Eventually, HUD relented and the city was able to acquire and demolish the structure.

Eight owners controlled land on the site for the Flagstar development. Instead of using condemnation proceedings, which might have resulted in unacceptable delays, the city chose to negotiate with each of the property owners. While the city was able to acquire most of the parcels on the site with minimal difficulty, the time constraints on the city and the publicized process gave the property owners leverage in the bargaining situation, and a very small number of them decided to take advantage of that leverage. As a result, the city had to spend more than the $1.05 million in CDBG money it had for land acquisition. With the city lacking sufficient funds to complete the assembly, Spartan contributed an additional $750,000 for land acquisition.

By early September 1988, the city had assembled all the necessary parcels and the site was ready for construction. The city sold the parcel to Spartan for $1.8 million (including the $750,000 already spent by Spartan). Fortunately, with the exception of two small parcels, the city already owned the block where the parking garage would be sited.

Because of the importance of the entire project to the future of downtown Spartanburg, both Richardson and the city wanted the facades of the building and the

parking garage to be complementary. The garage was designed and constructed simultaneously with the Flagstar project. Architects Dalton, Moran & Shook of Charlotte, North Carolina, designed a modern, multilevel, concrete garage whose facade complemented the modern, formal lines of the Flagstar building.

Despite the magnitude of the project, involvement on the part of the public and local businesses was minimal. Partly because the project was in a distressed area, and partly because of the good faith exhibited by Spartan, no referenda or public debates were held regarding the project's development. Quite simply, the public and the local business community were thrilled to find a major corporation willing to make such a significant investment in their city. When the building and parks were dedicated with a public ceremony in the plaza on October 14, 1990, nearly 5,000 Spartanburg residents participated in the event, which included a tour of the building.

What Should It Look Like?

In developing the new corporate headquarters, Spartan—and, more specifically, Richardson—wanted to create a landmark for the city, which would help to reinvigorate Spartanburg civic life. The job of designing the new headquarters was awarded to Clark Tribble Harris & Li of Charlotte, North Carolina. Spartan officials and members of the architectural team did extensive research on corporate headquarters throughout the country. According to Peter Schaudt, landscape architect for the project, "there was a strong desire to produce a meaningful landscape design." One of Richardson's only requirements to the designers was that the project include a plaza and a public park.

The building ultimately took the form of a 19-story tower. According to project architect David Wagner, this design allowed Spartan to create a significant landmark in a city with few structures more than three stories tall. The vertical design, as opposed to a more suburban, "campus" design, also left a significant amount of space available to satisfy Richardson's requirement that the project include a plaza and public park. The tower and plaza were to comprise a one-block corporate garden. Across the street, on the back side of the building, a less formal public park was to be developed on land donated by the city. The site of the building, at the corner of Converse and Broad Streets, is just two blocks from historic Morgan Square, once the crossroads of the city. The two greenspaces were meant to act as links along Main Street, between the project and Morgan Square.

The design of the 193,000-square-foot tower, the plaza, and the park reflects Richardson's concern for both Spartan employees and the city of Spartanburg. Each of the tower's 10,000-square-foot floors is only 65 feet wide, allowing all offices to be arranged around the perimeter and to enjoy natural lighting. All offices are also afforded views of the parks and surrounding hills. The slender tower has been likened to a sporty pocket calculator. A grid of deep windows set in a concrete frame graces the facade of the building, while two arcing balconies flank the executive floor. The mechanical and elevator cores are located at the ends of the tower, creating a large, transparent, ground-floor lobby that allows pedestrians to see through the building and

visually connects the public park with the corporate plaza. The transparent lower level also creates a visual connection with the first floors of surrounding smaller buildings, reducing the scale of the building in relation to its neighbors. A 200-seat, state-of-the-art auditorium is located on the top floor, beneath the tower's vaulted roof. When not in use, the auditorium is donated to the Kiwanis Club, the March of Dimes, and other local civic groups for meetings and fundraisers. To encourage employees to fan out into the community, the building was intentionally developed without a cafeteria, fast-food counters, or a health club.

The tower opens onto a formal plaza reminiscent of that in front of Biltmore House in Asheville, North Carolina. The rectangular plaza, designed primarily for the use and enjoyment of Flagstar employees, employs layers of space moving inward from Main Street to a *tapis vert*, or green carpet, of perfectly manicured lawn in the center, sunk 18 inches below the plaza level. Surrounding the 80-foot-long *tapis vert* is a water canal; the walls of the canal are lined with bronze waterspouts. The outermost edge of the plaza consists of a 150-foot-long pergola that simulates a building wall. The pergola was designed with columns to help bring a sense of scale to the tower's relationship with surrounding streets, which feature mainly two- and three-story buildings.

The park also features a dramatic lighting system that highlights both the building and the plaza. Traditional pole-lighting lines the perimeter of the plaza, while the perimeter of the building and the pergola feature dramatic uplighting that shoots light to the top of the tower; uplighting also illuminates the water canal. There is no

Elliptical lawns, benches, and colorful foliage in the public park evoke a more traditional Southern neighborhood park and act as a counterbalance to the modern formality of the plaza.

signage dictating any regulations attached to the plaza, but it is considered to be open during daylight hours.

The public park sits across the street, on the opposite side of the building, at the western terminus of the central business district. Spartan developed the park on land owned by the city; the city of Spartanburg then dedicated it to Richardson, designating it the Jerome Richardson Park. The triangular park, 150 feet wide on each side, features a simple fountain and two elliptical lawns surrounded by flower beds and benches, and is meant to counterbalance the strict formality of the corporate plaza. The park is enclosed by a serpentine brick wall and an ornamental wrought-iron fence that evoke a more traditional Southern neighborhood park and stand in contrast to the modern lines of the plaza. The public park does not feature the dramatic uplighting of the plaza but is illuminated by the same type of lampposts used along the plaza. Like the plaza, the public park lacks any signage, with the exception of a plaque bearing the name of the park's benefactor.

Keeping It Green

Flagstar manages and maintains both the plaza and the public park. As owner of the public park, the city contracts with Flagstar for park maintenance. Flagstar employs a full-time professional horticulturist and assistant to manage the parks, including cutting the grass and pruning the trees to maintain the park's elegant appearance. Because of the heavy clay soil found in this region of the country, keeping the rich landscaping in good health requires special effort, including the use of a sophisticated irrigation system installed underneath the major trees. Twice each year, in April and October, the flowers in each of the parks are changed to maintain harmony with the seasons. The Flagstar staff is also under contract to maintain the landscaping at the Broadwalk project across the street from the plaza, which allows for consistent landscape management of the plaza, park, and adjacent Broadwalk development.

The corporate plaza was intended to provide a serene, stress-free environment for employees. Toward that end, Flagstar management does not allow the use of landscaping or other machinery between the hours of eight a.m. and five p.m. While the plaza and park are both open to the public, Flagstar discourages loud or boisterous use of the park during business hours.

Part of providing a comfortable environment is creating a feeling of security. The project is located just two blocks from Spartanburg's main police station. Additionally, surveillance cameras cover the plaza, park, and parking facility and are monitored 24 hours a day by a security staff in the basement of the Flagstar building.

A low serpentine brick wall and an ornamental iron fence surround the public park, which features red maples, gingkos, azaleas, and Southern magnolias.

Using the Plaza and Park

The development of the plaza and park has turned attention to the central business district (CBD) as a site for public events. From the project's inception, both the plaza and park were conceived of as public spaces available for the community's use. While many programmed events are held in the plaza and park, neither was designed for active recreational use; instead, the plaza and park are meant to be gathering places where local employees and downtown visitors can repose in pleasant and peaceful surroundings. The perfectly manicured lawns, bright colors, and gentle water features offer an ideal environment for calm reflection or relaxed social interaction. These features have made the public park a popular site for weddings: about 20 wedding ceremonies are performed in the park each year.

One of the first programmed events conceived of for the plaza was a Christmas-tree-lighting celebration. By deciding to include a tree well (hidden by brick pavers laid on top of a steel plate) in the design of the plaza, Olin Thomson "created" this event even before construction of the project began. Each year, Flagstar erects a 50-foot blue spruce Christmas tree and sponsors a holiday celebration that routinely attracts more than 5,000 people. A "Dickens of a Christmas" festival is also produced in the plaza each year.

According to Jerri Greene, director of the Spartanburg Development Council, the Flagstar development "has worked to centralize the location of traditional Spartanburg festivals." A Spring Fling that features arts and cultural activities and an annual Austrian and Swiss Festival are now also held at the plaza and park. Prior to the park's development, many such festivals were held in various locations both within and outside the city. The project has also attracted new events to the city—such as the Miss South Carolina Pageant, which now stages portions of the competition in the corporate plaza.

The development of the Flagstar building and parks has clearly reawakened interest in downtown Spartanburg. When students at Spartanburg's Wofford College wanted to become more involved in the downtown by sponsoring a musical program, their first thought was to approach the city and Flagstar about using the plaza and park. Twice a month from April through October, the plaza or park is the site of Music on Main—public performances by a variety of musical artists. The Carolinas' effort to acquire a National Football League franchise offers another example of a reorientation toward downtown. Organizers chose the plaza as the site for a "Panther Party" to demonstrate South Carolina's support for a professional football team. The event drew 10,000 people.

Such extensive use of the park and plaza would not be possible without the cooperation and support of the Flagstar Corporation. Although Jerry Richardson left Flagstar in 1994, the company has continued to display its support for the city of Spartanburg. Said Karen Randall of Flagstar, "We have continued our commitment to the city. Representatives from Flagstar sit on most of the festival committees and the company is an active sponsor of many of the events." In addition to the festivals, the company sponsors an annual career day for local students.

What the Project Has Done

The development of the Flagstar project has had a tremendous impact on downtown Spartanburg. Tim Kuether, director of community development for the city, estimates that "the city has enjoyed a payback of about 30 to one in terms of private versus public dollars expended." Of course, one of the most immediate effects was the relocation of 300 employees—and thus potential customers —to downtown. Additionally, BB&T Bank, the largest non-Flagstar tenant, occupies the first level of the building, bringing more employees to the downtown.

Since construction of the Flagstar project began in 1988, more than $250 million in development has flowed into downtown. One of the first projects, developed coincidentally with the Flagstar building, was Broadwalk, a 58,000-square-foot office and retail project. A local developer held an option to build a commercial center on a site across the street from the plaza. Upon learning of Spartan's decision to locate downtown, the developer formed a partnership with two other local developers and increased the size and scope of the Broadwalk project. The developers worked with Spartan on the center's development, including a 120-foot underground tunnel

Bronze waterspouts grace the wall of a water canal surrounding the plaza's *tapis vert*. The *tapis vert* itself is sunk 18 inches below the plaza level.

that links the center to the Flagstar building and allows easy access for employees. Shortly after its development in 1991, a significant portion of the Broadwalk space was leased to Spartan to accommodate additional employees brought to Spartanburg when the company's Denny's division was transferred from Irvine, California. Unfortunately, that left little space available in the Broadwalk center for retail tenants.

Flagstar also inspired renewed vigor and community spirit among downtown businesses. When the long-defunct downtown merchants association was reorganized shortly after the Flagstar development, one of its first actions was to work to remove a Main Street pedestrian mall installed in the 1970s. The mall had closed the city's main shopping district to all vehicular traffic and has been blamed in large part for the decline in downtown business. The area is now open to two-way traffic, with diagonal on-street parking. While not much new retail development has occurred downtown since Flagstar's arrival, the existing establishments have been strongly affected, with some businesses reporting sales increases of more than 100 percent.

Residential development around the project has enjoyed a resurgence, helped along by already existing economic incentives. The city of Spartanburg offers tax credits of $6,000 per unit to developers who convert upper-floor space in downtown commercial buildings into apartment units. More than 50 of these upper-floor apartment units have been developed within a three-block area of the Flagstar project. Demand for apartments near the parks has been strong—evidenced by rental rates that have more than doubled, from an average of $250 per month to $550 per month. With continued residential development, city officials feel confident that retail development will eventually follow.

The average value of nonexempt property in the central business district increased 325 percent from 1983 to 1993. Property values in downtown Spartanburg are among the highest in the county, quite a feat in a county that has been enjoying a major economic boom: reportedly, the county has recently seen a larger influx of foreign investment capital than any other county in the country, most of it outside the city of Spartanburg.

The development of the plaza and park, according to Jerri Greene, has created a focal point for marketing the downtown for office development. Several new development projects have been completed near the Flagstar project, including two new local bank branches. Much of the previously vacant commercial space near the project has been absorbed by professionals newly interested in a downtown address. More significantly, a new master plan for downtown recommends development of the historic Morgan Square and targets new development in the CBD between the square and the new public park. An immediate result of this plan has been the development of a new public library near Morgan Square, just one block from the Flagstar project. This development is particularly significant, as a suburban site had originally been considered for the library.

The Flagstar project also demonstrates the success that can be achieved through public and private cooperation. Officials and business leaders are confident that the recently proposed $100 million redevelopment plan for downtown Spartanburg, dubbed The Renaissance Project, will succeed largely because of private sector involvement. Local officials have tried several times to lure a major hotel downtown. But as Mayor James Talley explained, "This time it is not the government initiating the project." Developers have obtained options on about 98 percent of the property needed for the project and are working to build public support. The proposed amenities will include a luxury hotel; a conference center; an exhibition hall; and new office, retail, and residential development. And the inventory of downtown open space will be increased by the development of a new four-acre public park, a public green, and a nine-hole, par three golf course.

Conclusion

The Flagstar Corporation, and more specifically Jerry Richardson, sought to bring a new identity and sense of place to downtown Spartanburg. In many respects the effort has been successful. The Flagstar project has worked to reorient civic life toward the downtown. The inclusion of the parks as a significant part of the project helped to do so in a way that merely placing a building downtown could not. The project also sought to revitalize the downtown economically, and has indeed gone a long way toward achieving that goal as well. But no single project can turn around a declining downtown.

City officials are continuing revitalization efforts that build on the success of the Flagstar project. The Flagstar development is one of the focal points of the recently commissioned master plan for the downtown. The impact of the project, said Jerri Greene, "has caused us to rethink our plans for the downtown" and take into consideration a new array of possibilities. In developing their plans for the future, officials are mindful of their city's history. Greene pointed out that in the early part of this century, Spartanburg was known as "the city of parks." The Flagstar development provided officials with a reminder of the important role that parks can play in a city.

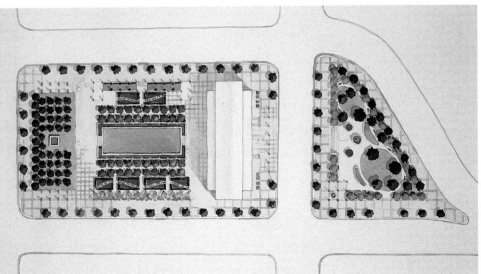

The Flagstar project features a large, formal, rectangular corporate plaza, open to the public, and a smaller, less formal public park.

Peter Lindsay Schaudt

Hawthorne Park

Kansas City, Missouri

Terry Jill Lassar

Like many other municipalities, Kansas City had been diligently following the federal guidelines for developing parks that were accessible to disabled users. But in the early 1990s, the city decided that complying with the requirements of the Americans with Disabilities Act (ADA) was not enough because the ADA is aimed primarily at persons in wheelchairs and addresses only a small portion of the handicapped population. Kansas City leaders had loftier ambitions and set out to design a park that would address a much broader range of physical and developmental disabilities, far exceeding ADA guidelines. This decision was motivated in part by the special interest of the park commissioners—two of the three commissioners had children with disabilities.

The revenue stream for parks improvements in Kansas City was greatly boosted in the late 1980s, when the city passed a half-cent sales tax increase for capital improvements. Whereas the city parks and recreation department had been refurbishing one or two parks and playgrounds a year, five to ten renovations became the norm. With a population of approximately 450,000 (1.5 million within the metropolitan area), Kansas City maintains 192 parks—including 60 playgrounds—on 10,500 acres of land.

The site ultimately chosen for the special park was Hawthorne Park, a two-and-a-half-acre park at 27th Street and Gillham Boulevard in midtown Kansas City. Hawthorne Park had been neglected and underused over the years and was a good candidate for renovation. Located in a part of the city that had been steadily gentrifying, the park occupied a full city block bordered by commercial and institutional development and single-family residential neighborhoods. Although the effort took longer than a quick-and-dirty renovation would have and involved far more participants, the final, precedent-setting product has already become the model for another similar park to be developed in Kansas City, and will undoubtedly receive close attention from other cities as well.

A Completely New Kind of Park

Park leaders envisioned a park that would provide high-quality recreation for all children, both those with and without physical and mental disabilities. They also wanted a plan that would promote interactive play between children with disabilities and other kids. Because there was no prototype for this type of fully accessible, integrated playground, the Board of Parks and Recreation Commissioners held an international design competition in the spring of 1992 to brainstorm for new ideas.

More than 60 responses came in, but park staff were disappointed that almost every design proposal dealt only with children in wheelchairs and failed to address a broader spectrum of physical impairments as well as cognitive developmental issues. And because the competition was not site specific, the submissions were highly conceptual. In the end, although few details could actually be used from the winning design, it was "useful in getting people to think out of the box," says parks commissioner Sheila Kemper-Dietrich.

Because the design competition did not generate any new approaches to accessible design, park staff decided to include health professionals and child rehabilitation experts in the initial planning stages. This decision to bring in therapeutic experts was probably the most important one in ensuring the success of the park.

Hawthorne Park had been selected as the site for the city's first fully accessible playground in part because of its close proximity to a number of children's medical, rehabilitation, and educational facilities, including Children's Mercy Hospital and the Children's Therapeutic Learning Center. Representatives from these institutions were invited to participate on the 30-member Hawthorne Park Planning Committee. Parks commissioner Kemper-Dietrich, whose daughter has severe physical disabilities, was particularly knowledgeable about key individuals to include. Other health professionals on the planning committee came from such organizations as the Children's Center for the Visually Impaired, the Marillac Center (for children with emotional disabilities), the Mayor's Office on Disabilities, the Easter Seal Society, the Kansas City Pediatric Alliance, the University of Kansas Medical Center, and United Cerebral Palsy. Department heads of the spina bifida and Down's syndrome clinics at Children's Mercy Hospital were also included.

In addition to the many health professionals involved in the planning process, representatives from neighboring institutions, such as Hallmark Cards, Inc., and the Jackson County Family Court, also participated, as did representatives from the two neighborhood homeowners associations—Hawthorne and Longfellow. (Hallmark's corporate headquarters, with 6,000 employees, borders the west edge of Hawthorne Park.)

Because the park was sorely in need of repair, the neighborhood welcomed the refurbishing plan. A main concern was that the park continue to serve the neighborhood by providing recreational opportunities for the entire family. "This was one of those things we needed to be educated about," noted parks commissioner Kemper-Dietrich, "to make sure we were representing the interests of the neighborhood." For example, although the initial plan was to remove the two tennis courts, residents persuaded the parks department to retain them. Residents also pushed for barbecue grills and family picnic areas. As a result, the park will feature an "adult garden," with lush landscaping, sitting areas, and game tables for family outings.

Neighboring institutions and residents were also concerned about security issues and the juvenile detention facility across the street from the park. Because a basketball court in the original park had apparently been a hangout for teenagers on their way to family court or the juvenile detention facility, the parks department decided to remove the basketball court and specifically target the playground to children ages two through nine.

Doing What's Never Been Done

The first development phase, completed in the fall of 1994, entailed construction of the younger ability play area and parking area, and renovation of the existing rest rooms. The second phase, completed in the fall of 1996, featured a water theme area with fanciful inter-

The deck of the Spanish galleon was built extra wide to accommodate children in wheelchairs. Ramps and handrails allow children to move from one part of the structure to another. Changes in color and texture delineate safety zones around moving play equipment and slides. The many types of play structures found in the park are all on soft, resilient surfaces.

active play elements, including a sea dragon and a Spanish galleon.

An overall strategy was to create a variety of different play opportunities to meet the needs of all children, whether disabled or not. In traditional playgrounds, which are typically linear in design, children must often wait their turn to use equipment. At Hawthorne, the equipment is arranged so that children have more freedom to play at their own pace, depending on their particular developmental stage.

The younger ability play area is geared to younger children, mentally challenged children, and children who are slow to develop their motor skills. Play equipment is located close to the ground, and changes in color and texture delineate safety zones around slides and moving play equipment. A main play feature is a low-slung "turnaround" that works much like a merry-go-round. Because of potential liability problems, merry-go-rounds have been removed from many play areas, and Kansas City parks staff initially balked at the idea. However, some of the therapeutic specialists on the planning committee pointed out that the sensation of spinning and twirling is important for cognitive development because it helps children experience their relationship to their physical surroundings; it is also an experience that many children with disabilities miss out on.

To address this need, park staff selected a turnaround called Snyder the Spider from *Gametime*, a playground equipment catalog. The piece was equipped with a special hydraulic limiter that controls how fast the children can spin. "This was one of those situations," said

Custom-designed cars in the "Route 66" play area have lights on the dashboard and steering wheels that turn. Route 66 is a linear path for bikes, wheelchairs, and roller skates and is intended to promote interactive play between children with and without disabilities. Along the way are areas that one might encounter on a highway—a café, a bank, a train depot.

Kemper-Dietrich, "where we successfully married two competing concerns. We came up with a piece of equipment that addressed the cognitive developmental needs of children without being a liability nightmare for the parks people."

Therapeutic advisers also emphasized the importance of encouraging disabled children to develop their upper-body muscles and improve their motor skills. A special slide was installed with transition return rails that function

This custom-designed slide has transition return rails (pictured in yellow), which function like parallel bars, allowing children to leave their crutches and walkers at a transfer deck, go down the slide, then pull themselves along the rail, and return to their starting point.

Seven cartoon figures—in the forms of rabbits, a squirrel, a bear, elves, and a monkey—sign the word *welcome*. The letters are also hand-signed on their bodies, which have Braille markers for visually impaired children.

like parallel bars. Children can leave their crutches and walkers at a transfer deck, slide down, then pull themselves along the rail and return to their starting point.

City landscape architect Robin Frye noted that none of the equipment was "textbook." According to Frye, off-the-shelf equipment was used whenever possible, "then reassembled in a manner to meet our particular needs." Although much of the play equipment featured in catalogs is described as being in compliance with ADA and purportedly caters to children with disabilities, it is generally aimed at children in wheelchairs and does not target the broader range of disabilities that are addressed at Hawthorne Park. Thus, a number of the pieces at Hawthorne Park had to be custom designed by local manufacturers.

For example, at the main entry to the park stand seven custom-made cartoon-animal figures, each signing one letter of the word *welcome*. The letters also appear in Braille on the animals' bodies, so that visually impaired children can read the welcome message. The sea dra-

The merry-go-round or "turnaround" is low to the ground and has a special mechanism that limits how fast the children can spin it.

gon and the Spanish galleon, also custom designed, have especially wide decks to accommodate wheelchairs. And in areas where the play equipment moves, the texture of the surfacing is changed to alert children walking with canes that moving pieces are nearby.

"Route 66," a linear concrete path for bikes, trikes, wheelchairs, and roller skates, is designed to promote interactive play between children with and without disabilities. To provide opportunities for imaginative role playing, the play area includes several elements that one might encounter on a highway—a café, a bank, and a train depot. The two cars, which have lights on the dashboard and steering wheels that turn, were custom designed.

Although ADA contains specifications for rest room design, they are limited to adults. Thus, new specifications for disabled children had to be developed for the refurbished rest rooms at Hawthorne Park. The facility offers equal features for both sexes, including stainless steel changing tables, both adult- and child-sized toilets, and accessible fixtures. Drinking fountains are slanted so that they can easily be reached by people in wheelchairs. To improve access, the front door was removed and replaced by a steel roll-up door (and privacy wall) at the entry that is open during the day and locked overnight.

One of the most costly construction items was the surfacing. Most surfacing materials used in traditional playgrounds to cushion children from falls—such as bark mulch and sand—impede wheelchairs and walkers and were thus inappropriate for Hawthorne Park. The main surface at Hawthorne is a two-inch foam shock pad on a compacted gravel base. A green turf material is then glued on top of the pad. When the park was first planned, the foam pad, which is laid down like a carpet, was the most cost-effective material available. An alternative poured-in-place rubberized material was used in selected areas, but it was too expensive to use for the entire playground. (Since then, the cost has come down. Because this rubberized surfacing is easier to install and probably more durable than the foam pad, it is likely to be used more extensively in future playgrounds for children with special needs.)

Some sand areas will be provided in the final development phase of the park. However, because sand tends to migrate and would eventually ruin the foam carpet, the sand components were confined to discrete locations completely separated from the foam surfacing.

Although it is a neighborhood park, the unique design of Hawthorne Park draws children from a larger radius, so additional accessible parking was developed on the west side.

The final development phase will contain two garden areas, one for adults and one for children. The adult garden, in the style of a formal European garden, will feature passive greenspace with water features, seating, game tables, and family picnic areas. The upper garden will offer gardening opportunities to children as well as raised sand- and water-tables for imaginative play.

Although crime had not been a problem in the neighborhood, the close proximity of the family court and several juvenile detention facilities raised some concerns about security and potential vandalism of the costly new playground equipment. Landscape architect Robin Frye had safety in mind when he chose to keep shrubbery low, creating open sight lines both into and out of the park. A low planting bed was created on the western edge as a protective barrier from traffic on the four-lane Gillham Boulevard. To create continuity and character, Frye used a deliberately limited plant palette—mainly ground-cover juniper, ornamental grasses, spreading yews, and spireas, as well as trees for shade.

As part of the strategy to keep teenagers from taking over the park, the original basketball court was removed and replaced with mini-sized basketball hoops intended for young children. Because some teenagers continue to play basketball in the play areas intended for younger children, there has been some talk of removing the basketball apparatus altogether.

Paying for the Park

Although passage of the half-cent sales tax in the late 1980s was a tremendous boon to the city's park system, park projects must still compete with other capital improvement projects. Michael Malyn, manager of the parks department, emphasizes the importance of the public/private funding approach taken at Hawthorne Park and notes that the significant commitment of private dollars made it easier to secure the public allocation.

Parks commissioner Sheila Kemper-Dietrich spearheaded the fundraising campaign. A main strategy was to identify those agencies and foundations that were positioned to benefit directly from the park, including some of the nearby health facilities. Kemper-Dietrich also targeted local companies that manufactured play equipment for children with special needs. Hallmark Cards, Inc., was another major contributor. An additional $250,000 is now being raised to complete the final phase and start a park endowment fund.

More Parks for Every Child

Hawthorne Park was initially envisioned as a pilot project to experiment with new design approaches and serve as a prototype for future fully accessible playgrounds in the Kansas City park system. The project also offered a unique opportunity to research and test new play equipment custom designed for children with special needs. The overwhelming success of the park has encouraged the city parks department to plan additional playgrounds of this type. For example, plans are now in the works

The renovated rest room facility features innovative design. The facility is symmetrical, offering equal features for both sexes, including fixed, stainless-steel changing tables, adult- and child-size toilets, and accessible fixtures.

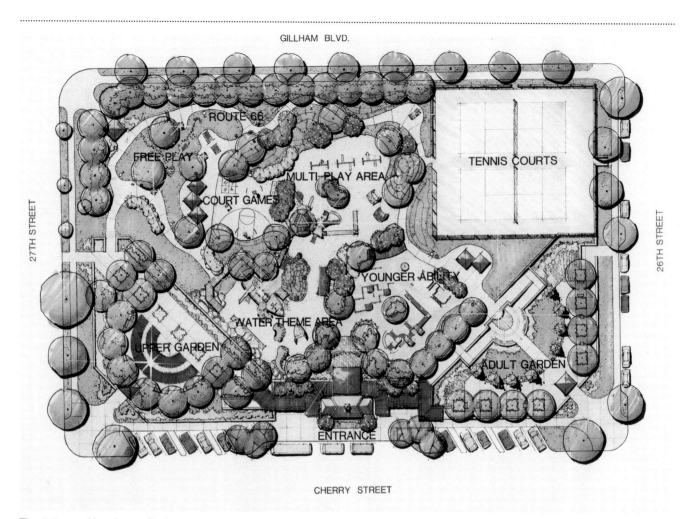

GILLHAM BLVD.

ROUTE 66

FREE PLAY

MULTI-PLAY AREA

COURT GAMES

TENNIS COURTS

27TH STREET

26TH STREET

YOUNGER ABILITY

WATER THEME AREA

UPPER GARDEN

ADULT GARDEN

ENTRANCE

CHERRY STREET

The 2.5-acre Hawthorne Park occupies a full city block in midtown Kansas City at Twenty-Seventh Street and Gillham Boulevard. Hawthorne Park was selected as the site for the city's first fully accessible playground in part because of its proximity to a number of children's medical, rehabilitation, and educational facilities.

to include fully accessible play areas as part of the renovation of Penguin Park on the north side of the city. To keep down costs, there will be less custom designed equipment than at Hawthorne. However, Kemper-Dietrich predicts that as more cities develop fully accessible playgrounds, creating increased demand for this specialized equipment, manufacturers will offer these pieces as part of their regular merchandise and the costs will come down.

Parks department manager Malyn emphasizes the importance of involving health professionals in the planning process from the start. "They brought a level of experience that was critical to the success of the park," says Malyn. For example, without their input about the importance of spinning and twirling for cognitive development, safety and liability concerns would likely have prevented park planners from installing a merry-go-round. In earlier parks, accessibility consisted mainly of ramps to get children in wheelchairs to the play equip-

ment. However, health professionals said it is more important to get children *out* of their chairs so that they can strengthen their muscles. Play equipment should be designed so that children in wheelchairs can leave their chairs and if necessary scoot around on their behinds. Likewise, therapeutic specialists educated city staff about the importance of providing ample shaded areas, water fountains, and seating. Children with certain physical conditions have difficulty cooling down after exercising.

As Commissioner Kemper-Dietrich noted, one of the main goals was "to create a playground that accommodated all kids with all needs, not just a playground for kids with special needs. A common concern is that playgrounds geared for the disabled are necessarily boring for able-bodied children." Hawthorne Park, which is extensively used by children who reside in the neighborhood, dispels this myth.

Project Data • Hawthorne Park

Development Schedule

Planning started	1991
Design competition conducted	Spring 1992
Master plan approved	Spring 1993
Phase I construction started	Spring 1994
Phase I construction completed	Fall 1994
Phase II construction started	Spring 1996
Phase II construction completed	Fall 1996

Financing Information

Private sources	
Phase I	$274,000
Phase II	137,000
Total private sources	$411,000
Public sources	
Phase I	$221,600
Phase II	231,800
Total public sources	$453,400
Total funding	$864,400

Development Cost Information

Phase I	
Rest room renovation	$125,000
Play equipment	130,000
Surfacing	112,600
Shelters	8,000
Trellis	20,000
Sidewalks	50,000
Parking	50,000
Total	$495,600
Phase II	
Play equipment	$60,000
Surfacing	142,800
Cartoon figures	10,000
Ship	60,000
Serpent	35,000
Fire engine	8,000
Cars	14,000
Boat	7,000
Water feature	10,000
Tunnel	15,000
Total	$361,800
Phase III (estimate)	
Adult garden	$110,000
Sand/water/plant garden	125,600
Total	$235,600
Total development costs	$1,093,000

The handicapped parking spaces have bright yellow rails designed to assist users.

Hudson River Park
New York City

Gayle Berens

Model composite courtesy of Quennell Rothschild Associates

Manhattan is known as a city of extremes—the tallest buildings, the hottest fashions, the trendiest restaurants, the densest population (over 52,000 per square mile—compared to Atlanta, for example, with 2,990 per square mile). The world watches Manhattan for trends because, like it or not, whatever starts there goes elsewhere in some form or another.

So it's not surprising that when the city and the state began taking another look at the Hudson River as an amenity, after ignoring it for so long, their vision was on a grand scale. The ambitious new plan for the Hudson River waterfront will create a continuous five-mile trail along the river, dotted with parks and recreational and educational facilities, providing residents and visitors with some 550 acres of open space. And the plan's success depends on active private sector involvement in the public realm—a risky approach when one looks at the Hudson River's history as the focus of internecine wars that have delayed or eliminated projects, costing the city, the state, and private developers countless dollars.

Scheduled to be completed by about 2003, the proposed waterfront revival has the potential to do for New York City in the 21st century what Central Park did in the 19th. This grand effort involves many different entities, but the primary facilitator of the process is the Hudson River Park Conservancy (HRPC), a state agency created specifically to oversee the revitalization of the waterfront. And unlike many previous efforts, the Hudson River Park Conservancy's plan depends on generating money from select commercial ventures within the park and using those revenues to help fund park construction, maintenance, operations, and programs. Hudson River Park is designed to make approximately $10 million annually through "appropriate commercial development within the park" to pay for its maintenance and management. When complete, the entire length of the park will have a waterside esplanade, 13 public recreation piers, and a continuous bicycle path. The proposed park will contain a variety of active and passive recreational facilities; maritime activities, including ferries, water taxis, and boat launches; and a range of educational, ecological, and historic features. The waterfront will also retain its function as a working harbor.

The first large-scale commercial venture completed along the site is a dramatic new privately developed recreational facility. Chelsea Piers Sports and Entertainment Complex is a privately funded, 30-acre sports and recreational facility built in long-neglected pier sheds, each the size of an 80-story building turned on its side.

Much of the waterfront has been poorly maintained and in a state of disrepair for many years, yet people are drawn to the water and have continued to go to the river to sunbathe and stroll. The Hudson River Park Conservancy recognizes people's natural tendency to gravitate toward water and enjoy the view that the waterfront affords.

While many of the other efforts are in various stages, plans are in place; the community has been involved every step of the way; and despite the many players and the gridlock that often accompanies projects in New York City, there is evidence of movement. Most important, the vehicle for building the park is in place.

Although this case study looks at one major effort underway on the Hudson River, it does not present the complete story of this great waterfront. For example, development of Battery Park City and its 1.5-mile riverfront esplanade in lower Manhattan was a long, complex—and ultimately successful—process not covered in depth here. Likewise, the plan for the waterfront between 59th and 72nd streets—which is outside of HRPC's purview and in the hands of a private development group—has undergone innumerable iterations, and although a final plan has been agreed on, other issues continue to be discussed. And from 72nd Street to 153rd Street, Riverside Park, an Olmsted-designed linear park, has stretched along the waterfront since 1910. But since 1937, when the six-lane Henry Hudson Parkway was cut through this publicly owned park, the park has never quite recovered. Various possibilities for its resuscitation are being explored. With all these elements, it becomes apparent that the full story of the Hudson River waterfront contains much more material than it would be possible to cover in a single chapter of this book.

Hudson River Park Conservancy

Developing a Plan Everyone Could Live With

Attention began turning toward the Hudson River as early as 1966, when the Lower Manhattan Plan recommended the development of what ultimately became Battery Park City (see feature box). This new city within the city, created by a 92-acre landfill project, was intended to stop the decline of lower Manhattan, which had been ongoing since World War II.[1] The landfill preparations were completed in 1976, but a fiscal crisis postponed development of Battery Park City until 1979.

In the meantime, another project was drawing attention to the Hudson River. A plan had been set forth to demolish the elevated West Side Highway (Route 9A), which had collapsed in 1973, and to construct in its place the Westway Highway. Westway was to be a 178-acre landfill project with an underground, six-lane highway extending just over four miles along the western edge of lower Manhattan. The original plan called for 82 acres of the proposed project to be for parks and open space.

The Development of Battery Park City

Battery Park City's development was the result of a bold plan by the state to revitalize a sinking neighborhood—lower Manhattan—by filling in an area along the Hudson and creating a whole new community that would bring the neighborhood new life—both residential and commercial. And like all development projects in New York City, it was not without its problems.

In 1968, the state legislature created Battery Park City Authority, a semiautonomous entity with the power to issue bonds, to oversee the development. The 92-acre landfill project proceeded apace, and in 1976 it was ready for development. However, a major fiscal crisis hit and development was postponed.

When the project began again in earnest, a precarious financial situation forced the state to reassess the original master plan, which depended on housing subsidies and heavy infrastructure financing. In 1979, Alexander Cooper and Stanton Eckstut completed an entirely new master plan for Battery Park City, drawing on the elements of New York that are the most beloved. The original plan called for superblocks that would hold massive, large-scale projects, including several high-rise office and apartment buildings; the new master plan proposed traditional-sized city blocks that would be divided into parcels for moderate-sized buildings. The designers took care to extend the patterns of existing streets, to maintain water views, and to create something that felt like it was part of New York. In addition, simply moving the site of the commercial buildings, among them the World Financial Center, allowed the existing infrastructure to be more easily extended to Battery Park City and saved millions of dollars. The new master plan called for 42 percent residential use; 9 percent commercial use; 30 percent parks, open spaces, and a riverfront esplanade; and 19 percent for streets and avenues.

Now Battery Park City is highlighted by a stunning, 1.5-mile riverfront esplanade that's framed by interesting sculptures, benches, parks, gracious lighting,

Alexander Garvin (1994)

and activity. The city within a city has taken on a life of its own, as well as the life of the city it's part of. With each year, each element that's added to the city is better than the last. Robert F. Wagner, Jr., Park, completed in 1996, was called by Paul Goldberger of the *New York Times* "one of the finest public spaces New York has seen in at least a generation." Some 4 million people visit Battery Park City annually, many to catch the ferry that will take them to the Statue of Liberty and Ellis Island.

While the plan underwent several iterations, an environmental fight, led by activist Marcy Benstock, succeeded in stopping the project. Citizens waged a ten-year battle against the project, and a judge ultimately ruled the environmental impact statement to be invalid because of possible harm to the striped bass caused by the proposed landfill and demolition of a Hudson River pier.

In 1985, the Westway project was essentially put to rest.

In 1986, after the Westway project had died, the 22-member West Side Task Force, chaired by Arthur Levitt, Jr., was charged with making recommendations for the reconstruction of the highway and establishing guidelines for future development of the waterfront. The task

Countless workshops and community meetings were held to ensure that residents were given the opportunity to voice their concerns and preferences and to help HRPC conceptualize the grand plan for the riverfront.

force recommended that the Westway be made into a six-lane boulevard and that a "broad public esplanade containing a continuous walkway, a bicycle path, and other active and passive uses" be built.

Those recommendations led to the formation of the West Side Waterfront Panel in 1988. Created by the governor and the mayor and chaired by Michael Del Guidice, the panel began to develop design guidelines and a financing mechanism for a Hudson River esplanade and to make recommendations for the piers and the waterfront area. The two-year effort involved government, business, labor, environmental, civic, and community leaders who, in 1990, released *Vision for the Hudson River Waterfront Park*. This vision statement recommended the formation of an organization that would oversee the planning, design, regulatory approval, and construction of a large-scale waterfront revitalization effort. On the basis of the panel's recommendations, the Hudson River Park Conservancy was created in 1992 to continue the planning process for the waterfront, secure regulatory approvals, and ultimately develop the waterfront park. HRPC is a subsidiary of the state's development authority and has an independent board of directors appointed by the governor, the mayor, and the Manhattan borough president.

One of HRPC's first efforts was to issue a request for design proposals, which resulted in the hiring of Quennell Rothschild Associates/Signe Nielsen as the master design consultant. The designers were charged with assembling and managing a team that would include designers, urban planners, engineers (civil, struc-

tural, and mechanical), marketing and economic consultants, environmental scientists, an art adviser, and a historian.

Starting in September 1994, the design team, along with HRPC, conducted a series of design charrettes, community workshops, and meetings with the residents of Tribeca, Greenwich Village, Chelsea, and Clinton, to get their ideas for the shape of the park. The first meeting in each neighborhood was mostly a brainstorming session with Community Board members and a wide variety of experts. A second meeting of residents, businesses, and community groups generated a new set of suggestions.

To assist in the design process, "community design liaisons" (landscape architects) were also made available to residents of Tribeca, Greenwich Village, Chelsea, and Clinton. The information gathered at the community meetings was taken back to the technical team, evaluated, and incorporated into two different schemes, which were then presented in November and December 1994 to the same group of people. The participants worked in small groups to reach consensus on "educational and recreational options, revenue-generating ideas, and overall land use patterns."

Throughout the process, the design team and HRPC kept the community informed through mailings and advertisements in local newspapers updating residents on the process.

From over 130 meetings with the design team, the conservancy, and residents, the master design consultant eventually came up with a single concept plan. HRPC's concept plan was on display at the Municipal Art Society Urban Center for several months, and a panel discussion was held in which visitors could provide their critiques and suggestions. Other opportunities for community members to present their opinions have been ongoing.

The Elements of the Concept Plan

The plan, which the conservancy considers to be a work-in-progress until all of its elements are finally approved and constructed, is an ambitious effort. To facilitate community understanding and interpretation, the team divided the many parts of the plan into three discrete units: structural elements, themes, and facilities. According to HRPC, "Structural elements are the features that define and shape the park. Themes give it flavor. Facilities—from boat launches to beaches, and from performance spaces to dog runs—are what will make people come back again and again."

Then the design team presented six identifiable "structural elements":

1. Ten major gateway entrances will be developed and delineated by a unifying maritime element (perhaps a lightship beacon), a Hudson River Park concession, and a public plaza. Minor entrances will be located every three blocks.
2. A continuous paved waterside esplanade extending five miles along the Hudson will allow unimpeded access to the waterfront.
3. Over 90 acres of the project will be dedicated to recreational uses (e.g., tot-lots; playgrounds; dog runs; basketball, tennis, and volleyball courts; and baseball diamonds).
4. Of the 34 piers within the designated Hudson River Park Conservancy area, which occupy an enormous part of the total 550 acres of open space, 13 are slated for public recreation; the other 21 piers will feature maritime, municipal, ecological, or commercial use.
5. Five expanded park areas will be found at Pier 40, the Gansevoort Peninsula, Piers 62 and 63, 42nd Street, and 55th Street.
6. When the New York State Department of Transportation completes reconstruction of Route 9A, it will be a landscaped urban boulevard with frequent signaled crosswalks, planted medians, and landscaped buffers, all designed to accommodate pedestrian access to the Hudson River. In addition, a continuous bikeway/walkway will be constructed along the boulevard from Battery Park to 59th Street.

The four themes that make up the plan are somewhat more esoteric: edges, channels, motion, and islands. The *edges* signify the point where the land meets water. The *channels* are a reminder of the many roles the river has played in New York's history. The *motion* of sun, rain, weather, tides, and currents is incorporated into the park through wind sculptures and water-play areas. And the *islands*—from Manhattan to Ellis Island to the wildlife islands—have been shaped by the Hudson River.

The facilities to be found along the Hudson River include an incredible array of recreational uses—from

One of the first parts of the effort includes a bikeway/ walkway/skateway along the water. The entire length of the park will have a waterside esplanade as well as a continuous bicycle path.

passive lawns to baseball to golf—as well as water uses, education and entertainment facilities, and concessions ranging from kiosks to full-scale restaurants.

And for many critics of the plan, it is proposed uses such as entertainment facilities, full-scale restaurants, and various other money-generating schemes that are the most unacceptable aspects of the plan. Essentially, HRPC will lease two designated piers (as well as the already completed Chelsea Piers) to private developers of park-related uses to generate money for park maintenance. Leases will require the developer/investor to build, maintain, and operate the site and the accompanying public space in accordance with state regulations. Chelsea Piers, profiled in the next section, is one of the first examples of such efforts.

Despite the optimism of HRPC, much of the plan is just that. Nothing can be built until a successful environmental review has been completed, and much is predicated on the reconstruction of Route 9A (what would have been the Westway project). While Route 9A is being reconstructed, land intended for park use will need to be temporarily paved to redirect southbound traffic.

The Hudson River Park project is on a six-year plan scheduled to be completed in 2003. This $300 million project depends on the state and the city each contributing $100 million; the remaining $100 million is intended to come from a variety of sources—such as surplus operating revenue, accumulated property revenue, private fundraising, and federal grants.

Project Data • Hudson River Park Project
Ten-Year Capital Plan (in thousands)

Basic Program	Cost Estimate (1995 dollars)	Cost Estimate (inflated @ 3%)
Capital costs		
Land area and esplanade	$127,700	$154,354
Bulkhead	25,000	30,213
Public piers	82,850	98,523
Planning and environmental impact statement	9,300	11,338
Total	$244,850	$294,428

Funding Sources

State funds	$100,000
City matching funds	100,000
Surplus operating revenue	24,576
Accumulated property revenue	23,490
Private fundraising	13,181
Federal grants such as ISTEA and Wallop-Breaux	13,181
Savings realized through interagency coordination	20,000
Total	$294,428

The following program elements will be pursued if additional funding sources become available (funding sources to be determined).

Pier 42	$13,400	$14,874
Area adjacent to Route 9A	16,750	20,013
Total	$30,150	$34,887
Grand total	$275,000	$329,315

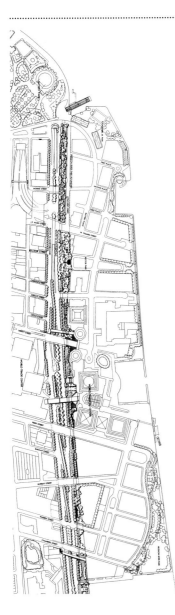

Battery Park City

Hudson River Park begins at Battery Park, on the southern tip of Manhattan. The portion of the park in lower Manhattan includes the only section not at the water's edge. Battery Park is the connecting point for residential Battery Park City and the financial district of lower Manhattan.

Next to Battery Park is the newly constructed 3.5-acre Robert F. Wagner, Jr., Park, named after the former New York deputy mayor, board of education president, city planning commission chairman, and city council member. This new park was designed by architects Rodolfo Machado and Jorge Silvetti, landscape architect Laurie Olin of the Olin Partnership, and garden designer Lynden B. Miller. The building in the park houses a café in the lower level and elevated platforms above, from which to view the scenery. One of the distinguishing features of the park is a hexagonal Holocaust memorial museum, designed by Kevin Roche, that borders to the north.

A 1.5-mile esplanade extends the entire length of Battery Park City. When the esplanade was completed in 1985, it became the first public waterfront park built in New York City since 1954, when the Brooklyn Heights Promenade was completed.

Belvedere Park is a 1.6-acre park that serves as a transition between the Battery Park City open space and the mammoth office towers that make up the World Financial Center.

North of Wagner Park, in Battery Park City, the board of education will be constructing a new grammar school with a playground that will be open to residents after school hours.

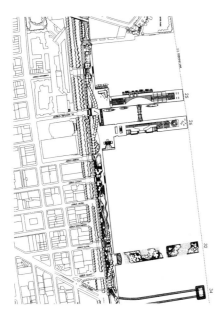

Tribeca

In Tribeca, the public will have access to two piers—25 and 26—which will be connected by a suspension bridge. Pier 25 will hold a large play area as well as several multiuse courts. In addition, it will be the location of a public boat dock, a water taxi stop, and food and rental concessions. Pier 26 will focus on education and research activities through demonstration gardens and an estuarium.

Pier 32 is severely decayed and will be made into a nesting platform to attract waterfowl, osprey, and harbor seals. Pier 34 is built over the Holland Tunnel and was rebuilt recently as two linked finger piers. The south finger is a public pier, and the north finger is used for service and emergency access to the tunnel vent shaft. The Port Authority of New York and New Jersey and the New York State Department of Transportation control that pier.

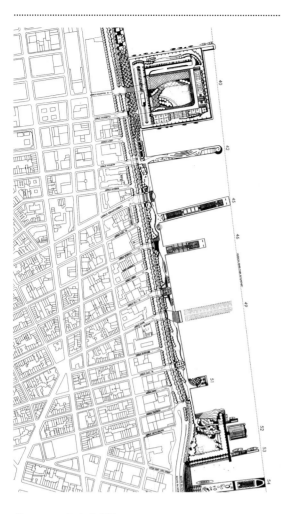

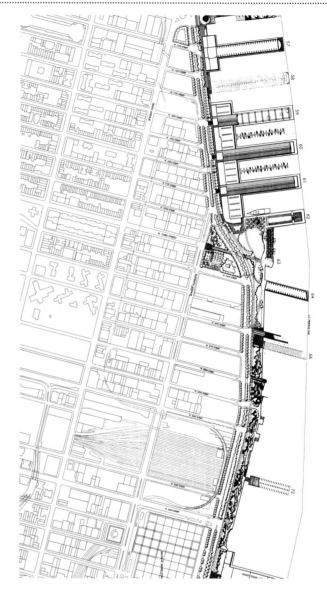

Greenwich Village

The 1.6 million-square-foot Pier 40 is a parking area for some 2,000 cars. A huge existing structure will be renovated and adapted to several new revenue-generating uses, including Manhattan's flower market and related retail facilities. The courtyard and roof will become a 10.5-acre public park, and a public walkway will be constructed around the perimeter of the entire pier. Residents wanted the structure on Pier 40 to be torn down because it obstructs views of the river, but HRPC retained the structure in order to protect the revenue stream.

Plans call for using Pier 42 as a concourse for in-line skating, Pier 45 for sunbathing and relaxing, and Pier 46 for volleyball courts. Pier 49 is currently just piles that serve as habitats for aquatic life and other flora and fauna. Pier 51, a short pier, will become a water-play area.

The Gansevoort Peninsula (Piers 52 and 53) is currently the location of a garage for the New York City Department of Sanitation. If HRPC succeeds in getting the department of sanitation to relocate, this peninsula will probably become a ball field and a beach.

Pier 54 will be the site of remnants from passenger and cargo ships in commemoration of the departure of the *Lusitania* and the return of the survivors of the *Titanic*.

Chelsea

Within Chelsea, nine piers can be found along the river. Pier 56 is in disrepair, and much of it will be removed; the remaining fragment will allow pedestrians to walk out onto the river to view wildlife. Pier 57 contains a 1957 art-deco construction now used to park municipal buses. Piers 59 through 62 house the Chelsea Piers Sports and Entertainment Complex. Chelsea Waterside Park, intended for Pier 62 and what's left of 63, will provide ten acres of passive and active recreation. A two-story shed on Pier 64 will double the amount of space available for free recreational, cultural, and community facilities.

North of Pier 64, the last remaining railroad float bridge in the Hudson River will be restored; an accompanying exhibit will recall the Hudson's historic role in moving cargo. Pier 66, another wildlife pier, will have its deck removed so that the pilings and the extensive plant and animal life that they support will be visible. Between Piers 64 and 76, the shoreline will be the focus, allowing users to appreciate the natural habitats and simply be near the water.

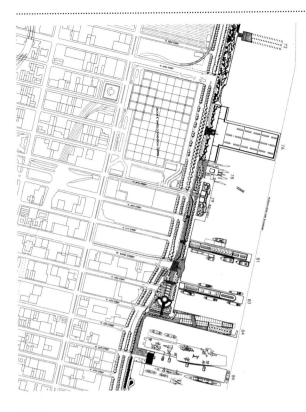

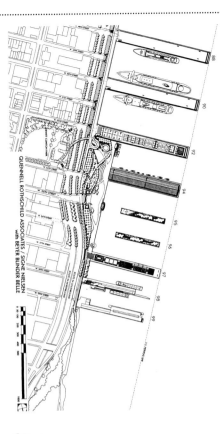

Midtown

Midtown is a densely populated area of Manhattan, and its proposed uses are therefore intended to be urban in character and to emphasize maritime activities. HRPC is proposing the addition of a new ferry terminal building at 42nd Street for use by commuters and tourists. At the south side of Pier 72 (a field of piles), a beach will bring people closer to the water and to the plants and aquatic life found in the Hudson.

Currently, Pier 76 is well known among Manhattanites as the tow pound for the New York City Department of Transportation. It is not currently under HRPC's jurisdiction, but HRPC is working with the city to relocate the pound and pursue other commercial uses on the site. Among the proposals being considered is moving the heliport from its current site on the waterfront to this pier.

Pier 78, the only privately owned pier in Manhattan, is owned by New York Waterways and serves as the embarking and disembarking point for 20,000 people who commute by ferry. Pier 79 is the site of an interim ferry terminal for service from Yonkers, Rockland County, and Staten Island. A permanent ferry terminal is being considered for that site.

Proposed maritime activity on Piers 81, 83, 84, and 86 will build on current commercial maritime uses.

Clinton

The final neighborhood under HRPC's purview is Clinton, also known as Hell's Kitchen. Famous for its concentration of impoverished immigrants, the Clinton neighborhood, while still attractive to immigrants, is being revived by residents who like the area for its convenience and relatively affordable housing. Piers 88, 90, and 92 are currently passenger-ship terminals and not under HRPC's jurisdiction; 88 and 90 will continue to function as such while the city explores new commercial options for Piers 92 and 94. Wildlife islands will be located at Piers 95 and 96. Clinton Cove Park will be constructed along the river between Piers 94 and 96. Pier 97 will be available for passive and active recreational uses and will hold a playground for children. Piers 98 and 99 will still be used by Con Edison and the New York City Department of Sanitation.

Chelsea Piers Sports and Entertainment Complex

A Great Place to Be a Kid or Act Like One

Within the Hudson River Park Conservancy's purview are the Chelsea Piers, a 30-acre sports and film center located on the Hudson River between 17th and 23rd Streets and one of the first new commercial enterprises on public land. Each of the four finger piers reaches more than 840 feet into the Hudson River; Piers 60 and 61 are covered, and Piers 59 and 62 are vast open spaces, each offering a different sports activity. Developed by the private sector, the piers are already complete, viable, and contributing to future park expenses.

How Chelsea Piers Came To Be

Entrepreneur and investor Roland Betts's young daughter was a figure skater, and the only place she could skate was at Sky Rink, which at the time was New York City's only year-round indoor ice rink. Located on the 16th-floor rooftop of a building on West 33rd Street, the rink was substandard, yet it was in great demand, which meant that Betts had to take his daughter to practice at four a.m. Betts was asked to be on the board of Sky Rink and improved conditions as much as possible, but he still thought that a new home for the facility, large enough to hold two rinks, was the only solution. In his search for a new location, he was led to Chelsea Piers. The huge spaces (120 feet wide, 840 feet long, with no columns) were ideal for the purpose. In early 1992, Betts and one of his subsequent partners, David Tewksbury (a development professional for Cushman & Wakefield whom Betts had met at Sky Rink), submitted a proposal to the real estate division of the New York State Department of Transportation (DOT), which owns the site. The plans called for just one pier—Pier 61—to be converted into two skating rinks on the upper level, with parking on the lower level. Even though their contact at the DOT liked the plan, he couldn't offer them more than a 30-day lease.

The 30-acre sports village was built on four 840-foot piers, located between 17th and 23rd streets and along the Hudson River. The esplanade that fronts the Chelsea Piers is 1.2 miles long, making the Chelsea Piers Maritime Center the largest marina in New York City.

Beck's Studio

Chelsea Piers before the renovation was a waterfront eyesore. Rollback cargo doors have been replaced by giant picture windows that feature spectacular views.

At about the same time, in April 1992, the state of New York decided to seek proposals for a development plan for three piers. Although it was more than Betts had bargained for, he pulled in his business partner, Tom Bernstein, with whom he'd been very successful in the film financing business. Upon investigation, Betts, Tewksbury, and Bernstein decided that it might be worthwhile to make a bid for the piers. They planned to retain and expand the two soundstages used by the television series *Law and Order*, and after a little market research, they concluded that there was enough demand for sports other than ice skating to justify turning the three piers and the headhouse that connects them into multipurpose recreational facilities with amenities such as restaurants and sports equipment stores.

According to Tom Bernstein, "We found out that New York City is starved for competitive sport space. Before we started the project we met with the eminent developer Jim Rouse, who told us that we would be overwhelmed by the response because we were programming into a vacuum. But we did pick the sports carefully. For example, there are no tennis courts because Manhattan already has enough tennis courts."

The proposal submitted by Betts, Tewksbury, and Bernstein offered the state of New York lower monthly rents than it would have received under the other ten proposals ($157,000, adjusted annually for inflation), but seemed to the state to present a more viable long-term use. The state signed a 20-year lease (later extended to 49 years) with the partnership, and thus began the Chelsea Piers Sports and Entertainment Complex.

The Facilities

Chelsea Piers provides an array of activities for adults and children. One of the most unusual parts of the complex is the Golf Club at Pier 59, where a little bit of sub-urbia can be found in the middle of one of the most urban settings in the United States. A newly constructed, shingled clubhouse is home to a pro shop, locker rooms, meeting rooms, a bag storage area, and the Chelsea Brewing Company, a 300-seat waterfront microbrewery and restaurant.

But beyond the country-club atmosphere is one of the most technologically advanced driving ranges and teaching centers in the world. The four-tiered structure provides 52 heated hitting stalls that can be used no matter the weather. Surrounding the fairways and the tiered structure is a 155-foot-high net, supported by 12 steel towers positioned on top of steel piles, some of which extend almost 300 feet into the bedrock. "The piers are capable of accommodating substantial vertical loads, but are incapable of sustaining any bending or twisting," said James G. Rogers III, of Butler Rogers Baskett, project architects. "With a net 150 feet in the air, you create a sail, and the pier has effectively no capacity to resist that bending movement. The result is that the towers that support the net are not supported by the piers or pier structure. Rather they are supported by individual structures of 280-foot steel piles. We sawed holes in the pier deck and drove hollow-ended steel piles until we hit bedrock. Each cluster of piles (six at each tower) has built on top of it a concrete pile cap, and the base of each tower is bolted on top of that."

But even that structure can resist bending motions and lateral forces only to a point, so the nets, controlled by a sophisticated computer system, lower automatically when winds reach 50 miles per hour. If the nets were to ice up in sleet or freezing rain, they would essentially become solid, and with high winds would be quite dangerous.

The 150,000-square-foot Sports Center at Pier 60 could alone be the centerpiece of such a project, as it features premier equipment; a banked, six-lane, 200-meter com-

With Japanese technology programming the driving range, golfers need never bend down or touch a golf ball. Each of the 52 heated and weather-protected hitting stalls has a computerized ball tee-up capability that raises the ball from the ground level according to how the golfer has programmed the tee height.

petition indoor running track; a 4,600-square-foot rock-climbing wall, the largest in the Northeast; and a 10-by-60-foot bouldering wall. This 880-foot-long and 120-foot-wide center is the length of three football fields. The workout area alone encompasses 20,000 square feet. In addition, the sports center offers 4,000 square feet of studio space; a six-lane, 25-yard swimming pool; a whirlpool; a boxing ring; and an 18,000-square-foot flexible infield that accommodates track and field events as well as volleyball, indoor sand volleyball, and other special events.

In addition, the sports center houses a sports medicine and performance center operated by a New York hospital and an Origins Feel-Good Spa (an Estée Lauder company). The spa provides an array of services, from lymphatic drainage massage to acupressure facials to treatment for jet lag.

All this is housed in the second level of Pier 60, one of two buildings standing when Chelsea Piers Management, Inc., began development. To add visual appeal to the interiors of the nondescript structures, the developers and architect punched out the roll-up door walls and supplanted them with floor-to-ceiling windows offering dramatic views of the Hudson. With the river view and the sense of the outdoors coming into the space, the sports center feels almost like a vacation resort.

The same could be said of Sky Rink at Pier 61. Floor-to-ceiling windows in the two ice rinks offer spectacular views of the Hudson. "I've played hockey all over the country," said Betts, "but until Chelsea Piers was finished, I'd never played with a window at all. You can't believe what a different feeling it is."

In addition, the new facility provides high-quality locker rooms; a pro shop; skate rentals; food service; meeting rooms; and seating for 1,600, including two skyboxes. An array of adult and junior programs is offered, from hockey clinics to skating school to figure skating to open skating.

Roller skaters also have a spot at the plaza entrance to Chelsea Piers. The roller rinks, located on Pier 62, feature two outdoor, regulation-sized, professionally sur-faced, in-line and roller skating rinks for general skating, hockey, and lessons. The roller rinks offer many programs for adults and youths, including roller hockey leagues and classes and in-line instructional and fitness classes. At the water end of Pier 62 is a public park paid for and maintained by Chelsea Piers Management, Inc. Pier 62 will become a public pier at the time of the Hudson River Park construction.

The plaza entrance, where the buses stop and the taxicabs wait, has a small parking lot where cab drivers can park for 20 minutes for free, use public rest rooms, and stop for a soda or to make a phone call—a real luxury in Manhattan.

The headhouse stretches from 22nd Street down to 18th Street and accommodates the management offices, offices for Silver Screen Studios (where two television series are produced by DreamWorks, whose New York office is also located at Chelsea Piers), a pro shop, a skate rental facility, a logo-wear shop, a café, Pier 59 studios, the Surfside 3 Marina, and a motorboat dealership.

Also in the headhouse is a 90,000-square-foot field house. Located between Piers 61 and 62, the field house contains an array of athletic facilities: a 23,000-square-foot gymnastics training center, a rock-climbing wall especially designed for children and adult beginners, two basketball courts, two artificial-turf playing fields, and four batting cages.

The gymnastics facilities are the only ones in New York City sanctioned for competition by USA Gymnastics. The facility features at least two sets of equipment for each of the men's and women's Olympic events, as well as sunken trampolines and tumble tracks. The newest addition to the complex is a 40-lane, state-of-the-art bowling facility with food service, a bar, and party rooms.

In total, 550 parking spaces are available on the first levels of Piers 59, 60, and 61. A 600-seat, $7.5 million seafood restaurant, The Crab House, has opened below Sky Rink. The Chelsea Brewing Company, a restaurant/microbrewery in Pier 59, seats 300; another large-format restaurant is planned for Pier 60.

How Did They Do It?

One of the most amazing aspects of the Chelsea Piers complex is that the developers were able to complete their project in four years, from bidding to opening. Tewksbury attributes the speed of completion to "a matter of timing and luck and relative inexperience. We had no track record and no bad stuff. And no buildings were actually constructed."

The last point is the critical one. Although the developers had to get an extraordinary number of approvals and zoning changes (the chairman of the Board of Standards and Appeals has been quoted as saying that the proposal involved the most comprehensive series of zoning changes in the history of the city), the absence of new construction greatly reduced the number of community groups that had to be involved in the process. The developers took care to involve Community Board 4 in the discussions and planning and review, but the board had almost no formal role in the process. And as expected, there were some objections from the private sector, but for the most part, the public sector embraced the plan from the start.

A full environmental impact assessment was conducted and showed almost no problems. One of the biggest concerns was traffic, but it was already heavy because of the highway—and in the end, the concern wasn't strong enough to stop the project.

The basic structures are fairly simple buildings, distinguished only by enormous steel truss work: the steel girders that support the second floor are five feet deep and reach 60 feet to either side. Architect Jim Rogers retained the original steel truss work throughout. Instead of fighting the architecture with cuteness, he simply de-

signed each facility to look different from the others. The various facilities are connected by virtue of being located in one enormous structure on the waterfront, but according to Rogers, "This is not architecture for the architectural purist. It has to do with being appropriate to the energy and sense of action that is so much a part of the facilities. While all are part of the same entity, they're very different and for very different markets. The gymnastics facility is used mostly by kids and is painted in primary colors. The ice skating rink is all about moving fast and quick reactions to things and bright colors and blue-and-white-diagonal checkerboard, what I'll call high-energy coloration. The health club is more sophisticated, not directed toward children but toward adults

The sports center—the length of three football fields—houses one of the longest indoor tracks in the world (one-half mile) as well as a banked, 200-meter competition track. In addition to the many other workout facilities, the sports center houses 15,000 square feet of locker rooms fully equipped with saunas, steam rooms, and other amenities. Massages, facials, and other mind and body therapies are available.

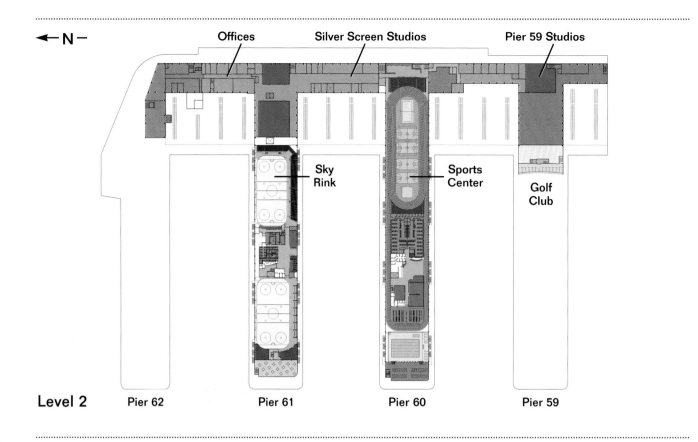

Level 2

← N →

Offices   Silver Screen Studios   Pier 59 Studios

Sky Rink

Sports Center

Golf Club

Pier 62   Pier 61   Pier 60   Pier 59

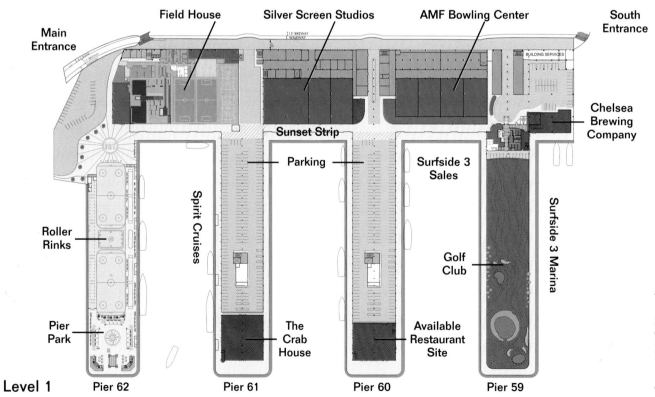

Level 1

Main Entrance

Field House   Silver Screen Studios   AMF Bowling Center   South Entrance

15' BIKEWAY
WALKWAY

BUILDING SERVICES

Sunset Strip

Chelsea Brewing Company

Roller Rinks

Spirit Cruises

Parking

Surfside 3 Sales

Surfside 3 Marina

Golf Club

Pier Park

The Crab House

Available Restaurant Site

Pier 62   Pier 61   Pier 60   Pier 59

Sonnenblick–Goldman Company

Piers 60 and 61, the enclosed piers, primarily house the sports center and the sky rink. The open piers, 59 and 62, are the sites of the golf club and the roller rinks. At the western end of Pier 62, Pier Park is open to the public, providing benches, picnic tables, and a wooden shade structure for visitors to take advantage of the spectacular river views. A five-block-long building called the headhouse connects the piers and houses additional athletic facilities, retail stores, and restaurants, as well as film, television, and photography studios.

The new twin-rink facility on Pier 61 operates 24 hours a day, seven days a week, year-round, and is available to skaters of all ages and ability. With party rooms that overlook the Hudson River, Sky Rink is a popular spot for birthday celebrations and other gatherings.

Fred George

who are prepared to spend a substantial amount of money and time working on themselves."

In order to finance the project, the partners and investors put up $17 million of their own money, and Morgan Stanley issued $45 million in mortgage bonds. But because the project was a relatively untried concept, money was hard to get, and the loan ended up being an expensive one. Betts said that "financing was a harrowing experience." Once the project was finished and was deemed a success, Chelsea Piers Management, Inc., wanted to refinance $55 million of short-term, high-interest debt; to do that, the corporation sought an extension on the 20-year lease, which was ultimately extended to 49 years.

The final cost of the project was $90 million, with $25 million in improvements made by subtenants. (It had originally been budgeted at $25 million in 1992 and at $60 million in 1994). Revenues come from a variety of sources—memberships, user fees, rental fees, percentages from restaurants. Sponsorships are an important revenue source. The field house, for example, is plastered with banners from sponsors such as Reebok, ConEd, Pepsi, and IKON. Employees wear sponsor clothing; logos decorate collateral materials.

While critics might long for the piers to be all public parkland, Chelsea Piers is a realistic compromise that generates needed revenue for the state and provides a missing link along the Hudson. Tewksbury says, "We've taken our lumps in the community, but before we developed Chelsea Piers it was surrounded by an eight-foot-high chain-link fence. This water has been inaccessible for a long time. Now our project is almost too good to criticize."

The renaissance that was going on simultaneously in Chelsea has probably also been a factor in the success of Chelsea Piers. It wasn't just the procession of new superstores that moved into Chelsea—among them Filene's Basement; Barnes & Noble; Old Navy Clothing; and Bed, Bath & Beyond—that changed the neighborhood virtually overnight. It was also a gradual movement of galleries, artists, and designers who left SoHo as it became more and more expensive and commercial.

But Betts is convinced that the Chelsea Piers complex alone has enhanced the neighborhood, apart from the renaissance in Chelsea: "It changed real estate values across the street. Residential prices have doubled in four years. Warehouse space is becoming the new SoHo. It accelerated a trend already begun."

Even without using the sports facilities, pedestrians can walk all through the project along Sunset Strip, a walkway that runs parallel to the river. From there they can enter any of the commercial spaces—the stores, the café, the seafood house, the microbrewery. They can watch the outdoor sports, including the roller rink and the golf club, they can sit in the park at the end of Pier 62, and they can sit on any of the benches that dot the

The 23,000-square-foot gymnastics center features column-free competition spring floors, deep foam training pits, tumble tracks, and in-ground trampolines, as well as multiple sets of bars, beams, rings, horses, and vaults.

esplanade. Chelsea Piers brings in some 8,000 to 10,000 visitors daily, and is now a stop on New York Apple Tours. As of early 1997, the sports center had some 4,000 members.

The complex is kept immaculately clean, one of several management ideas that the developers freely admit they stole from Disney. Badges for all 600 employees bear only a first name—and that goes for owners and managers as well as the 150 part-time employees. And while Chelsea Piers has its own security force, the limited entrances provide natural checkpoints, and Bernstein says, "We tell our employees, 'You're all part of the security force.' Guest services and security go hand in hand. So in a sense we have a 600-person security force. However, security hasn't been a real problem. Since all venues have a water view, people don't feel like they're in New York, so they don't act like it either."

The owners are convinced that programming is their key to success. And they try to make Chelsea Piers a place where people don't go for 50 minutes to work out. They go for two, three, or four hours to enjoy what's going on. Betts said, "We're tapping into the lifestyle thing. Good healthy sports. Most other entertainment complexes are sedentary—restaurants, retail, gimmicky things. We have almost no retail at Chelsea Piers. When we first started this, we were barraged by virtual-reality people. But it didn't interest us. We think competition

fits the New York lifestyle." Bernstein added, "We believe this gives us staying power and that we'll stand the test of time where others might not."

Conclusion

For many years, New Yorkers shunned the polluted Hudson River. Yet the Hudson River waterfront has some of the most spectacular vistas in the world—across the river to the Statue of Liberty and inward toward the Manhattan skyline. Fortunately, a change in environmental regulations led to 25 years of intensive effort to clean up the river, which now bears new aquatic life and has been deemed swimmable for the first time in many years.

Now, 50 years after New York City turned its back on the river, the Hudson River Park Conservancy has developed a plan to reawaken the waterfront and create a park on a vast scale. "Once in a century, a city gets a chance to reclaim its heritage and endow its future with a signature park," declares the Hudson River Park Conservancy's concept and financial plan. "This time around, on the Hudson, New Yorkers also have an opportunity to do something brand-new: build a great park that they themselves have designed. And, at the same time, build a great park that will forever pay its own way." This large-scale effort will be one for many people to watch.

Project Data • Chelsea Piers Sports and Entertainment Complex

Operating Information

Revenues

Golf	14.23%
Sports center	17.07
Sky rink	19.55
Roller rinks	3.49
Fieldhouse	9.96
Studios	8.65
Marina	2.87
Parking	4.16
Restaurants	3.66
Sponsorship	5.79
Special events	2.67
Office leasing	3.83
Company store	1.18
Other revenue	2.90
Location shoots	0.00
Total revenues	**100.00%**

Expenses

Golf	5.14%
Sports center	15.02
Sky rink	9.16
Roller rinks	2.29
Fieldhouse	7.50
Studios	0.34
Marina	0.20
Parking	1.99
Restaurants	0.00
Sponsorship	0.40
Special events	0.66
Office leasing	0.00
Company store	0.52
Location shoots	0.04
Total operating expenses	**43.27%**

Overhead expenses	36.65%
Net income	20.09%

Construction costs[1]

Sports center	24.39%
Golf	16.37
Sky Rink	15.33
Studios	11.07
Service areas	10.86
Fieldhouse	4.87
Roller rinks	2.36
Marina	2.16
Other hard costs	2.12
Total hard costs	**89.52%**
Total soft costs	**10.48%**
Total construction costs	**100.00%**

Note

1. Figures are based on total construction costs of approximately $80 million.

Note

1. For an excellent discussion of the Westway project and the development of Battery Park City, see Alexander Garvin, *The American City: What Works, What Doesn't* (New York: McGraw-Hill, 1996), pp. 302–307.

Mill Race Park
Columbus, Indiana

Steven Fader

Mill Race Park is a park of high ambitions. Its planners and designers intended to reclaim a floodplain and toxic waste site for community use, to provide support for downtown revitalization efforts, and to leave a legacy to the community on the 500th anniversary of Christopher Columbus's voyage to America. And if those ambitions were not enough, the park's planners were determined to match the "world-class" level of design for which Columbus, Indiana, is nationally known, and to accomplish all of these goals without major capital funding from the city.

The resulting 85-acre park, located at the west end of downtown Columbus, substantially succeeds in its ambitions. Dedicated in

1992, the park is now a focal point for concerts and community activities and a source of civic pride. The design of the park has attracted national attention, and the once swampy and sleepy bottomlands have been recalled to life with minimal public investment.

Located "at the meeting of city and river," as project landscape architect Michael Van Valkenburgh described it, the park's built forms and landscapes range from urban to wild, and its uses from communal to solitary. Along the park's urban edge, the landscape and hardscape tend to be rectilinear—parking lots framed by the remnants of old concrete floodwalls, rows of Kentucky coffee and hackberry trees, and an 80-foot observation tower, axially sited in line with the primary entry into the park and the downtown area. The urban edge soon gives way, however, to softer forms, terminating in the natural vegetation of the meandering riverbank, which borders the park on three sides. Taking advantage of the site's proximity to water and the gravel pits left on the site from an industrial past, the landscape design also includes two lakes: the 450-foot-diameter Round Lake, and the previously existing North Lake.

Interspersed throughout the park is a series of red-painted structures designed by architect Stanley Saitowitz—an amphitheater stage, an arbor, picnic shelters, fishing piers, a boathouse, and rest rooms. Park facilities also include a playground, a basketball court, a horseshoe pit, a wetlands interpretive area with a raised boardwalk, a wildflower area, and the scenic Riverwalk that connects to the city's People Trail outside the park borders.

From Death Valley to City Park

Mill Race Park is located on a plain where the Flatrock and Driftwood rivers merge to form the east fork of the White River. Long known as Death Valley for its swampy, pestilential character, the site floods annually and was used intermittently from the mid-19th century onward for industrial purposes: a tannery, gravel pits, brick manufacturing, and similar enterprises. The tannery dyes would make the river run red, and the smell cast its pall over the entire city. Eventually, squatters' dwellings—often with dirt floors and without running water—grew up on the plain.

According to former mayor Bob Stewart, it was a land of "big mosquitoes and barking dogs."

By the 1960s, the tannery had closed, and there was substantial community support for clearing the site and making it into a park. It was a "cancerous situation," recalled Carl Miske, head of the River Rats, a group that spearheaded volunteer efforts on behalf of the park. "If we didn't eliminate the cancer, it would spread."

During this period, the city acquired most of what is now Mill Race Park, named in honor of the site's early industry, and cleared the remaining structures. Over time, the Mill Race Playhouse was built on the site and an old covered bridge was relocated to the park. The ethos remained volunteerism, however: "If we couldn't bum it, we didn't need it," recalled Miske.

While the park was clearly an improvement over the prior use of the land, by the 1980s the park was subject to vandalism and had acquired a reputation as a site for nighttime sexual assignations. In addition, the park suffered from inadequate lighting and a lack of playground equipment. As a result, family use of the park had declined, and the flatland by the river was once again considered a civic problem.

The current incarnation of Mill Race Park was spawned in the mid-1980s. A citizens' group called 1992 Columbus was formed to plan and organize the city's 1992 quincentennial celebration of Christopher Columbus's voyage to America. It was determined that as part of the celebration, something of a permanent nature should be created—a legacy—as a gift to the city. Renovation of Mill Race Park was the obvious choice.

The choice was confirmed through an informal process of community input. The late Paul Kennon, a noted architect who was the architectural adviser to 1992 Columbus, conducted surveys and informal conversations with residents at Columbus's downtown shopping mall. Heading the list of desired civic improvement projects was Mill Race Park.

The new Mill Race Park was enlarged by the donation of a 17-acre parcel by the Cummins Engine Foundation. This parcel, which had for a time been an unofficial dumping ground, tested positive for petroleum and other toxic residues and had underground tanks that had to be removed. The abatement process, which took about six months, was managed by the Cummins Engine Foundation, which then transferred the site to the city.

In addition to permits from the Indiana Department of Environmental Management for the hazardous materials cleanup, park development required permits from the Army Corps of Engineers (for the river channels) and the Indiana Department of Natural Resources (floodway protection and wetlands remediation). Among the requirements imposed by these agencies was a 24-hour right-of-access to the river (for fishing purposes) and a general prohibition on any construction that would substantially obstruct floodwaters.

Funding for the renovation came from several sources, some quite unusual. Of the $8.4 million total, the city provided just $944,000 in cash, budgeted over several years from the parks and recreation department's capital and operating funds. Hutch Schumaker, co-chair of the 1992 Celebration Committee, commented, "In this community you are asked to contribute your time, your money, or your talents."

The largest portion of funding (approximately $5 million) came from cash donations from Columbus residents, businesses, and foundations. Of this, approximately $3.6 million came from just six major donors and was raised in three weeks. According to Jim Baker, the former chief executive officer of Arvin Industries, fundraising was done "personally, informally, and quickly." He adds, however, that the Paul Kennon survey, which

The park site circa 1942, when it was known as Death Valley and lined with squatters' dwellings.

Mazo Lomax, *The Evening Republic*

clearly showed communitywide support for the project, was persuasive to potential donors. As part of the major giving program, four local foundations pooled resources and set up a two-to-one matching grant fund. In addition, a number of "donor opportunities" were devised, ranging from park benches to the amphitheater structure.

Among the major donors was the Cummins Engine Foundation (see feature box), which provided a grant to cover the design fees for the landscape architect, structures architect, and related engineering consulting and testing. The Cummins Engine Foundation also paid for the hazardous materials abatement of the parcel it donated to the city. In total, the value of the Cummins Engine Foundation donations to the project exceeded $1 million.

Donated Job Corps labor and equipment was another primary source of project support. The Job Corps is a national program that trains disadvantaged inner-city youth in construction trades. Some 200 student Job Corps trainees, from the local Job Corps training center and elsewhere, were brought in to perform a variety of construction tasks under the supervision of Job Corps advisers and local contractors. The value of this donated labor has been estimated at over $2 million. As part of this effort, the U.S. Department of Labor, which runs the Job Corps program, provided $80,000 in grants to cover the cost of heavy (earth-moving) equipment required for the project.

Additional, outside-the-budget support came from donated services and materials. Each of the five local general contractors involved in the project "adopted" a structure or element on the basis of expertise or interest. All five provided construction labor to the project at cost and donated their construction management services. Similarly, local vendors provided most of the construction materials at cost.

Designing for Nature

According to landscape architect Van Valkenburgh, designing Mill Race Park was a matter of editing the landscape. "It was both additive and subtractive, like putting paint down on a canvas and taking it up," he said. The design process included a four-month master-planning period, in which the landscape architect met with community leaders, interested citizens, groups such as the River Rats, and even elementary-school children. The very public consultations and design presentations "allowed people to feel an involvement in the process" and aided in creating a vision for the park.

With the site's riverfront location and long history, there were a variety of positive elements and memories

A covered bridge, moved to the site long before the park's renovation, is one of four bridges found scattered throughout the park. The park's designers sought to make a strong statement through the structures in the park as well as the landscape features.

to draw upon, as well as "found objects" that had been brought to the site over time. To maintain a sense of continuity with the past, the old tannery floodwalls were retained, as was an old gravel-pit lake. Similarly, four old bridges representative of early wood and steel bridge technology, which had been brought to the site, were incorporated into the design.

Despite its rich history, Mill Race Park was "like the Tin Man looking for a heart," commented Van Valkenburgh. To remedy this, he designed a new lake in the shape of a grand circle, formally ringed by old-fashioned lampposts and ornamental trees. The "civically scaled" and "democratic" Round Lake, as it has come to be known, stands in deliberate contrast to the nearby river and North Lake.

In addition to the lake, several landscape mounds were added to the site. One crescent-shaped mound forms the amphitheater, with terraced, concrete-and-grass benches carved out of the slope, facing the stage. A second grassy mound flanks a basketball court, giving the court a strong presence in the otherwise flat and open plain. The mounds echo those built by Native American tribes indigenous to the Midwest. They also served as disposal sites for earth excavated in the construction of the lake.

The principle of "editing" was applied to the landscaping as it was to other park features. Over 700 trees were planted at Mill Race Park, while some 200 were removed. Some of those removed were dead or diseased; others were removed or pruned to open up vistas and to make connections to the water. New trees were added

An open sluice, designed to visibly demonstrate the connection of the river to the lake, returns lake water to the river.

Michael Van Valkenburgh Associates, Inc.

strategically to complement the existing landscape, to protect park structures from flood-borne logs and debris, and to create the formal landscapes desired for Round Lake and the "city" edge of the park. Native sycamores were planted along the Riverwalk, while red maple, Kentucky coffee, hackberry, and other species were planted elsewhere. The common denominator of the landscape palette was tolerance of flooding.

The flood-prone character of the site was accommodated in other aspects of the site design as well. Drainage was carefully planned to minimize ponding and retention of floodwaters; pathways were made strong enough to resist flood scouring and wide enough to accommodate standard cleaning machines; and off-the-shelf playground equipment was selected because it would be easily replaceable in the event of flood damage.

Accommodation to the annual flood cycle was also a principal requirement for the park's structures. Designed by Stanley Saitowitz, a series of red-painted structures populates the landscape, standing in sharp contrast to the park's greenery. The structures, which serve a variety of purposes, share many of the same materials, including steel tubing, wire mesh, perforated metal, concrete, and glass blocks. The design intention, according to Saitowitz, was to "establish a family." Though each structure is specific in function, "all share the same genetic structure." The "family" includes three picnic shelters, the Custer-Nugent Amphitheater structure, an arbor, a boat pavilion, two fishing piers, rest rooms, and the lookout tower near the park entry.

The picnic shelters are all circular in form, though each varies in detail from the others. "The marking out of a circle," explained Saitowitz, "is the most primitive and universal way of claiming territory." Within the circle, the picnic tables, benches, barbecue pit, and trash-can receptacle are all poured-in-place concrete. Roof coverings over the shelters are designed as warped planes supported on red metal tubing.

The amphitheater has both architectural and landscape components and resulted from a collaboration between Saitowitz and Van Valkenburgh. The open stage structure, which is topped by a red steel canopy shaped like an inverted curve, plays on one side to the concrete and grass terraces, which seat approximately 600. On the opposite side, the stage plays to an open lawn capable of supporting 10,000 or more concert patrons.

The design of the rest rooms addresses not only the threat of flooding, but also the more routine problems of bringing light and air into spaces more typically known for their dampness and darkness. The rest room walls are made entirely of glass blocks, which permit light to penetrate to the interior. These curved walls of glass blocks are raised approximately eight inches off the ground to allow floodwaters to drain out of the structures more easily. At the top, the glass-block walls stop short of the roof, maximizing natural ventilation within the rest rooms. In a bit of whimsy, the steel-tube and corrugated-metal roof structure is bent into the shape of a "W" on one side and an "M" on the other.

Like the park structures and the landscape design, the construction process was anything but routine. Traditionally, a municipality will bid a project and then give a single general contractor responsibility for completing it on time and on budget. At Mill Race Park, no one general contractor had ultimate responsibility for the project. Instead, construction was orchestrated by an informal management group consisting of the director of the city's department of parks and recreation, a construction manager retained by the city, several local contractors who donated their time, and volunteers from 1992 Columbus. Similarly, whereas subcontractors are generally hired by and report to a single general contractor, at Mill Race Park the work was split among

The Architecture of Columbus, Indiana

Columbus, Indiana, a city of approximately 33,000 one hour south of Indianapolis, is nationally known for a wealth of public buildings designed by distinguished architects and designers. Though well into Indiana farming country, this small city has since the 1950s become home to approximately 50 schools, firehouses, and other public and private buildings designed by a "Who's Who" of American architecture. For many years a pilgrimage site for students of architecture, the city has become a tourist destination, its architecture heavily promoted by the local chamber of commerce. So significant has Columbus become in the world of contemporary architecture that it was the site for the 1994 awards ceremony for the Pritzker Prize, architecture's highest honor.

This rich heritage of contemporary architecture originated in the unique insight and interest of J. Irwin Miller of the Cummins Engine Company. Headquartered in Columbus, Cummins is among the world's largest producers of diesel engines. In the years after the Second World War, Miller recognized that for Cummins to flourish, it would need first-rate managers and technicians, and that to compete for talent with the big urban centers, Columbus had to have something special to offer. That "something" was quality of life. Toward this end, Miller formed the Cummins Engine Foundation in the 1950s.

Combining his concern for quality of life with his lifelong interest in architecture, Miller offered a deal to the local school district: if the district would choose distinguished architects for its new school buildings, the Cummins Engine Foundation would pay the architects' fees. Given the sharp increases in enrollments created by the post-war baby boom, the deal proved highly appealing to the school district. A few years later, on the basis of the program's success in the school district, the foundation expanded its architecture program to include fire stations, libraries, and other public buildings. Since the first grant in 1957, the foundation has funded buildings by a host of well-known architects and architecture firms, including I.M. Pei and Partners; Richard Meier and Partners; Skidmore, Owings, & Merrill; and Robert A. M. Stern.

The primary requirement for participation in the Cummins Engine Foundation architecture program is that the client (which must be a public agency in Bartholomew County, Indiana) must agree to choose an architect from a list offered by the foundation. The list typically includes four to six names supplied to the foundation by a disinterested, anonymous panel of distinguished architects. There is no permanent list; a new list is created for each request, appropriate to the prospective commission. Once an architect is selected, the public agency negotiates a contract with the architect. The foundation monitors the execution of the contract but is not involved in the client-architect relationship.

Though the architecture program is the most well-known activity of the Cummins Engine Foundation, the foundation extends grants for other related purposes and in other locations in which the company does business. Grants are provided in the areas of youth and education, equity and justice, quality of life, and public policy.

As the foundation's architecture program has flourished, it has inspired numerous corporations, churches, and individuals to look to notable designers for corporate headquarters, manufacturing plants, churches, golf courses, residences, and other nonpublic buildings. Today, more than half of the buildings on the *Architectural Tour Map of Columbus,* issued by the Columbus Visitors' Center, were built without help from the Cummins Engine Foundation—attesting to an architectural sensibility that has blossomed communitywide.

St. Peter's Lutheran Church—designed by Gunnar Birkerts, Architect—is one of many notable buildings in the small city of Columbus, Indiana.

Bold red structures, designed by Stanley Saitowitz, are found throughout the park. The rest rooms pictured here are designed to let in air and light through the use of glass blocks and the separation of the walls from the roof. The eight-inch space between the bottom of the wall and the floor accommodates flooding.

six entities—five general contractors, each of whom brought in a set of subcontractors and workers, plus the Job Corps contingent, managed by the Job Corps training center.

As Chuck Wilt, director of the Columbus Parks and Recreation Department, commented with notable understatement, "The most challenging task was working with different groups to keep each moving toward the final objective—completion of the park in time for the 1992 celebration. Contractors, unions, trainees, federal bureaucrats, local funders, and city government all had expectations and constraints which had to be addressed and balanced. Even the weather proved uncooperative by sending a 100-year flood at a critical point in the construction phase."

The flooding was not to be the only unpredictable force. Because the Job Corps students were trainees rather than experienced construction workers, the pace of work was slower than normal and difficult to predict and control; on top of this, the students were rotated in and out of jobs and in and out of the program itself.

Despite all these difficulties, the park was dedicated as planned in October of 1992, during the quincentennial celebrations. The park's opening to the public was, however, delayed until the spring of 1993, and park construction was completed in 1994.

Programming the Park

According to the master plan objectives, the design of Mill Race Park provides a broad range of recreational

environments and experiences, from solitary river walks and contemplation to rock concerts for 10,000. Facilities are provided that appeal to children (playground), teens (basketball court), and families (picnic shelters). Several facilities, such as the amphitheater, the boat rental, the fishing pier, the lakes, and the trails, attract a wide range of users.

In sheer numbers, it is the highly popular amphitheater and programmed events that attract the largest number of park visitors. From June through September, nearly every weekend is programmed. The amphitheater is the site of the Mill Race Park Live Concert series, which includes rock concerts, country-and-western concerts, and performances by the Columbus Philharmonic and entertainers such as the Woody Herman Band and Count Basie. The amphitheater is also the site of a noon concert series for kids and the Family Film series. The Family Film series is "like going to a drive-in," said Chuck Wells, marketing and event coordinator for the Columbus Parks and Recreation Department. Recent events held at the park include the Chautauqua of the Arts (20,000 visitors over two days), the annual Scottish Festival (8,000 visitors), and the holiday-time Festival of Lights (50,000 visitors from Thanksgiving through the first week in January).

In addition to the concerts, films, and major events, the park hosts several other smaller programs and camps. These include the annual Fishing Derby, a Native American crafts camp, and the Mill Race Players (a link to the original Mill Race Players, who performed in the park in the 1960s).

Responsibility for planning and staging the myriad events and programs resides jointly with the Columbus

Some 200 Job Corps trainees were brought in to assist with the construction of the park, gaining hands-on experience. The landscape architect had to design the elements in such a way that inexperienced crews could construct them.

Arts Council, a nonprofit organization, and the Columbus Parks and Recreation Department. Funding for events and programs comes from several sources: parks and recreation department operating funds; arts council fundraising; private sector sponsorship; foundation support for various series, such as the Family Film series; and admissions fees to concerts and major events. Volunteers help to defray the cost of maintenance. "The intention is to keep fees to the public as low as possible," according to Kimberly Proffett of the arts council, "while at the same time keeping operations self-supporting."

Interest in the amphitheater offerings has far exceeded expectations. There had always been the intention of providing a replacement for the destroyed Mill Race Playhouse, but the planning committee had not envisioned how popular the amphitheater would become as a concert venue, nor were there sufficient funds to undertake more than a relatively simple stage and performance setup. As a result, the amphitheater lacks a waterproof roof covering and a rear backdrop, access for large trucks, a stage lift, and full theatrical sound and lighting systems, all of which are required for the larger and more elaborate concerts and productions. With the true potential of the amphitheater now apparent, the city has retained the original designer, Stanley Saitowitz, to design these improvements.

Several other park features have also proven to be popular, though on a much smaller scale. The three picnic shelters, which rent for $20 a day on weekends and holidays, are always in demand, and are typically completely booked in the summer. Paddleboat rentals are also popular, although the rentals do not earn enough to pay for the staffing of the paddleboat rental structure. Of the free facilities, the children's playground is the most actively used.

Park operating hours are from sunrise until 11 p.m. The boat ramp is open 24 hours a day, as required by state agencies regulating river access. In part because of the required river access, the park boundaries are not fenced. Enforcement of the park operating hours and responsibility for safety and security in general is the task of the Columbus Parks and Recreation Department Park Patrol. The park patrol visits the park periodically throughout the day and night, as one stop on a route that includes all of the city's parks. Extra city police are assigned to the park on a temporary basis for special events, to assist with traffic and access.

Though there are no full-time staff stationed on park grounds, little significant vandalism or crime has occurred in the park since its rededication in 1992. In one of the few exceptions, a rest room was broken into (via the slot between the floor and wall that is used to drain floodwaters), and the plumbing and the walls were damaged.

Despite this incident and a few others, the parks department does not consider vandalism or crime to be a significant problem. On the contrary, as park usage increases, vandalism and crime appear to be decreasing. As Chuck Wells succinctly described it, "The more activity, the less vandalism." Page Gifford, chairman of the parks board, echoed this sentiment: "A high level of activity is the cheapest security there is."

Managing and Maintaining a Floodplain

Periodic flooding is the most significant management and maintenance issue for Mill Race Park. The river tends to flood in spring but sometimes floods in winter as well. In the spring of 1996, flooding in the park nearly reached the bent metal roofs of the rest rooms and the globes of the streetlights ringing Round Lake.

Sometimes the flooding deposits a layer of silt (runoff from upstream farms), which is actually beneficial

Kris Medic

The tube-shaped steel arbor, one of the park's most whimsical structures, is essentially an alley with seats that directs visitors from the center of the park to the riverfront.

The amphitheater's concrete seating is a terraced berm. A steel canopy slopes over the stage, which is used for outdoor performances. The landscape architect created mounds throughout the park to symbolize those built by indigenous Native American cultures.

to growing conditions for the park's vegetation. At other times, the flooding deposits sand and rubble, which must be removed as best as possible. In all instances, however, a mixture of tree trunks and limbs, rocks, and debris washes over the site, which can damage structures and facilities, both hardscape and landscape.

A checklist of actions to be taken before and after flooding guides the parks department's response. Usually, sufficient advance warning allows certain precautionary steps to be taken. All floatable objects, such as trash cans and boats, are removed to safety. Barricades are used to limit access to the park, and the elevator is sent to its highest station. Power to the park is shut off, in part manually and in part automatically (a float valve in the river automatically shuts off power to much of the park when the river reaches a predefined flood stage).

As the flooding recedes, cleaning begins on the high ground. Undertaken primarily by staff of the parks and recreation department, the cleanup includes removing debris, hosing down the rest rooms and other structures, and plowing the silt and sand. Silt that remains dries to the consistency of fine dust and is removed with a rotating broom.

The most difficult task is the fine-cleaning of all the electrical equipment, which is easily fouled by dust. Though some electrical equipment in the park was deliberately placed above flood level to avoid this problem, Kris Medic, director of park operations for the parks and recreation department, advises that this issue should be a design priority in other communities that intend to develop recreation facilities on floodplains.

For the most part, the landscape materials at Mill Race Park have well-endured the three flood seasons since their planting. This is attributable, states Medic, to the fact that the tree species were carefully selected for their hardiness—in this case, the ability to tolerate the extremely wet and extremely dry conditions typical of a floodplain. An exception is the ring of cherry trees the city selected to surround Round Lake. Chosen more for their aesthetic characteristics and symbolic associations than for their growing characteristics, the trees did not fare well and were replaced with red maples after one season.

Most maintenance tasks—flood-related and routine —are undertaken by parks and recreation department staff. Maintenance crews operate citywide, rotating through Mill Race Park at designated intervals; there are no full-time maintenance staff stationed at the park. Some relatively minor assistance is provided by unpaid workers (persons under court order to perform community service) and by volunteer groups such as the Girl Scouts or the River Rats, which occasionally undertake planting and other projects. Work that is contracted out includes elevator servicing, aerial tree work, and larger, construction-related projects such as the recently installed road to the boat ramp.

Although the park is generally well maintained, some maintenance difficulties are apparent. According to Kris Medic, several park structures and elements constitute "midlevel aggravations." The elevator, for example, frequently needs repair; the grass in the amphitheater access area often gets compacted by the trucks rolling over it; and the grassy mounds suffer from uneven sun exposure and water runoff, both of which make it difficult to keep the mounds lush and green. Other observable problems include areas where the grass and trails have been scoured away by flooding or covered by

The picnic shelters, which have proven to be popular beyond all expectations, are simply curved canopies made of red perforated metal that shelter concrete walls, benches, and tables.

Michael Van Valkenburgh Associates, Inc.

sand, and some minor rusting of the metal structures from exposure to rain or floodwaters.

The Park's Success

Mill Race Park is successful from several perspectives. Once avoided as "Death Valley," the 85-acre floodplain is now the most actively used park in the city in terms of total number of visitors. The amphitheater and special events account for most of the patronage, with individual concerts or events drawing upwards of 10,000 visitors. The park is popular with area residents for its other facilities as well. The picnic shelters, children's playground, and other recreational facilities are well used, as are Round Lake, the Riverwalk, and the other landscape features of the park.

The park is successful urbanistically, but perhaps not to the degree hoped for by its planners. The park has been successful in the limited goal of stabilizing the western border of downtown, and the degraded environment of the floodplain is no longer a limitation on the prospects for downtown revitalization. But neither has the park's development been much of a boon to downtown. While some office workers walk to the park at lunchtime, and while there is some cross-patronage between downtown and the park, the geography remains an impediment. From the downtown shopping area, one must cross two major thoroughfares and a set of railroad tracks—a two- or three-block-wide "no man's land"—to get to the park entry. To overcome this impediment and visually connect the park with downtown, the city has installed a "colonnade" of streetlights clad in red steel tubing along the connector between downtown and the park, echoing the design of the park's structures. While it seems to have raised awareness of the park, this architectural flourish has not been able to bridge the stretch of inhospitable land between the park and downtown.

Steven Fader

The 80-foot observation tower at the east end of the park includes an elevator to allow access to all visitors.

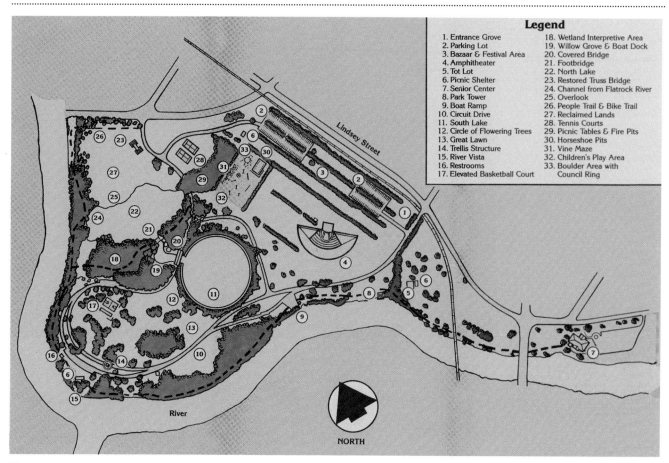

The site is designed to be mostly geometric on the city side, where grids and rows prevail. As the site moves toward the river, it becomes softer and more irregular in its forms.

Environmentally, the park's success is more clear-cut. Development of the park has removed inappropriate uses from the floodplain and rehabilitated lands that had become toxic. Further, the park now stands as an environmentally appropriate and viable example of floodplain use. The use of this flood-prone land is not without cost, however. Cleaning and repairing the facilities after each flood entail significant expense to the city over and above the normal costs of park maintenance.

Though the park is considered to be a great success both locally and nationally, the planners and designers of Mill Race Park note several ways in which the park could be improved or future efforts in other localities enhanced:

- The amphitheater should be designed for more intensive use, with a watertight roof, backdrops, full theatrical sound and lighting systems, stage lift, and truck access.
- Rest rooms should be closer to the amphitheater.
- Additional picnic shelters would be desirable, with varied sizes to accommodate larger groups as well as families.

- Additional lighting would increase safety and the sense of security.
- Additional shade trees would be desirable (though as the newly planted trees mature, the urgency of this need should diminish).
- Additional active recreation facilities, such as volleyball courts, would be of benefit.
- Given the difficulty of cleaning flood-soaked electrical equipment, further consideration of electrical service in floodplain projects is warranted.

Notwithstanding the potential for improvement, Mill Race Park stands as a model of what can be achieved on marginal lands—lands that flood or lands that have been abused. The park also demonstrates how environmentally sensitive land can support active urban usage without loss of environmental integrity. Finally, Mill Race Park demonstrates that a park can be more than simply a collection of recreational facilities: by design, building a park can be an exercise in placemaking and an opportunity to strengthen community identity.

Perhaps most important, Mill Race Park is a model of how we may build parks in the future. Given the

Project Data • Mill Race Park

Development Schedule

Initial site acquired	1960s
Planning started	1987
Master plan approved	1990
Construction started	July 1990
Construction completed	June 1993
Park opened	June 1993 (dedicated 4 October 1992)
Project completed	1994

Financing Information

Funding Source	Amount	Percentage of Total
Private		
Local foundations and community fund drive	$5,265,800	62.50%
Local		
Parks and recreation department	944,000	11.20
State		
Build Indiana Fund	72,000	.85
Federal		
Job Corps	2,143,400	25.40
Total	$8,425,200	100.00%

Development Cost Information

Site acquisition cost (17 acres donated)	$600,000
Site improvement costs	
Excavation/demolition	$156,182
Grading	500,000
Utilities (drainage)	813,775
Paving	207,495
Curbs/sidewalks/wall/amphitheater seats	1,590,000
Landscaping	379,776
Concrete	98,087
Total improvement costs	$3,745,315
Construction costs	
Structures	$1,980,565
Electrical	608,443
Elevator	91,200
Other (miscellaneous park equipment)	125,680
Total construction costs	$2,805,888

Soft costs

Architecture	$180,260
Landscape architecture	832,675
Engineering	119,941
Project management	104,321
Professional services	36,800
Total soft costs	$1,273,997
Total site acquisition and development costs	$8,425,200

Operating Information

Annual operating expenses

Taxes (FICA)	$2,800
Insurance	1,144
Repair and maintenance	55,575
Management	36,000
Utilities	14,000
Professional services	350
Rentals/boat dock	20,500
Miscellaneous	7,000
Park events (concessions)	27,200
Total	$164,569

Annual gross revenues

Boat dock	$3,000
Park events/concessions	32,700
Shelter rentals	1,500
Total	$37,200

competing needs for increasingly scarce public dollars, not many small municipalities are able or willing to take $8 million out of the public coffers for "dirt." Said Bob Stewart, former mayor of Columbus, "There was always a minority opinion that we should be spending this kind of money on people, not on parks." Though the park idea was popular, "We would have been run out of town if the city spent that kind of money on a park." Thus, for Columbus, and possibly for other localities, collaborating with the private sector and the community was both a spiritually and financially appropriate path toward community improvement.

The Park at Post Office Square
Boston

Peter Harnik

Bill Horsman

Boston, the city that in 1634 presented America with its very first urban civic space—the Boston Common—has broken new ground again, this time with an innovative park that has the potential to change public thinking about creating new greenspace among downtown skyscrapers.

At 1.7 acres, the Park at Post Office Square is barely large enough to hold all the awards it has won. Its conception and design have led it to be called "the perfect park," and it has become the focal point for the city's dense, serpentine financial district. Because the park has the feel of a comfortable living room, most visitors—and many Bostonians—have trouble believing that it hasn't always been there.

The park's centerpiece is a walk-through sculptural fountain so whimsically user-friendly that in summertime, office workers eating lunch often kick off their shoes to dip their feet in the fountain, unless an entire class of preschoolers has preempted them by stopping to splash. A couple of yards away is a 143-foot-long formal garden trellis, supported by granite columns, draped with seven species of vines and lit internally by computer-driven mini-bulbs that perform a subtle nighttime show. The jewellike Great Lawn, raised above the walkways by a granite curb, provides a relaxed retreat, even furnishing a ramped, grassy entryway for wheelchairs. One-hundred-twenty-five different species of plants, flowers, bushes, and trees can be found throughout the park. Post Office Square includes an airy, copper-and-glass garden pavilion that houses a year-round café (kosher, no less). It features one-of-a-kind, wrought-iron fencing and specially monogrammed drainage gates. Seating styles fit every posterior and mood—stately teak benches, curving steel settees, movable cast-iron café chairs with tables, hundreds of linear feet of inviting polished granite wall, and half an acre of lawn. And under it all are seven floors of parking spaces for 1,400 cars.

In an unusual twist, the Park at Post Office Square is supported —both physically and financially—by a 500,000-square-foot parking garage, the largest in Boston. And amazingly, the auto-arboreal relationship ("Park Above, Park Below") works.

"The garage functions like a gusher," wrote *Boston Globe* architecture critic Robert Campbell, "spuming people and activity continually upward." The garage gushes more than the 2,000 people who enter and leave the gazebo-covered escalators daily. It also generates the profits, about $8.6 million a year, to pay for the $76 million development of the park-and-parking-lot; its $2.9 million annual operation; its $1 million local tax bill; and, if things go well, a bit extra to contribute to a maintenance fund for neighborhood parks all over Boston.

"Post Office Square Park has changed Boston forever," mused the *Globe*'s Campbell. "The business district used to be an unfathomable maze of streets and buildings without a center. The park provides that center, and all around it, as if by magic or magnetism, the whole downtown suddenly seems gathered in an orderly array. It's as if the buildings were pulling up to the park like campers around a bonfire."

Perhaps even more enchanting is how the Park at Post Office Square came to be.

The Site: From Parking to Park

Until 1954, Post Office Square was an open cobblestone plaza crisscrossed by trolley tracks. That year, the city of Boston, concerned that the lack of downtown parking was contributing to the loss of retail business to the suburbs, signed a 40-year lease of the land for the construction of a four-story garage. The low-fee garage immediately became a dominant, quirky fixture in the neighborhood, warehousing 950 cars a day, producing major traffic jams on Congress Street, and generating huge profits for its operator, a garage and taxi magnate named Frank Sawyer.

By the late 1970s, the squat, 25-year-old concrete structure, trash-strewn and unmaintained, was, in many people's minds, a blight on the neighborhood. Many buildings on the square had shifted their entrance doors and addresses to other streets, symbolically dismissing Post Office Square as a backyard for auto storage.

Enter Norman Leventhal, a native Bostonian who had worked his way up from childhood poverty to become head of the Beacon Companies and one of the city's most prominent developers. Besides understanding the financial aspect of development, Leventhal was also an urban visionary willing to take astonishing risks.

When the Federal Reserve Bank of Boston moved out of its venerable Post Office Square location in the mid-1970s, the building sat on the market for several years, until Leventhal eventually proposed clearing half the site to construct a large office tower and renovating the historic bank as an upscale hotel. After a bruising battle with the city's powerful historic preservationists, he secured the necessary permits.

Two years later, in 1981, as he stood on the steps of the plush new Hotel Meridien and cut a ribbon with Boston Mayor Kevin White, he proudly surveyed the scene. Everything was perfect—except the view across Pearl Street.

"Mr. Mayor," Leventhal said, "that garage has got to go." The mayor agreed, but with the city locked into a lease until 1994, there didn't seem to be any recourse without Frank Sawyer's approval. And, with Sawyer netting over $1 million a year on the garage, he wasn't even returning phone calls.

Undaunted, Leventhal formed Friends of Post Office Square, Inc., in 1983 and sent invitations to some of his neighbors: Fleet Bank, Olympia & York, NYNEX, Eaton Vance Management, Equitable Life Assurance Society, State Street Bank, Harvard Community Health Plan, and FMR Corporation (Fidelity Investments). To make the best use of the board, Leventhal decreed two rules: only chief executive officers were permitted to attend (no surrogates allowed), and all meetings would begin at seven-thirty a.m. and end no later than nine a.m. That standard set the tone for the focused, high-powered attention that the enterprise required. Soon the Friends numbered 20.

"I told them we'd need a million bucks which they'd never see back," recalled Leventhal. Fortunately, the local economy was supercharged at the time and Bostonians were optimistic. Each Friend anted up about $50,000, enough to begin planning and to hire Robert Weinberg, a Leventhal associate and former director of the Massachusetts Port Authority, as president. The Leventhal-Weinberg team then swung into action to begin negotiations with Frank Sawyer.

The parking garage was a neighborhood eyesore that did little to enhance the surrounding office buildings. The dank, uninviting concrete structure failed to provided an attractive streetfront and was avoided by pedestrians. The parking garage was notorious for being ill kept and trash strewn, but it provided much-needed parking spaces and a steady income stream to its operator, who was reluctant to give it up for redevelopment.

The new parking garage with park created an oasis in Boston's financial district, providing a new geographic center and creating a strong point of reference for both pedestrians and drivers. The new park is primarily an open lawn with a canopy of large deciduous trees.

Steven Dunwell

A four-year legal and political struggle over the land ensued. Sawyer retained a former Massachusetts Supreme Court justice as his attorney, but the Friends nevertheless convinced the city that the decrepit building was a dangerous blight on the community and got approved as a "limited dividend corporation," a rare designation that includes the power of condemnation. When Sawyer realized that he no longer held the winning cards, he finally agreed, in 1987, to a $6 million buyout of his lease.

Meanwhile, Leventhal and Weinberg were also trying to find about $80 million from private sources, since the city of Boston and the state of Massachusetts had made it clear from the start that there were no public funds available for Post Office Square. So the Friends, many of whom were in banking and finance, did what they do best—and what may well be unique in the annals of park creation. They began to sell shares in the project. For $65,000, an investor could buy one share of the project, repayable in 40 years, with an interest rate of up to 8 percent.

In the middle of Boston's economic boom of the mid-1980s, an 8 percent return was not a particularly good financial investment. "But we threw in a sweetener," said Weinberg, with a faint smile. "Each share included

A 143-foot-long trellis covers the main walkway connecting the North and South plazas and provides a memorable architectural feature within the park. Supported by 26 granite columns, the trellis is covered with a rich assortment of vines and plantings.

Peter Vanderwarker

the guaranteed right to lease one parking space, at market rate, forever, in the best location in Boston, in the best garage in the city, maybe in the world."

In short order, 450 shares in the project were sold and the Friends had $30 million. A bit more salesmanship and they also had a $48.5 million loan (from a $60 million line of credit) from the Bank of New England.

But their troubles weren't over yet. Not everyone agreed that a square block in the middle of what was then the hottest downtown real estate market in the country should be merely a place for workers to sunbathe. Several developers dangled tantalizing proposals for a job-creating and tax-producing skyscraper for the site. (The garage at Post Office Square does pay taxes to the city, but not nearly as much as a 70-story building would have.) One New York architect, hearing that the powerful Boston Redevelopment Authority was adamantly opposed to the loss of any more sunlight in the financial district, submitted an architectural model made entirely of cellophane. "They said, 'See? It casts no shadow!'" laughed Shirley Muirhead, landscape designer for the redevelopment authority and self-proclaimed guardian of downtown solar access. "Eventually we convinced the mayor that a park would do a lot more for the city than one more skyscraper."

The mayor (by this time, populist Ray Flynn had succeeded Kevin White) was also lobbied by the city's park and environmentalist community, which had recently formed the Boston Greenspace Alliance. The alliance rallied around Post Office Square, both because the financial district was considered everybody's turf and because the Friends had pledged to contribute profits from the garage operation to a fund that would benefit all community parks in the city.

The final agreement yielded substantial financial benefits for the city. First, the city received $1 million for its ownership interest in the site. Second, the project pays annual property taxes of $1 million. Third, the city contributes no money to the operation of the park or the garage, and all net cash after debt service goes to the city for maintenance of neighborhood parks. And fourth, once all the debt and equity are repaid, ownership of the project will revert to the city.

In March 1987, the project was approved.

Getting the Park They Wanted

Although the garage was to be the economic engine, Leventhal knew that the project's ultimate success would depend on the park. If successful, Post Office Square could become as revered as the Public Garden and the Boston Common. Botched, it could become as scorned as the vast, failed space around Government Center, only a few blocks away.

In cooperation with the mayor's office, a park program/design review committee was established, made up of a cross-section of the community, both from the neighborhood and citywide. Not surprisingly, Leventhal was the committee chair.

The Friends first hired Skidmore, Owings & Merrill to investigate scores of urban parks—some with garages and many without—and to put together an armchair tour, with slides, of what they found—the good, the bad, the mundane, and the extraordinary. The culturally and economically diverse group then met repeatedly for facilitated discussions about what they wanted—and didn't want—in a park. They also chose a few key parks to visit in person and study. "Frankly, if this had been a public project we couldn't have done this—it would have been labeled a junket," said Charlotte Kahn, a design review committee member who was then head of Boston Urban Gardeners and is now on staff at the Boston Foundation. "It was extravagant, but the process was designed to get us all working together as a group, really communicating. And it was extraordinarily successful."

The committee made some basic decisions. Food in the park was okay, playground equipment was not, a water element was desirable but only if it didn't look empty when the water was shut off. (Boston is too cold for fountains for about half the year.) The park should include both formal and casual elements, including a trellis. The park should be lively and well used—often not the case in other urban parks the group saw across the country. The park should also be inviting from the ground level, not just something to be appreciated by a few company executives from their 50th-floor suites. Finally, the group agreed that the park did not have to be flashy or wild—that it could succeed best simply by being built on a human scale and by making references to authentic 19th-century Boston architecture.

Only after the program/design committee had completed its design document and adopted it unanimously did the Friends undertake a competition to select a landscape architect. "We told all the entrants that we were choosing a *designer*, not a *design*," said Weinberg. "We wanted to find a company whose attitude and approach we agreed with and then work with them."

Over 100 firms entered; the winner, ultimately, was the Halvorson Company of Boston, the firm that did the best job of offering to meet every suggestion and requirement spelled out in the design plan. "Basically,

we showed them how we would give them everything they wanted," said Chuck Kozlowski, principal designer of the park. "They wanted lots of different types of seating. We gave them wood, steel, the granite wall, places far from the street, and places near it. They wanted a feeling of rooms. They wanted places to meet people, to watch people, and to avoid people. They wanted the park half green and half hard surface. It ultimately came out 53 percent green and 47 percent hard, not including the ramps."

The auto ramps into the garage, two up and two down, were among the greatest challenge to the park's design. For one thing, they sap fully 14 percent of the entire surface area. For another, by squeezing the park in the middle, they made it hard to unify the north and south plazas. Viewed from above, they are jarringly visible, but from within the park they almost disappear, thanks to layers of natural screening—grasses, bushes, flowers, and trees—and an ornamental iron fence.

The survival of vegetation was by no means a given in Post Office Square. For one thing, the site is shadowed by numerous tall buildings; for another, the entire park is located on the roof of a garage. From the start, Halvorson had specified three feet of topsoil over the whole site, a requirement that would affect both the depth and the load-bearing capacity of the garage. During design, two complications emerged. The landscapers determined that they would need an additional six inches of soil, and the garage architect realized that the elevator motor would protrude an additional three feet, to just millimeters below the surface of the park. Fortunately, each team was able to accommodate the other. The elevator shaft was topped by a brick walkway rather than

The focal point of the park is the copper-and-green-glass fountain/sculpture located near the north end of the park and surrounded by rich plantings and low granite seat walls.

The park is surrounded by four one-way streets, and auto entrances and exits are provided on both the east and west sides of the park; entrances are separated from exits to ensure the smooth movement of traffic, which had been a significant problem for the previous parking garage.

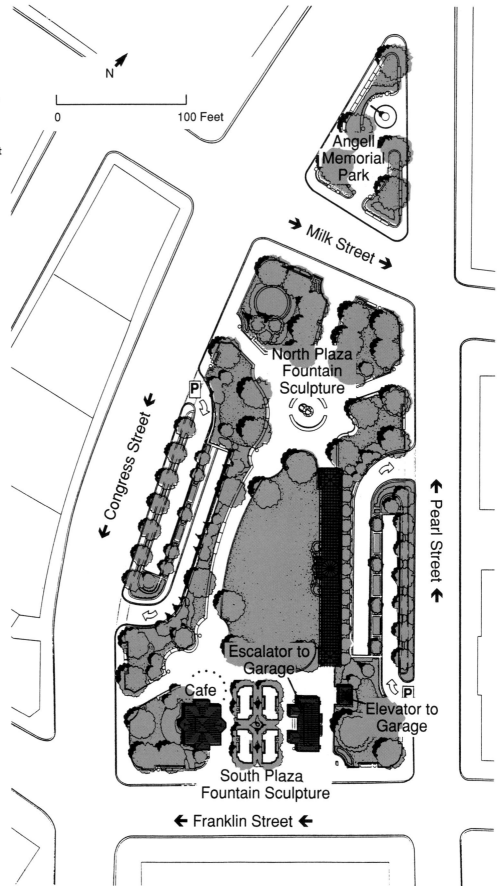

N

0   100 Feet

Milk Street →

Angell Memorial Park

Congress Street

North Plaza Fountain Sculpture

Pearl Street

Escalator to Garage

Cafe

Elevator to Garage

South Plaza Fountain Sculpture

← Franklin Street ←

by a tree sunk into thick loam, as originally planned; the luxurious topsoil now supports scores of trees, some of them nearly 30 feet tall—one of the factors that makes the park seem mature, broken in, and familiar. As for light, Halvorson did solar studies and placed the Great Lawn and the perennial flower garden in the two sunniest spots.

A year before the competition to choose the landscape firm, the Friends had contracted with Ellenzweig Associates of Cambridge to design the garage. "We were retained first," recalled Harry Ellenzweig, "to establish exactly where the ramps were going to be. But I think our most important contribution was persuading Norm Leventhal that the garage should operate like a first-class subway station—the money and everything else should be handled underground. We didn't want the garage administration to take up too much space in the park."

In addition to designing the garage, Ellenzweig designed two matching, gazebo-type structures on the surface, one to house the Milk Street Café, the other to serve as the escalator entranceway to the garage. Constructed of copper and glass, the café building is airy, yet movable doorways and glass panels make it flexible enough to handle the extremes of Boston's seasons. In warm weather the café is surrounded by cast-iron tables and chairs recalling those in Paris; in cold weather it serves hot soup and provides a refuge from the wind.

Even though the Ellenzweig firm was hired first, the Friends made an unusual decision to prove their commitment to the park: they assigned the role of prime contractor to the Halvorson Company—the landscape architect—and retained Ellenzweig as a subcontractor. Like almost everything else on the project, that relationship worked magically.

One of the Halvorson Company's subtlest but most satisfying solutions—accomplished jointly with the garage engineering firm, Parsons Brinckerhoff Quade and Douglas—came about in response to the air vent challenge. A half-million-square-foot garage generates a lot of pollution and requires a continuous supply of clean air. Parsons Brinckerhoff engineers calculated that they would need two vents, each 24 feet in circumference, to meet code. Moreover, a Boston public health ordinance requires that any vent in close proximity to humans must be at least eight feet tall. In short, what amounted to a pair of giant smokestacks had to be hidden in the park.

The team scoured the site. Since the intake vent was not a health threat, it could be located in a corner and hidden by a thick circle of evergreens. The exhaust problem, however, seemed intractable until the design team realized, in a flash of inspiration, that the hole need not be round. If it were long enough, it could be thin—and

One of the glass-and-copper park pavilions provides escalator access to the underground parking facilities and the other houses the year-round Milk Street Café.

just might fit into the narrow space between the up and down auto ramps. Not only would the vent be essentially invisible, it would also be as far as possible from any park user and, for the most part, eight or more feet above the slope of the ramps. The engineers rerouted the pipes; today, when Weinberg gives visitors a tour of the park, he delights in challenging them to find the eight-foot-high garage exhaust vent.

Weinberg also boasts of a marble lobby with fresh flowers; Mozart in the elevators; 24-hour staffing; a shoeshine; telephones and rest rooms in the lobby; a debit-card payment option; a car wash; vacuum and minor repairs downstairs; attendants who leave a note on your windshield if your inspection sticker is about to expire; a free phone connection to a traffic hotline; free downtown maps for tourists; video cameras everywhere; plus backlit walls for better visibility and security. "You can even give someone a gift certificate to park here," he said. "We have a couple of suburban-based repair companies that rent spaces for their service vans, use our phones, eat in the park, and don't even need an office in the city—they're just based at Post Office Square, a couple of minutes from everywhere."

Landscape architect Halvorson refers to Post Office Square as "a garden for all seasons." Through a careful selection of trees, bushes, and flowers, the landscape architects created a park that exhibits color every month: witch hazel blossoms in March, saucer magnolia petals and forsythia sprigs in April, numerous flowers all spring and summer, red maple leaves in October, and deep green Norway spruce needles and red holly berries in the snows of January.

Four of the park's biggest trees are on loan. In a major horticultural and public relations coup, the Friends learned that the Arnold Arboretum was seeking a place

Each parking floor is organized around a central elevator core that is distinguished by colorful neon, easily visible from anywhere on the parking level. The parking floors are laid out on flat grids, carefully planned for easy perpendicular parking. An internal express ramp is located at the north end of the garage to move motorists between levels.

to transplant six excess specimens that did not quite meet the botanical garden's exacting standards. A permanent loan was arranged, and although two of the trees turned out to be fatally diseased, the remaining four are doing fine.

Like virtually all new urban parks these days—and older parks that have been renovated—Post Office Square has had to conform to the reality of security needs. The park has no exterior wall and no high hedges or other midlevel vegetation to impede sight lines—and thus no truly secluded places. The park is also quite noisy, with the roar of trucks and the wail of sirens echoing off the surrounding building facades. Fortunately, the design, combined with the 24-hour staffed garage, has kept crime to a minimum. Even the level of vagrancy is dramatically lower than in other Boston greenspaces.

Halvorson's design had to deal with another modern urban menace—skateboards. Young hot-rodding skateboarders, who can traverse almost any surface at any angle, can cause thousands of dollars of damage to railings, benches, walls, and curbs, but enforcing a ban on skateboarders is not easy. In an attempt to protect the hundreds of linear feet of expensive marble wall, Halvorson had a one-inch chamfer cut into the corners and had the top and edge polished to a high hone, to reduce the chance of nicking and chipping (and, incidentally, to make the wall more comfortable for sitters). Thus far, it has worked.

To designer Kozlowski, the wall represents a special triumph. "I love the fact that this park never looks vacant," he says. "The key is the wall. When the park is crowded and the benches are filled, the wall functions

The entrance to the parking garage includes a gracious main lobby, with high-quality finishes, fresh plants, and bright lights—something often missing from parking garages. The garage is open and staffed 24 hours a day.

Peter Vanderwarker

as overflow seating. When the park is lightly used, people naturally prefer to sit on benches rather than on the wall. But an unoccupied wall isn't depressing like an unoccupied bench—it doesn't shout 'empty!' at you."

Another success is the fountain in the middle of the park's North Plaza. A piece so strong that it succeeds simply as a copper-and-green-glass sculpture during the five months when the water is shut off, it was designed by Providence, Rhode Island, sculptor Howard Ben Tre, with whom Halvorson worked for "zillions" of hours to make the art and the landscape come together—not only during the day, but at night, when the fountain is lit from below and within. Ben Tre's design, which includes scores of computer-controlled nozzles that respond to wind speed, pushed technology so far that no one could predict the exact shape of the water spray until the work was built and the fountain turned on.

Making the Park Pay for Itself

Ironically, the only reason there is a park at Post Office Square is that parking in Boston is so expensive. And the reason parking is so costly—more than $20 a day— is that Boston, responding to a U.S. Environmental Protection Agency mandate to control air pollution, instituted a freeze on the number of parking spaces allowed in the central business district. "Owning a parking space in Boston is like owning a taxi medallion in New York," explained Weinberg. "It's a closed market. And when we bought out Mr. Sawyer and made some other deals, we got 1,400 parking spaces, about 30 percent of the entire market in our neighborhood. If parking in Boston weren't so profitable, we couldn't have afforded to

go underground, which is more than three times as expensive as developing a space aboveground—and about ten times as expensive as surface parking." The final tab for constructing each parking space at Post Office Square was $34,000.

The economics of Post Office Square are complex. In one sense Boston was given, for free, a beautiful new park; but to get it, the city forswore the receipt of millions of dollars of tax revenue that would have been collected from the owner and tenants of a skyscraper. However, the economic value of the buildings, shops, and hotels on and near the park has risen because of the amenity of Post Office Square—raising city tax receipts and possibly even inducing some firms and residents to remain downtown.

The bottom line is mixed. After five years of operation, Friends of Post Office Square, Inc., was earning enough to cover all expenses (for the garage and park), pay its taxes, and pay the interest on its loan. It was not making enough, however, to pay a dividend to its stockholders or to pay anything into the fund for Boston's neighborhood parks. "If back in 1988 we'd been able to borrow money at 8 percent rather than 11, we'd be right on target today," said Weinberg. Nevertheless, the financial picture continues to brighten as the parking fee ratchets upward without loss of patrons: from $16 a day at the time of opening to $25 by mid-1997.

The Verdict

The number of "firsts," "mosts," and "bests" connected with the park and garage at Post Office Square is almost laughable: deepest excavation in the city, biggest garage,

Users take advantage of the many types of seating found in the park, which can accommodate as many as 1,000 people during the peak hours of use. Seating includes 20 wooden garden benches under the trellis and in the South Plaza, 35 steel benches in the park and along its perimeters, and 700 linear feet of sculptural granite wall.

Peter Vanderwarker

Parks Built Over Parking Facilities

Union Square, San Francisco (1850,1940)

Considered in its pioneer days to be the center of San Francisco, the park, given to the city in 1850, derives its name from demonstrations held there in support of the Union during the Civil War. The park was originally 2.6 acres of green lawns and shrubbery that surrounded a 90-foot-high granite naval monument dedicated in 1903. In 1940, the monument was removed and the lawns dug up to install underground parking; after completion of the garage, the monument and landscaping were restored.

Mellon Square, Pittsburgh (1953)

Inspired by Union Square in San Francisco, Mellon Square was built in 1953 as part of the city's Renaissance I redevelopment effort and was considered at the time to be the centerpiece of the city's revitalization.

Portsmouth Square, San Francisco (1963)

Located in the Chinatown section of San Francisco, Portsmouth Square was the site of many significant episodes in the city's history. The square dates from 1833, when it housed a Mexican customs house, a flagpole, a speakers' platform, and a cow pen. The park was a grassy plaza until 1963, when it was torn up to accommodate the Portsmouth Square parking garage underneath. In 1994, the park was renovated to allow more sunshine and better delineate areas for children and seniors.

Market Square, Alexandria, Virginia (1967)

Market Square sits on the site of a colonial marketplace. For several decades prior to development of the park, the site served as a farmers' market. Market Square features a Southern-style formal garden with magnolia trees, boxwood, crape myrtle, and azalea plants. A self-park garage beneath the park accommodates 236 cars.

O'Bryant Square, Portland, Oregon (1971)

Donald C. Sloan bequeathed the park to the city in 1971. The dominant feature of O'Bryant Square is a bronze fountain in the shape of a rose, surrounded by rosebushes. The park is scheduled to be redeveloped by 1999 with new irrigation, lighting, and park furniture.

Memorial Plaza, Cleveland (1991)

The site is one of three sections of a historic mall designed by Daniel Burnham at the turn of the century. The Fountain of Eternal Life, designed by Marshall Frederick, is one of the plaza's most prominent features. The park was redeveloped in 1991 to house a 900-car parking garage underneath. The fountain was restored and the area newly landscaped. Four other memorial sculptures have since been placed in the plaza.

---

most expensive park, first privately financed park. Even the site is special; the post office at Post Office Square was the first in the 13 colonies.

The critics, the politicians, the corporate neighbors, and the users all love it. Even headline writers relish it: "They Pulled Down a Parking Lot and Put Up Paradise"; "Call It Garage Mahal."

Whether it could be replicated is another matter. Norman Leventhal is dubious. "What we had here in Boston in 1988 was a very special situation. The economy was terrific. The big companies were making a lot of money and they could afford to throw some at this even if it wouldn't have worked. Plus, how often can you assemble a whole square block by acquiring one old garage?" Then there is also the issue of parking rates, although Leventhal concedes that other cities might be able to compensate somewhat with lower land prices and cheaper construction costs.

Of course, Post Office Square is not the first park built over a downtown parking garage—San Francisco; Pittsburgh; Alexandria, Virginia; and other cities did the trick earlier (see feature box). It isn't even the first privately built such facility—Cleveland has one, too—although it is probably the first that used absolutely no public funds. And it is certainly the first to sell stock and offer investors interest.

The success of Post Office Square, and the public interest in it—Weinberg regularly gives tours to delegations from around the country and even from Europe and Asia—makes it likely that the experiment will be repeated and embellished, at least in such high-density, high-parking-fee locales as New York, San Francisco, and Chicago, as well as cities in other countries.

Project Data • The Park at Post Office Square

Land Use Information

Site area: 1.7 acres

Gross building area (garage): 519,057 square feet (parking and parking related)

Gross building area (café): 1,000 square feet (separate structure in the park)

Number of parking levels: 7

Total parking spaces: 1,400

Land Use Plan

Components	Acres	Square Feet	Percentage of Site
Landscaped areas	0.76	33,189	44.8%
Walkways	0.65	28,077	37.9
Structures	0.04	1,772	2.4
Garage ramps	0.23	10,188	13.8
Exhaust/supply vents	0.02	826	1.1
Total	1.70	74,052	100.0%

Development Schedule

Site purchased	March 1987
Planning started	1981
Construction started	October 1988
Leasing started	Spring 1990
Garage opened	October 1990
Park opened	Spring 1991
Project completed	June 1992

Financing Information

Initial stockholder contributions	$930,000
Preferred stock offering[1]	29,250,000
Debt[2]	60,000,000
Total[3]	$90,180,000

Development Cost Information

Site acquisition cost (to operator)	$4,772,879
Site improvement costs	
Payment to city	$1,000,000
Initial site improvements	520,641
Demolition	503,144
Park and café	5,581,493
Total site improvement costs	$7,605,278
Construction costs	
Structure	$28,799,497
Heating, ventilation, and air conditioning (HVAC)	949,040
Electrical	1,812,192
Plumbing/sprinkler	816,918
Elevators and escalators	957,374
Finishes	1,743,300
Fees/general conditions	6,181,077
Other/unallocated	3,061,870
Total construction costs	$44,321,268

Soft costs/fees

Architecture and engineering (garage)	$4,970,434
Park design	1,635,987
Project management	2,976,377
Professional services	1,031,082
Marketing	607,400
Permits, licenses, and surveys	1,057,079
Taxes/insurance	933,657
Construction interest and fees	5,599,384
Total soft costs/fees	$18,811,400
Total site acquisition and development costs	$75,510,825

Operating Information (1996)

Average number of cars parked per day	1,918
Parking rates	
All-day rates	$25.00
Average daily ticket	$18.47
Monthly rate	$330.00
Annual gross revenue (1996)	
Parking revenue	$8,549,782
Leasing income	64,280
Other income	20,391
Total	$8,634,453
Annual operating expenses (1996)	
Taxes	$1,000,000
Insurance	151,451
Professional services	50,301
Repair and maintenance	210,952
Management	302,815
Utilities	168,223
Marketing	85,325
Garage and park operations	995,808
Total	$2,964,875

Notes

1. Four hundred fifty shares of preferred stock were sold as a private offering at $65,000 per share. Each share is entitled to a cumulative 8 percent dividend and has the long-term right to rent a monthly parking space at the prevailing monthly rate. Because of the scarcity of parking in the financial district, the long-term parking right helped create a demand market for the private offering.

2. A ten-year note was provided by the Bank of New England in 1988. The loan was assumed by Fleet Bank of Massachusetts when it purchased the failed Bank of New England from the FDIC. The nonamortizing, interest-only note serves as a line of credit that can be drawn on throughout its term to cover the development, construction, and operating requirements of the project.

3. Total project funding exceeds project cost. This excess funding is held in reserve in a line of credit.

Philadelphia Green
Philadelphia

Peter Harnik

Most urban parks are relatively small, planned parcels of nature and open space carved out of the concrete fabric of the city. In America's biggest cities, these green domains are few and far between. Yet in urban neighborhoods across the country, the deterioration of the built environment has left much unplanned and unmaintained vacant land where buildings once stood.

Where abandonment and demolition are outpacing development and renewal, communities are struggling to deal with the proliferation of unplanned and unbudgeted vacant land. In Philadelphia, the nation's acknowledged leader in the greening of low-income neighborhoods, some viable strategies are beginning to emerge.

Like most older industrial cities, Philadelphia has been buffeted by job loss, population decline, housing decay, and other problems. With the loss of about half a million inhabitants since the 1950s, areas of the city are so severely depopulated that vacant lots outnumber buildings, and many of the structures still standing are empty. But in a major campaign to keep depopulated neighborhoods green and alive—and hopeful—Philadelphia is undertaking one of the most ambitious community gardening and greening programs in the nation.

The Pennsylvania Horticultural Society

The driving force behind Philadelphia's greening effort is a remarkable institution called the Pennsylvania Horticultural Society (PHS). Founded in 1827, the society, primarily composed of and led by suburbanites, produces the world-famous Philadelphia Flower Show; yet PHS undertakes an astonishing array of programs for low-income residents and has more staff working on inner-city issues than on garden showcases for the leisure class.

The horticultural society was not originally created for the purpose of saving the inner city. Until the late 1970s, most PHS activities were focused on its membership. Since then, the society has engaged in publishing, information dissemination, public education, lectures, and horticultural displays through the flower show and harvest show, and it has served as a focal point for every kind of horticultural activity in the Delaware Valley.

Nevertheless, the society's urban program, known as Philadelphia Green, is the largest, most ambitious private city beautification effort in the country, with a staff of 45 and a budget of $3 million. While some of the programs are clearly aimed at the city's public face—landscaping the gateway route from downtown to the airport, for instance, or redesigning the four-acre Azalea Garden behind the Philadelphia Museum of Art located in Fairmount Park —the majority focus on communities that are desperate not only for greening but also for jobs, housing, retail establishments, medical care, and schooling. "Philadelphia Green's approach is to help residents implement a wide range of green projects, from window boxes and flower barrels to street tree plants and community gardens," said J. Blaine Bonham, PHS vice president and head of

Philadelphia Green. "We also provide the technical assistance that's needed to ensure long-term maintenance and sustainability of these projects. Our special interest is to work with community-based housing organizations to incorporate the use of vacant land into their overall revitalization plans."

Dire Straits

What is happening to much of Philadelphia's built environment is startling. Between 1970 and 1990, over 21,400 residential structures were demolished—and on four out of every five of those sites, nothing was rebuilt. In 1992, the city identified 15,800 vacant parcels and an additional 27,000 long-vacant residential buildings (structures that are essentially abandoned). Using conservative numbers, the City Planning Commission estimated that the vacant parcels totaled 522 acres; if all the abandoned properties were included, the total came to 1,414 acres, an area larger than all of the Center City district of Philadelphia. Of the 23,000 publicly owned properties in the city, 9,500 of them (41 percent) are vacant land. While Philadelphia's suburbs and its central business district remain vibrant, the neighborhoods within three or four miles of downtown are in dire straits, having lost more than 33 percent of their residents between 1950 and 1990.

While converting derelict inner-city land to gardens seems simple and obvious, subtle challenges arise: legal issues of land ownership; horticultural issues of appropriate plant materials; financial issues of acquisition of seeds, seedlings, soil, and fences; logistical issues of lot cleanup and preparation; and sociological issues of management, security, plot assignment, and compliance with rules. And one of the biggest challenges is the complete dependence on volunteers—a resource that is finite. Moreover, gardens are not all cut from the same mold: some are operated by individuals in lots adjoining their houses; others cover an acre or more and serve scores of residents who must comply with a litany of rules. Some feature vegetables, others flowers; still others are oriented toward children or have special themes—peace, ethnicity, a religious motif. Others are sites for artwork, murals, performances, and community gatherings.

While it is unlikely that community gardens can save Philadelphia, they may provide what the city's beleaguered residents need to tame the urban wilds. Gardening, according to its proponents, can provide people with a sense of purpose and accomplishment, a renewed sense of community, practical skills to tackle tougher challenges—and, ultimately, hope and optimism, perhaps the inner-city's greatest need these days.

A West Philly Garden

A case in point is the Warrington Community Garden, located in West Philadelphia in a struggling working-class neighborhood dotted with vacant land.

Sometime after the oil shortages of the 1970s led to sharp increases in produce prices, some neighbors began to tend small gardens on a vacant, one-acre parcel of private land along Warrington Avenue. The landowner was supportive, and in the mid-1980s, when he wanted

The community vegetable garden shown here, known for its leader, Jessie Carter, is one of the most successful gardens in the Philadelphia Green program and a frequent winner in the annual city gardening contest.

to divest himself of the property, he offered to donate the land as a community garden. At the time, however, there was no existing nonprofit entity capable of legally accepting it. Ultimately, an urban land trust, the Neighborhood Gardens Association (NGA), was incorporated, but it was too late; by then the land had already been sold. The new owner allowed the gardeners to remain, but the land was soon sold again, this time to a developer for a townhouse project.

When the developer requested the necessary zoning variance to begin development, what would ordinarily have been a routine application suddenly became controversial: local residents demanded to know why their beloved garden had to be destroyed when there was so much untended, trash-strewn land available in the neighborhood.

"In the city, vacant land equals trash," said Claire Power, director of the NGA. "It's called 'short dumping' —people from outside the community come in at night with junk furniture or truckfuls of concrete and in no time the neighborhood looks blighted. It's not only dangerous and unsanitary, it creates a real feeling of helplessness among the residents. What we're engaged in is a land reclamation effort, securing the land and letting the gardens flower."

Philadelphia Green's work on horticultural programs at several thousand sites is supplemented by NGA, which steps in to handle the legalities and the political struggles that sometimes ensue. At any given time, NGA and Philadelphia Green are working in partnership on 40 or 50 sites.

The citizens were successful in stopping the zoning variance, but they knew that the Warrington Garden's days were numbered unless they could acquire formal title to the property. Fortunately, by this time the NGA was up and running and began negotiating with the owner. While the talks dragged on for two years, the neighbors threw themselves into a fundraising campaign and eventually raised $15,000. Impressed with that show of commitment, the NGA raised $20,000 in foundation money to complete the deal.

The garden was saved in perpetuity, but that's not the end of the story. A few years later, a tragic fire destroyed an apartment building adjacent to the greenspace. Instead of allowing the newly vacant lot to become a local eyesore and dumping ground, the community is working to expand the garden, create a revenue-generating tree nursery, and develop other community-related activities. Even better, thanks to new-found space for a totlot and a small off-street parking area, the local church can now offer the community a performing arts program and a badly needed daycare center. Furthermore, recognizing that their working vegetable garden did not

The mural being painted in the background depicts local community leaders and heros who were important to the greening of that community. The project is one of many beautification projects of the Philadelphia Mural Arts Program (formerly known as the Philadelphia Anti-Graffiti Network), which works with groups like Philadelphia Green to paint murals in areas riddled with graffiti.

always present the most attractive vista to their supporters and friends across Warrington Avenue, the gardeners raised money to install a more appealing fence, break up some of the concrete, and plant a flower garden on the street frontage.

A Careful Balance

With more than 20 years of experience under its belt, Philadelphia Green has evolved a sophisticated program that carefully balances a community's needs with its indigenous abilities. "We don't make gardens for residents, we help them create gardens themselves," said Bonham. "We started out back in 1974 spending a small chunk of our flower show earnings and establishing ten small gardens on old playgrounds and vacant lots in low-income parts of town. Back then we practically had to beg people to garden—it was unheard of. Now, with more than 2,000 garden sites throughout the city, there are waiting lists everywhere and the phone doesn't stop ringing."

The core of Philadelphia Green's funding stems from the PHS's Philadelphia Flower Show, a mighty financial engine. More than 300,000 people attend the week-long extravaganza, making it not only the largest indoor flower show in the world but also the single largest tourist event in Philadelphia. It nets the PHS nearly $1.4 million, money that is supplemented by foundation grants, government contracts, and individual contributions.

"We like to brag that Philadelphia is the country's horticultural center," said Bonham. "The father of American horticulture was John Bartram, an early-18th-century explorer who came to Philadelphia from England and discovered and identified plants native to the Eastern United States. The climate and soils are conducive to growing many plants that America is famous for—azaleas, dogwoods, rhododendrons. We've got dozens of estate gardens developed in the 19th century, including Longwood Gardens created by the DuPonts."

Moreover, there was William Penn himself, who cared so deeply for things sylvan that he named his state Pennsylvania—Penn's Woods—and left explicit instructions as to how Philadelphians should design and build their city. "Build," he said, "in the middle of the lot so as to leave ground . . . for gardens, or orchards or fields that will be a greene countrie town which will never be burnt and always be wholesome."

Glenwood Green Acres, started in 1984, is one of the most successful community gardens in the city. Located in North Central Philadelphia on the edge of a Greene Countrie Towne, the garden even includes demonstration plots of tobacco, cotton, and peanuts.

Pennsylvania Horticultural Society

A "greene countrie towne." At the time of the industrial revolution, when the city's population was mushrooming, fortunes in real estate were there for the making, and William Penn was long in the ground, the admonition was ignored; but 100 years later, Philadelphia Green picked up the rallying cry and initiated the Greene Countrie Towne program, an ambitious effort to go one step beyond block-by-block greening.

"The Greene Countrie Towne is where we tried to put together everything we learned," explained Bonham. "The 'towne' is really a neighborhood where people receive assistance with everything from window boxes to street trees to community gardens to park revival. It involves a formal application, and if we accept a neighborhood we give it intensive greening attention for three to five years."

Putting It Together: The Fall and Rise of Norris Square

Of eight Greene Countrie Townes, the most successful is Norris Square, a 35-square-block neighborhood about two miles from downtown, in the city's devastated Lower North. Norris Square was also the toughest, because of a pernicious drug trade that held the community in its grip. Eileen Gallagher, a project manager for Philadelphia Green's community greening program, has been knocked down, robbed of her camera, cursed and threatened in the line of duty, all because of her commitment to gardening.

"I wasn't trained in community organizing," she said. "But that's about 90 percent of what my work turns out to be. We use neighborhood greening as a way to build people's confidence, increase community cohesion, give people hope. We don't do anything *for* them, but we enable them to do things for themselves. We may deliver a load of mulch or a pile of stones, but they've got to do the planning and the spreading. We learned a long time ago that if the local people aren't involved in every aspect of the garden from the very beginning, they won't own the project; and if they don't own it they won't defend it."

Until recently, defending the garden meant defending it against drug dealers. At one of Norris Square's community gardens, drug dealers tore down the fence seven times, and each time the community rebuilt it—both to protect the crops and to provide one less route for dealers to use to escape from police. The seventh time, one of the dealers walked over and helped with the repair. "Somewhere, deep down, even the dealers feel something of the community's pride," said Gallagher.

Norris Square historically operated as a self-contained urban village within the Philadelphia metropolis, owing its economic vitality not to the downtown financial dis-

Norris Square Park before and after. Because of the efforts of the residents and Philadelphia Green, Norris Square Park was transformed from a decaying, drug-infested park into the proud center of the Norris Square Greene Countrie Towne, the eighth such project in the city.

trict but rather to the hulking textile, carpet, lace, hosiery, and haberdashery factories that lined American Street to the west and the Kensington district to the east. The center of the small, human-scale community was Norris Square Park, 5.8 acres of manicured greenery, stately trees, benches, and a fountain. Surrounded by a wrought-iron fence, the park faced fashionable homes and a formal streetscape dominated by the sandstone Gothic spire of St. Boniface Catholic Church.

By the mid-1800s, following the industrial revolution and the resultant building boom, Norris Square was the sole nugget of greenery that remained from a vast tract that William Penn had given his good Quaker friend Isaac Norris back in 1693. Officially deeded to the city as a park in 1848 and constructed in 1859, Norris Square was for about 100 years carefully and attractively maintained and compared favorably to Rittenhouse Square, the city's peerless plaza for the downtown elite.

"Norris Square Park is a wonderful space," said Richard Tyler, historic preservation officer for the city of Philadelphia, "beautifully defined by the buildings that surround it—late-19th-century brownstones of large proportions that proclaim a solidly affluent, upper-middle-class square. It's one of the few 19th-century squares that still retains the historic character of the city."

Designed to 19th-century standards and sensibilities, the park is a flat square with a low, central circular wall that formerly surrounded a fountain. Facing the wall is a circle of benches. Walkways radiate to the edges and corners of the square. At the streetside entrance to the walkways are old concrete gateways that have been enlivened with colorful mosaics created by neighborhood children under the leadership of Philadelphia Green staff. Surfaced largely with grass, the park has nearly 100 trees, including sycamores, ashes, lindens, cherries,

honey locusts, and silver bells; some massive trees date back to the park's creation, while others were planted recently to replace dead and diseased specimens removed over the years. On the east side of the park is the so-called Pavilion, a modest, newly constructed, brightly colored sitting-and-gathering area with plantings, a trellis, concrete tables, and chessboards. At the center of the park, where the fountain used to be, is the community's pride and joy—a new playground.

In the 1960s, Norris Square hit bottom. A wave of factory closings robbed the community of jobs and income, and ethnic tensions prevented the residents from working cooperatively to save their neighborhood. In a few short years, thousands of homeowners relocated, often losing the entire value of their homes, and leaving behind a community rife with vacant buildings and inhabited mostly by low-income Puerto Rican immigrants.

As the neighborhood deteriorated, it became attractive to drug dealers, who took advantage of empty buildings and abandoned cars to store contraband and used vacant lots for quick getaways. The Norris Square area became the city's number one drug market, with the 2200 block of Palethorp Street alone serving five different heroin gangs.

Amid this bleak scene of urban misfortune, a tiny beacon of hope and inspiration appeared in 1972. Natalie Kempner, a 48-year-old Quaker activist who had spent many years doing development work in Africa, began a second career as a public elementary school teacher and was assigned to the W.F. Miller School on Norris Square. "In my class," said Kempner, "I had 37 kids, only three of whom could read. I took them to the park and showed them that everything there had a name. Not only names like 'oak' and 'pine,' but things like 'trunk' and 'branch'—they didn't know that. Suddenly they

Neighborhood senior citizens plant flowers in Norris Square Park. Philadelphia Green depends on volunteers, particularly from the ranks of retirees, to carry out their programs throughout the city.

wanted to read. Finding out that things have names and labels gives children a tremendous sense of power."

W.F. Miller, the second-oldest school building in the Philadelphia system, was decrepit and overcrowded, with average test scores to match. Kempner was an enthusiastic teacher, but the circumstances were impossible. "You couldn't explore the streets or the park with that many kids. My principal understood. So I got a small environmental education grant and created the Miller Mini Nature Museum with all the things we found in Norris Square Park. The neighborhood was rough and the park was dangerous, but the kids were thrilled with what they learned."

One day in 1974, Kempner heard about a course on indoor classroom gardening called "Room to Grow," signed up for it, and was introduced to the Pennsylvania Horticultural Society. Over the years, as Kempner formalized her program into the Norris Square Neighborhood Project and as the PHS's work turned more and more toward the inner city, the two entities began collaborating. In the 1980s, when Philadelphia Green was seeking a new neighborhood for "Greene Countrie Towne" status, Norris Square seemed the perfect site. Except for the drug problem.

By 1986, the Norris Square Neighborhood Project had moved into its very own townhouse on the square (complete with solar greenhouse), the W.F. Miller School had been torn down, and Kempner had retired and moved to Maine, but the effort was still very much alive and well and operating almost like the ward headquarters for Norris Square. And ward healer par excellence was Sister Carol Keck, a former principal of St. Boniface Catholic School who first served on Kempner's board and later as director. "In 1986 we got a grant to hire an intern, who interviewed everybody in the neighborhood to find out what they liked and what they disliked. The drug problem came up as the number one problem."

"We'd been conducting a quiet, secretive drug battle," she continued, "encouraging people to give tips to the police, but it wasn't working. Everyone was afraid. So we went public. We organized United Neighbors Against Drugs. We held a prayer service rally in Norris Square Park. We marched together to a nearby open market and stayed there all night, ending with a community breakfast. We held vigils every other Friday night for four years. To keep up the interest we had a cleanup vigil and a cookout vigil and a poetry vigil and a games vigil. We got the police to bring in searchlights. We harassed people trying to buy drugs. We gathered information and shared it with the police and with the U.S. Attorney."

Finally, on August 8, 1992, at four a.m., an unprecedented federal and city police force descended on the neighborhood. Armed with search warrants, tow trucks, and bulldozers, they arrested 70 drug dealers, towed away 26 abandoned cars, and demolished several abandoned buildings that were being used as crack houses.

The drug trade's back was broken, and instead of attracting dealers, Norris Square drew other visitors—including, over the years, President George Bush, Tipper Gore, Attorney General Janet Reno, and Andrew Cuomo, then Assistant Secretary for Housing and Urban Development.

Finally, Norris Square could officially become a Greene Countrie Towne—the first one ever in a Hispanic neighborhood. Today, the Norris Square neighborhoods are dotted with more than 70 community greening projects, including vegetable and flower gardens, miniparks, street tree blocks, and garden blocks. Many of the greening projects are located in communal lots that include paths, sitting areas, patios, and colorful murals painted by the Philadelphia Mural Arts Program (formerly known as the Philadelphia Anti-Graffiti Network). There's a display garden for herbs, vines, and perennials. There's the *Raices* children's garden—Spanish for roots—with a large mural depicting Puerto Rican history. There's a composting and recycling garden. The biggest garden, *Las Parcelas* (the parcels), has a *casita*, a small Caribbean shack symbolically furnished with shrines and used for children's gardening classes.

The gardens not only beautify and give value to the neighborhoods' vacant lots, but also provide the first tentative link between the community development movement and the environmental movement in the inner city. That, says the horticultural society's J. Blaine Bonham, is where the greening movement must head next. "To be effective, our work has to be part of a larger community revitalization effort," said Bonham.

"That's why we're now beginning to cast our lot with the community development corporations that are working on housing, jobs, retail, and other infrastructure in these neighborhoods."

A National Movement

The vitality of the community gardening movement across the country is indicated not only by the numbers —about 200 associations in cities nationwide—but by the exuberance of the groups' names: Boston Urban Gardeners (BUG), Garden Resources of Washington (GROW), Green Guerrillas (New York), the San Francisco League of Urban Gardeners (SLUG). The oldest and largest single group is Philadelphia Green, although New York City, with many different organizations and a stronger local government commitment, has the most gardens.

The community gardening movement began in Detroit just before the turn of the century. When the Panic of 1893 led to a serious economic depression, Mayor Hazen S. Pingree provided some of the city's destitute and unemployed residents with garden plots on municipally owned and privately donated vacant land. By 1895, Detroit was providing 455 acres of garden plots. (By modern standards the plots were very large—between one-quarter and one-third of an acre each; today's plots are frequently 1,000 square feet, or 1/44th of an acre.) Pingree's experiment, known as the Potato Patch, received extensive media coverage, particularly when his Poor Commission reported that its $5,000 appropriation resulted in $28,000 worth of produce.

Philadelphia quickly picked up on the idea. By 1897, almost 100 indigent families were working 27 acres of public land; six years later, the program had grown to 200 families and 800 acres. The fostering agency was not the Pennsylvania Horticultural Society (which was weak and almost bankrupt at the time) but the Vacant Lot Cultivation Association, an organization that would be characterized as a workers' and civil rights organization in today's parlance.

Unfortunately, the potato patch movement didn't survive. As the economy revived, speculation and rising land prices led the plots' owners to reclaim their

Norris Square Park playground before and after. The new playground equipment is designed for children of varying ages and abilities.

parcels for sale or more profitable development. Three times more in the first half of the century—during the Depression and the two world wars—the nation saw the resurgence of large-scale urban gardening. The lowly garden achieved its all-time greatest power in 1944; with the population mobilized for winning World War II, 20 million Victory Gardens yielded 40 percent of the fresh vegetables consumed in the country.

The century's final burst of enthusiasm for community gardening started in the mid-1970s, in response to

A 1992 National Gardener Survey conducted by Kansas State University showed that community gardens supplement budgets for unemployed people, students, and retirees. The survey reported that 24 percent of those earning less than $5,000 annually saved in excess of 5 percent of their incomes by raising produce. In addition, well over half the gardeners valued the physical and psychological well-being that came from working outside. Here, residents are tending the Johnson Homes Vegetable Garden, at one of several public housing sites that Philadelphia Green works with.

an environmental and economic movement that began with Earth Day and the oil crisis. At the same time, most central-city neighborhoods were finding themselves in a deflationary spiral that was generating a huge supply of vacant land. By 1982, according to a Gallup poll, 10,000 community gardens were serving 3 million gardeners.

Two more progardening factors were at work. Beginning in 1977, Congress gave a special appropriation for urban gardening to the Agriculture Department's Cooperative Extension Service, and over the next 15 years about $50 million was funneled to community gardens in 23 major cities. Although the program was significantly reduced during the Clinton Administration, more than a dozen cities have been using Community Development Block Grants from the U.S. Department of Housing and Urban Development (HUD) for garden programs. Philadelphia Green, for instance, receives an annual HUD grant of $350,000.

The other new development that began in the 1970s was the establishment of land conservancies and trusts, legal entities capable of acquiring, owning, and transferring land to protect it for environmental uses in perpetuity. Most prominent is the Trust for Public Land (TPL), whose New York office led the way in promoting the concept of publicly owned garden spaces (and which also provided the technical support needed to establish Philadelphia's Neighborhood Gardens Association in 1987). Through aggressive negotiation and fundraising, TPL has transferred more than 100 publicly or privately held sites, many of them gardens, to neighborhood land trusts and city park agencies in New York; Boston; Newark, New Jersey; and Oakland, California. Other urban land trusts working to save garden plots operate in Pittsburgh, Denver, Seattle, and elsewhere.

Gardens and Parks

Even though community gardens and parks both bring greenery to the concrete jungle, they are vastly—perhaps diametrically—different. As TPL's Lisa Cashdan explained, "Community open spaces are usually low cost, small scale, locally controlled, and user-oriented, in contrast to traditional open spaces, which tend to be higher cost, larger scale, publicly controlled, and maintained by professionals or corporations. Though both types of open space have a role in cities, the growing movement toward resident development and management of neighborhood parks, playgrounds, gardens, and open spaces has occurred, in part, because of reduced capabilities of local governments."

Community gardens are, however, somewhat less "public" than traditional parks. While they provide the nongardening public with some of the benefits of traditional open space, they are in effect semiprivate, members-only enclaves. Most community gardens are fenced, gated, and locked, with keys distributed solely to the gardeners themselves. (Only in New York City are publicly owned gardens required to be open to the public at certain times.)

With city agencies struggling to maintain Philadelphia's large public parks, Philadelphia Green has become almost an alternative private park agency, filling in some of the gaps in the public program. PHS has been phenomenally successful at landing multimillion-dollar grants from both the William Penn Foundation and the Pew Charitable Trusts, as well as sizable gifts from others.

Another de facto problem facing community gardens is the age of the gardeners, who tend to be older women and schoolchildren. Despite their hard work and diligence, the physical frailty of some of the older volunteers often leads to instability in the garden's political structure—if the captain suddenly dies or becomes infirm, there is often no crew to fill in. More than one garden has suddenly withered and collapsed for lack of leadership. The ideal solution, according to TPL's Cashdan, is a partnership between private citizens' groups and city agencies, whereby each brings its strengths to the relationship. "We need to bring in the agencies and have them play an active role in supporting private citizens' volunteer activities," she said.

The Next Phase: Gardens and Housing

Under a $2.75 million grant from the Pew Charitable Trusts, Philadelphia Green is now exploring its newest challenge: combining greening with housing development and other community development efforts. Working with the New Kensington Community Development Corporation in a 150-square-block neighborhood just east of Norris Square, the experiment involves an ambitious, five-year program to develop a neighborhood open space management plan in partnership with an organization that has traditionally focused on residential construction.

"New Kensington has a lot of vitality," said Michael Groman, community greening manager for PHS, "but it is absolutely blighted by unclaimed, unmaintained vacant lots where large and small factories used to stand. We're trying to get the care and maintenance of those abandoned parcels into someone's hands—either an adjoining neighbor, a community association, or a land trust. That's what we mean by open space management."

Philadelphia Green holds a series of after-school gardening programs for more than 250 youths. Students from Pastorius School Ecology Club (shown here) have been regular contestants in the city gardening contests.

In 1973, in response to the glut of vacant, abandoned, tax-delinquent lots, Philadelphia created a vacant property review committee and a process whereby neighbors and others could apply to acquire nonproductive parcels for a variety of uses, including side yards, gardens, and off-street parking. However, because of poor records, inefficient procedures, and understaffing, the process of acquiring such lots took an average of five years. Now, thanks to pressure from Philadelphia Green and a concerted effort by a consortium of city agencies, the city is working to shorten the process to six months.

"Perhaps most interesting, New Kensington has officially declared itself 'blighted,' thus qualifying for urban renewal and allowing unkept property to be condemned," said Groman. "This will allow new housing, new open space, and new job opportunities—some even in the greening business. We're hoping to create a neighborhood horticultural resource center, bringing in compost from Fairmount Park and providing plants and other resources to support the neighborhood gardeners."

"Frankly, this is a big challenge for us," admitted Bonham. "For the first time we have to adapt our proven way of doing things to meet the needs of the community organization in order to achieve a common set of goals. It's an exciting aspect of the collaboration and one that we hope will yield lasting results." It may also finally answer an important question: Can a garden save a neighborhood?

Pinellas Trail
Pinellas County, Florida

Peter Harnik

A new 60-foot-wide linear park on the coast of west-central Florida is becoming the community back porch of a sprawling, 292-square-mile county encompassing 24 political jurisdictions and a fractious population of 890,000. The abandoned railroad track, conceived as a kind of low-speed pathway, may have consequences far beyond those originally intended; already dubbed the "Peace Trail" by one politician, the trail may be beginning to break down the psychological barriers between towns that have never before had a forum for collaboration.

Pinellas County occupies a grand peninsula between Tampa Bay and the Gulf of Mexico on the state's west coast. Home to

St. Petersburg and Clearwater, the county has miles of prized beaches and beachfront hotels and unending fast-food emporiums along busy, multilane roads. It also retains many isolated fragments of the lush, subtropical environment that formerly stretched from horizon to horizon. The county now also has one 35-mile-long strip of green called the Pinellas Trail.

The Pinellas Trail is a rail-trail: a car-free, public pathway developed from an unused rail line. Like other rail-trails, the park evolved from a complex set of circumstances involving geography, commerce, land deals—and, ultimately, the changing economics of transportation. And like other rail-trails, it began as a rather simple notion and grew into something much greater than the sum of its parts.

The Trail Experience

Pinellas Trail, an asphalt treadway nestled within a vegetated parkway never more than 100 feet wide, stretches from St. Petersburg north through the level terrain of South Pasadena, Seminole, Largo, Belleair, Clearwater, Dunedin, and Tarpon Springs. It then leaves the railroad corridor and hooks east and south to the Brooker Creek Preserve and Oldsmar. A total of 342 acres, this long, narrow ribbon weaves its way through a mass of low-density housing and high-volume roads.

Although conceived mostly by bicyclists and designed mostly by highway engineers, Pinellas Trail actually provides distinctly different experiences, depending on the speed of the user.

At the velocity of a bicyclist or an in-line skater, the trail serves as a wonderful introduction to manmade Pinellas, with the sights, sounds, and smells of civilization flashing by. Since Pinellas Trail is a former railroad track, there are industrial remnants, old downtowns, "right side" and "wrong side" neighborhoods, new developments; there are also bayous, orphan fields, and occasional stands of unmolested trees.

At slow speed—the three miles per hour of the walker—the trail teaches about nature, offering birds, trees, bushes, and flowers to be admired. Florida's magnificent environment has been sorely reduced, but Pinellas Trail allows a precious fragment of it to flourish and be appreciated.

Pinellas County Department of Public Affairs

Pinellas Trail was created primarily from an abandoned railroad corridor that stretched the length of the county. The last train ran in September 1986. After many meetings and fundraising activities, ground was broken on the new trail in January 1990.

All together, just over 1 million people use Pinellas Trail every year. Faced with the needs of so many different users, the designers opted for generous treadway width: 15 feet total, ten feet for wheeled users and five for walkers. Wherever corridor width permits, these two treadways are further separated by a grass median strip and sometimes by a row of trees.

A motley combination of vegetation, fencing, and grade dropoff defines the margins of the trail. At its loveliest, the boundary is marked by a homeowner's weathered wooden wall or a woven wire fence festooned with trumpet vine and shaded by a gnarled live oak or a cabbage palm. At its plainest, the boundary consists of a highway-type guardrail and a grassy drainage ditch.

Every half-mile, on average, a road or street crosses Pinellas Trail. Most other rail-trails have far fewer interactions with the surrounding streetscape, but Pinellas Trail makes the best of a bad situation through bollards, signs, rumble strips—and, increasingly, through impressive new bridges that lift the trail above the worst of the road crossings.

How the Trail Came About

The Pinellas Trail grew out of two tragedies. The first was human: in 1983, 17-year-old Bert Valery III was hit by a car and killed while bicycling on one of Pinellas County's causeways. His devastated father, Bert Jr., vowed to make cycling safer in the state and undertook a whirlwind media campaign throughout the county in favor of bike trails.

The second tragedy was economic. On September 26, 1986, after the last train ran on the old Western Rail Line track, CSX Corporation received government permission to abandon the corridor. The line had played an integral role in the county's history and development, not only bringing in hundreds of thousands of tourists and new residents but also serving the freight needs of the growing county. (The rail line even led to the naming of St. Petersburg in honor of the home town of Piotr Dementieff, the Russian émigré who went bankrupt building the original track in 1888.)

The abandonment came late in the county's development, when auto gridlock was already cause for widespread concern. The board of county commissioners quickly agreed that the corridor should be acquired so that it could be considered for some kind of public transit use, perhaps a monorail.

In 1986, the Florida Department of Transportation completed the $19.5 million acquisition of 35 miles of the corridor, the full route from St. Petersburg in the south to Tarpon Springs in the north, except for a gap in downtown Clearwater that had previously been sold to private interests in the city.

Meanwhile, the Bicycle Advisory Committee (BAC) of the county's Metropolitan Planning Organization (MPO), the committee that included Bert Valery, Jr., had been exploring every right-of-way in the county, including drainage ditches and power line corridors, in its search for possible off-road bike trails that would be safe and away from traffic. When the BAC learned of the partially abandoned CSX track, it quickly determined that the route would be nearly perfect. The committee, assisted by Dan Burden, of the Florida Department of Transportation, submitted a proposal to the MPO board that was swiftly dismissed on the grounds that rail transit should take precedence. In addition, the board expressed doubt that a sufficient number of cyclists would use a trail.

Although rail-trails were virtually unknown in Florida in 1986, the rails-to-trails conversion movement had begun as early as 1965 in the upper Midwest—Wisconsin, Minnesota, Iowa, and Illinois, principally. The movement has since been embraced with such exuberance that it has caught elected officials, park managers, and even open space planners by surprise. Enthusiasm for rail-trails has energized thousands of local activists, spawned a national organization based in Washington, D.C., and generated one of the most significant new park-creation forces in the nation. By early 1997, more than 885 rail-trails, with a combined total length of 9,000 miles, could be found throughout the nation. An average of 60 to 100 miles of trails are added to the system monthly.

Florida receives a steady stream of new residents, and two newcomers were particularly influential in the development of the Pinellas Trail: Ned Baier, one of Pinellas County's young planners, had grown up in Iowa and Minneapolis. Earnest Foster, a former Union Carbide executive, had started bicycling in Connecticut; upon retiring, Foster had plunged into leadership of the St. Petersburg Bicycle Club.

"The corridor was supposed to be used for rail transit," recalled Baier, "but the consultants came back with a report showing that there wasn't sufficient population density or enough large destinations to make a billion-dollar system worth building. When the MPO concluded that a light-rail system was possible but premature, it was clear that a bike trail would be less expensive and that it was needed. At the same time, the MPO's Bicycle Advisory Committee came out with a study showing that, over the previous five years, Pinellas County's per capita bicycle fatality and injury rates were in the top five in Florida and that the state, in turn, had the second-highest rate in the nation."

Armed with this information, in May 1988 the BAC again proposed a bicycle trail on the corridor. This time —partly to hold and preserve the corridor, partly to keep it from becoming a dumping ground and public nuisance—the county commission took the proposal more seriously. "As soon as the tracks were taken out the property started becoming a nuisance and a problem," said Joe Kubicki, director of transportation services for King Engineering Associates, the Clearwater-based company that planned the trail. "People were dirt-biking and dumping on the land. It was starting to be viewed as a liability."

The Advocacy Group

Despite growing support, it was clear that the trail would not come into existence simply because the planners and the BAC wanted it. Construction costs would be high, and there were not enough cyclists to justify a bike-only trail. In addition, because the trail passed through seven different cities and miles of unincorporated sprawl, it seemed to defy management.

Under the leadership of Valery and Foster, three important decisions ensued. First, it was resolved that the facility be named Pinellas Trail—simple and direct enough to give the fundraising campaign a focus, but broad enough to be inclusive of everyone in the county. Second, Foster insisted that the fundraising effort reach beyond bicyclists to all potential trail users and that it be spearheaded by a full-time, staffed advocacy group separate from the BAC. Finally, the trail advocates inside and outside government agreed that the trail would be run as a single county park rather than as a collection of separate pathways.

On December 16, 1988, the advocacy group, Pinellas Trails, Inc. (PTI), was incorporated with a broad-based board of 14 and Foster as president. PTI's ambitious goal was to raise $200,000 in private donations, $150,000 of which would pay for rest stops, water fountains, rest rooms, benches, and other amenities. In order to do this, the group hired Cuma Glennon, a noted organizer and

Pinellas County Department of Public Affairs

Every half-mile, on average, a road or street crosses Pinellas Trail. Bollards, signs, and rumble strips warn users to be cautious, and a series of flyovers allows them to continue without yielding to vehicle traffic.

Florida law requires everyone under 16 to wear a helmet at all times when riding a bicycle, be it on residential streets or bicycle trails.

fundraiser who had, among other things, put together Pinellas County's highly successful Diamond Jubilee celebration the previous year.

Glennon, Foster, and Valery were well connected in the county and were promoting a concept that touched a deep nerve, particularly among bicyclists and parents concerned about safety. The trail supporters offered tangible items—benches, water fountains, rest stops, bike racks—in return for contributions. Early on, a prominent St. Petersburg stockbroker (and member of the St. Petersburg Bicycle Club) pledged $2,500; the campaign immediately gained respectability, and people took out their checkbooks. Within a year, Pinellas Trails, Inc., had nearly 2,000 paying members and cash donations totaling $100,000.

Even more significant than the donations was a brief but momentous conversation Glennon had with Charles Rainey, chair of the Pinellas County Board of Commissioners. "I asked Chuck Rainey to give us some serious money for the trail," she recalled. "He said, 'We can't just go and spend $1 million on bicycles.' I said, 'Well, what should we do?' He said, 'Show us that the people of Pinellas really want something like this.'"

The "Penny for Pinellas" Campaign

The timing could not have been more fortuitous. A year earlier, the Florida legislature had responded to the crisis in local funding by allowing cities and counties to place before their voters a referendum on increasing the sales tax to pay for badly needed infrastructure improvements. So Pinellas County put on the ballot a "Penny for Pinellas" measure to "finance, plan, acquire, im-

prove, and construct . . . projects including transportation, parks and open space, jails, courts, drainage, and public facilities." Amazingly, a penny tax increase would translate into $110 million per year, $1.1 billion over the ten-year life of the act. Controversy over the measure was intense.

Glennon, Foster, and the county administrator quickly realized that the fate of the trail hinged on the tax measure. After gaining assurance that if the Penny for Pinellas campaign won, at least $6.1 million of the tax revenue would go for the trail, PTI plunged into the campaign with gusto, giving speeches, doing mailings, distributing flyers, leafletting on the trail, producing buttons. By the time the election rolled around, many residents were under the mistaken (but helpful) impression that the penny was for the trail, rather than largely for drainage canals, prisons, roads, and other more mundane purposes. When the smoke cleared on November 7, the sales tax was approved by 398 votes out of 135,000 cast.

The county administration knew that Pinellas Trails, Inc., had made the difference between victory and defeat. County Administrator Fred Marquis called the trail advocates to say, "I'm telling the engineering department tomorrow that the trail project is the first to come out of the chute."

Planning the Park

Converting the concept of a rail-trail into reality was not easy. Pinellas County Project Engineer Frank Aiello knew all about building roads, but no manual on trails existed at that time. How wide should it be? What surfacing material should be used? What about intersec-

Like all such trails, the Pinellas Trail must accommodate a wide variety of users. Although the trail was initially focused on bicyclists, the number of skaters is now about the same as the number of bicyclists.

At various points where corridor width permits, a separate treadway is available for walkers.

tions? Lighting? Keeping cars off? Signs? Moreover, there were no appropriate models anywhere in Florida.

Fortunately, through the national Rails-to-Trails Conservancy, Aiello and his team learned of Seattle's Burke-Gilman Trail, a groundbreaking urban rail-trail with a dozen years of operating experience, and arranged a site visit. Hundreds of photographs, thousands of feet of videotape, and many hours of interviews later, the team was able to adopt some of the best ideas from Burke-Gilman and avoid the most egregious pitfalls.

"Originally, we thought eight feet would be much too wide," laughed Aiello. "Then we started actually measuring—one bike, two bikes side by side, two bikes passing a pedestrian, two bikes and two pedestrians. We learned that even Burke-Gilman itself was too narrow for the use it gets. That's why we selected our generous configuration—ten feet of width for cyclists plus five feet for walkers, separated by a grass median wherever we have enough corridor breadth to do so."

With scores of road crossings, the handling of street intersections became a major issue during the design process.

"We probably argued bollards at least two months," said Aiello, referring to the design of the posts that keep cars off the corridor. Aiello and his team ultimately decided to install four red-and-white posts on the trail at each street crossing, spaced closely enough to prevent unauthorized vehicles from gaining access to the trail, but spaced widely enough to allow bikes, wheelchairs, and strollers through. Although all four bollards look identical, three of them are iron sunk in cement and one is removable plastic, in order to allow access for maintenance and emergency vehicles.

The bollards are placed 40 feet in from the edge of the pavement of the intersecting street. To alert speeding or inattentive bicyclists, Pinellas Trail adopted the European concept of changing the texture and color of the trail surface, the bicycle equivalent of the automobile "rumble strips" that are sometimes used on approaches to tollbooths. The strips consist of white concrete that contrasts with the black asphalt of the trail. Even though the concrete is smooth (ripples or ridges would be dangerous for in-line skaters) it is effective at rousing cyclists from any "cadence reverie."

In addition to the bollards, the designers had to deal with the road crossings themselves. For these they proposed five different solutions: stop signs on the trail, stop signs on the road, four-way stops, bicyclist-activated traffic signals, and grade-separated trail bridges over the busiest roads. Depending on local rules, traffic volumes, and funding availability, different solutions are instituted as appropriate; surprisingly, the most expensive solution —bridging over the roads—is gaining favor. Five overpasses have already been built and three more are on the drawing board, not including a mile-long, $2 million causeway across Long Bayou.

Constructing the Park

Most rail-trails have long, difficult gestation periods marred by controversy and dissension. Not so Pinellas. With the county and the citizen group working together as smoothly as a well-oiled machine, opposition barely surfaced, and the public was treated to positive press coverage, regular bulletins on exciting events, and a steadily lengthening trail. The January 1990 groundbreaking was a media bonanza, with a "Trailgate Party" that included 500 celebrants, music, and a glimpse of the future: two 100-foot demonstration sections of paved and landscaped trail located at opposite ends of the county.

With cyclists up and down the county clamoring for the trail, the only controversy arose over which section would be built first. Ultimately, the trail was begun mid-county and extended north and south as quickly as planning, engineering, and funding allowed. By mid-1996, the trail was virtually complete from central St. Petersburg to north of Tarpon Springs, and the final, 12-mile extension—alongside roads, since no rail line was available—was under construction.

One typical construction challenge that Pinellas Trail did not have to face was water management. "In this area the heavyweight regulatory agency is the Southwest Florida Surface Water Management District," said Aiello. "With the water table only inches below the surface and all the rain we get, nothing gets built without a water attenuation plan—a system to prevent additional down-stream runoff. But we asked them for an exemption."

"They couldn't believe their ears," he laughed. "'You're going to build something that causes absolutely no pollution?' they asked. I explained that we would be putting down pavement for 35 miles but that it would be over ground that was already packed down and water impervious because of the tracks—and that an excellent drainage ditch system was already in place, thanks to the railroad. Eventually they agreed. That saved us a lot of money. We were also fortunate in that there was very little contamination; less than 1 percent of the corridor needed cleaning up. Interestingly, what we found wasn't from the trains—it was from people illegally emptying oil from their cars and things like that."

A series of benches, shelters, picnic tables, and other conveniences can be found along the trail.

Jerry Cummings (left), manager of Pinellas Trail, and his staff of six park rangers patrol the trail on bicycles and serve as the "eyes and ears" of the trail. Also shown is Pinellas Trail ranger Bill Gagliardo.

Design, Security, and Maintenance

Not every aspect of the park's appearance is perfect. Since it was planned and constructed by the county's engineering department with little involvement of park professionals, it lacks some of the classic "soft" elements of the other handsome parks in the county. Railings are generally off-the-shelf highway materials, signs are metal rather than wood, fencing is unattractive chain-link, there is little use of visually appealing wood or stone materials. And despite a goodly number of cabbage palms, Southern red cedars, crape myrtles, live oaks, and sunflowers, plantings are still sparse in most areas.

"We've tried to do some screening in industrial areas," said Joe Lapartis, assistant parks director, "but we're being pretty judicious on the landscaping because of the constraints we're operating under. Unlike our other parks, this one has no irrigation on the trail, so it's hard to establish new plants—we have to go out there regularly with a tanker truck. With trees we also have to be careful—there are a lot of utilities with restrictions above and beneath the corridor. Also, we need to preserve good sight visibility at the intersections, we can't plant anything in the drainage ditches on either side of the trail, and our security people don't want trees or shrubs that people can hide behind."

From the moment the Pinellas Trail was proposed, attention was given to making it safe and secure, both for users and for nearby residents. Even before the trail was constructed, the county created the Pinellas Trail Security Task Force, chaired by the police chief of Tarpon Springs, a community that at the time included one of the seedier sections of the corridor. (Thanks to the trail, that stretch has since been markedly improved.)

The committee recommended various rules and regulations, including such items as prohibiting horses and nighttime use, setting a 20-mile-per-hour speed limit, and requiring dogs to be leashed. Under an agreement, the county parks department handles the easier enforcement issues, and each local police department and the county sheriff's department are on call for more serious problems.

Initially, only the town of Largo opted to use bicycle-mounted police to patrol the trail and the surrounding area; the county sheriff's office swore that its officers would never get out of their cars. However, the efficacy of bike patrols (not to mention requests from many officers themselves) has revolutionized the look of most of the departments, including the county sheriff's. Nearly 100 officers now patrol on bicycles.

"Not that the police spend much time on the trail," says Jerry Cummings, manager of Pinellas Trail. "There's no need to. There's virtually no crime here." In 1995, for instance, out of 13,066 reported crimes in unincorporated areas of Pinellas County, only 26 took place on the trail—less than 0.2 percent. "Interestingly, there is less crime on Pinellas Trail than in other parks within our system," says Cummings. "I think it's because we have no parking lots, more exercise, less picnicking and alcohol. Compared to other facilities we have absolutely no drinking problem on the trail."

More visible than the police are Cummings and his staff of six park rangers and 15 full-time volunteers—ambassadors of the parks department who provide information and directions, pick up glass, help repair bikes, and serve as the "eyes and ears of the trail," according to ranger Tim Costerman. "My friends are so envious of my job, they all hate me."

Cummings's staff can devote much of its attention to the public because a private company handles most of the day-to-day maintenance. Under a $229,000 contract, Spectrum Landscaping Company handles trail mowing, trash removal, insect and weed control, fence repair, tree trimming, and landscaping. Among numerous other stipulations, the trail corridor is mowed 32 times a year, trees are trimmed to provide a clearance of 12 feet above and four feet from the edge of the trail, trash is emptied weekly, 1,500 new trees and shrubs are planted a year, new cabbage palms (the state tree) are watered daily for 12 weeks until they are established, and missing signposts are replaced within 48 hours of notification (except stop signs, which are replaced immediately).

How the Park Is Used

Although the trail was initially conceived as a bikepath, "skating is where the growth is," said Cummings. "In 1990, there were about five bikes for every skater; now it's about even." (Skating presents a new set of challenges for park design and maintenance, requiring smoother pavement, longer "run-out" areas below the fast hills of the overpasses, and greater promotion of helmets and knee- and elbow-pads; some of the most serious accidents have involved skaters.)

With many educational institutions along the corridor, users are predominantly schoolchildren and retirees. About one out of three trips is for purposeful transporta-

Commercial activity of all kinds has increased substantially along the trail, much of it designed to accommodate trail users.

tion, although so far, commute-to-work trips are lower than anticipated. "This is a very good area to walk," said Cummings. "Our surveys show that people come from many miles away—they actually plan their trips around the trail."

Immediate neighbors are the heaviest users. "When the trail was first put in we saw some community nervousness," said Cummings. "Many fences and concrete walls went up. But next thing you know these same people were cutting holes in their walls and installing gates and doors so they can get right from their yards to the trail."

The Economics of the Park

Since linear parks have scores of entrances and exits, charging a user fee can be difficult. (Some linear parks in Wisconsin, Iowa, and elsewhere require users to purchase and display daily or annual use passes on their bicycles or snowmobiles, but Pinellas has not chosen to implement this system.) Nevertheless, Pinellas Trail, like all linear parks, has strong economic links to the surrounding communities.

For one thing, the retail climate along the whole length of the trail has improved—from items like soda, film, and sunscreen; to sit-down meals and bike and skate rental and repair; to bicycles, skates, jogging strollers, and sports clothing. A new McDonalds with a recreational theme has opened near the trail, a special connection was constructed from the trail to the Publix Store in the Caladesi Shopping Center, and some formerly marginal shops near the abandoned rail line

As part of the many opening celebrations for the trail, a race was held. Shown here are runners passing through St. Petersburg.

have been upgraded in response to the new clientele. In Ozona, adjacent to the trail, an upscale townhome community was developed that uses the word *trail* in its name.

In addition, although firm figures on the trail's impact on nearby property values are not yet available, anecdotal evidence points to higher prices, which would yield higher tax receipts for the county. "Both houses and commercial property along the trail are certainly more marketable," said Scott Daniels, president of Pinellas Trails, Inc. "Real estate ads mention proximity to the trail as one of the selling points."

Finally, and most dramatically, the private sector has become a source of enthusiastic support. PTI has raised about $150,000 for benches, plantings, water fountains, mileage markers, tables, bicycle racks, maps, and other items. Garden clubs have donated greenery and have even installed demonstration xeriscaping boxes showing residents which plant materials to use in order to minimize the use of water—both along the trail and in family backyards. In some cases, neighboring shops and institutions have paid to extend water lines and install drinking fountains for the benefit of trail users. In a few short years, the private sector has risen to the challenge of improving a trail that Pinellas County did not have sufficient park funds to develop fully.

The community that has seized on the Pinellas Trail opportunity with the greatest enthusiasm is the town of Dunedin. Originally settled by Scottish immigrants in the 1870s, Dunedin's human-scale downtown had been gradually undermined by the development of regional shopping centers, so much so that in 1988 the town created a community redevelopment district to try and save Dunedin's quaint core, where retail establishments were turning over every six to nine months.

The town of Dunedin in particular has embraced the trail and benefited from the users who pass through its downtown. The city now sponsors eight special musical and performance events on Main Street each year. Shown here are members of the citizens' group Pinellas Trails, Inc., at the Dunedin trail site.

The trail, passing through the middle of the redevelopment district and generating a continuous flow of people, helped give a focus to commercial efforts. "About 1,500 people come through town on the trail every Saturday and every Sunday," said Bob Ironsmith, director of community redevelopment for the city. "Not every cyclist immediately stops to eat or shop, but many of the trail users see stores or restaurants that catch their eye and promise themselves to return another day. The trail gave Dunedin's downtown an identity, a vibrancy. The retail near the trail is not going under any more, and there are no vacancies on Main Street."

The old Dunedin train station had already been converted into a museum run by the town's historical society, and in November 1991 the city completed a $350,000 reconstruction of two blocks of Main Street where it crosses the trail. Through a joint donation from the Dunedin Rotary Club and SunTrust bank, a new bicyclist and pedestrian plaza serving the Pinellas Trail has been constructed.

"Dunedin doesn't have notable architecture, but we do have urban design," explained Ironsmith. "By narrowing your streets, slowing traffic, making it pedestrian-friendly, you can create a lot of charm. That's what we're doing around our stretch of trail."

The Verdict

Although Pinellas County has an impressive system of natural parks and beaches, Pinellas Trail is the first county facility expressly devoted to active recreation. That, combined with its length, has caused it to become remarkably influential in a brief time. Not only has annual use exceeded the total population of the county,

Pinellas Trails, Inc., publishes a comprehensive guidebook that indicates distances and trail conditions as well as the location of public parking lots, rest rooms, gas stations, stores, restaurants, sightseeing points, and so on.

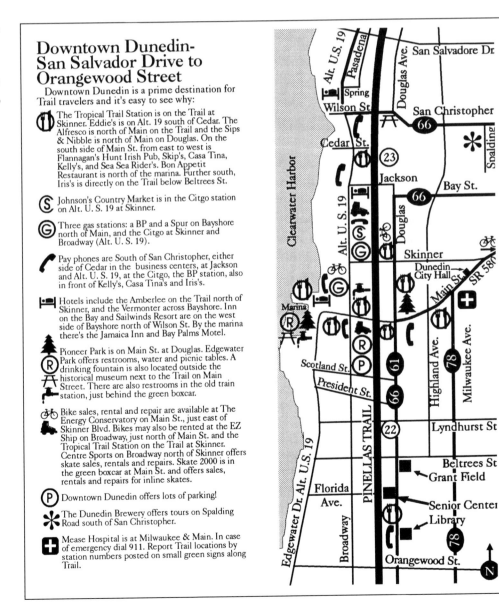

Downtown Dunedin-San Salvador Drive to Orangewood Street

Downtown Dunedin is a prime destination for Trail travelers and it's easy to see why:

The Tropical Trail Station is on the Trail at Skinner. Eddie's is on Alt. 19 south of Cedar. The Alfresco is north of Main on the Trail and the Sips & Nibble is north of Main on Douglas. On the south side of Main St. from east to west is Flannagan's Hunt Irish Pub, Skip's, Casa Tina, Kelly's, and Sea Sea Rider's. Bon Appetit Restaurant is north of the marina. Further south, Iris's is directly on the Trail below Beltrees St.

Ⓢ Johnson's Country Market is in the Citgo station on Alt. U. S. 19 at Skinner.

Ⓖ Three gas stations: a BP and a Spur on Bayshore north of Main, and the Citgo at Skinner and Broadway (Alt. U. S. 19).

☎ Pay phones are South of San Christopher, either side of Cedar in the business centers, at Jackson and Alt. U. S. 19, at the Citgo, the BP station, also in front of Kelly's, Casa Tina's and Iris's.

🛏 Hotels include the Amberlee on the Trail north of Skinner, and the Vermonter across Bayshore. Inn on the Bay and Sailwinds Resort are on the west side of Bayshore north of Wilson St. By the marina there's the Jamaica Inn and Bay Palms Motel.

🌲 Pioneer Park is on Main St. at Douglas. Edgewater
Ⓡ Park offers restrooms, water and picnic tables. A drinking fountain is also located outside the historical museum next to the Trail on Main Street. There are also restrooms in the old train station, just behind the green boxcar.

🚲 Bike sales, rental and repair are available at The Energy Conservatory on Main St., just east of Skinner Blvd. Bikes may also be rented at the EZ Ship on Broadway, just north of Main St. and the Tropical Trail Station on the Trail at Skinner. Centre Sports on Broadway north of Skinner offers skate sales, rentals and repairs. Skate 2000 is in the green boxcar at Main St. and offers sales, rentals and repairs for inline skates.

Ⓟ Downtown Dunedin offers lots of parking!

✳ The Dunedin Brewery offers tours on Spalding Road south of San Christopher.

✚ Mease Hospital is at Milwaukee & Main. In case of emergency dial 911. Report Trail locations by station numbers posted on small green signs along Trail.

The Pinellas Trail cuts through a 292-square-mile county encompassing 24 political jurisdictions and a population of almost 900,000. Just over 1 million people use the trail each year.

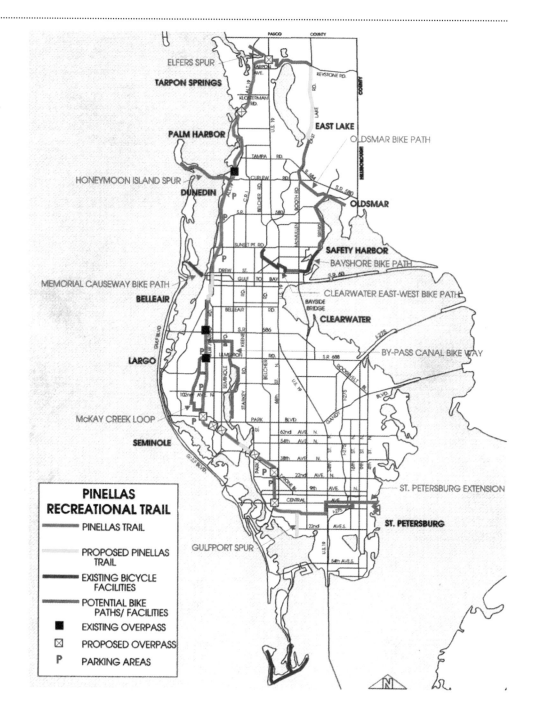

PINELLAS RECREATIONAL TRAIL

━━━ PINELLAS TRAIL

━━━ PROPOSED PINELLAS TRAIL

━━━ EXISTING BICYCLE FACILITIES

━━━ POTENTIAL BIKE PATHS/ FACILITIES

■ EXISTING OVERPASS

⊠ PROPOSED OVERPASS

P PARKING AREAS

but users have in a profound way extended and deepened their awareness of and connection to their county. And the landscape itself is responding.

The most immediate response has been the construction of several flyovers to separate the trail from busy roads and to maintain the trail's continuity. Although expensive, these bridges are being funded by ISTEA enhancement money; no other rail-trail in the nation is undergoing as ambitious a program to separate it from dangerous crossings.

Almost as dramatic is the trail's stimulation of private commercial enterprises, through both renovation and innovation, as entrepreneurs begin to comprehend the opportunity represented by the large new market of trail users. While small towns like Dunedin and Tarpon Springs have responded most quickly, the main centers of Clearwater and St. Petersburg are not far behind.

The third and most lasting change to the landscape is the parkland and greenspace that Pinellas Trail is fostering. County and local governments are busily linking Pinellas Trail to existing parks near and along the corridor and are planning new parks and trails adjacent to Pinellas Trail. Governments and private landowners are

Project Data • Pinellas Trail

Development Schedule

Initial site acquired	1986
Planning started	1989
Design competition conducted	1989
Master plan approved	1990
Construction started	July 1990
Construction completed	(estimated) 1998
Park opened	December 1990
Project completed	(estimated) 1998

Financing Information

Funding Source	Amount	Percentage of Total
Private		
Pinellas Trail, Inc.	$300,000	0.9%
Local		
Pinellas County	10,523,000	31.1
State		
Florida Department of Transportation (ISTEA funds)[1]	23,021,000	68.0
Total	$33,844,000	100.0%

Development and Construction Costs (in millions)

Project Phase	County	State and Federal	Total
Land acquisition	$.406	$19.000	$19.406
Engineering/planning	1.097	1.699	2.796
Construction	8.942	2.322	11.264
Miscellaneous	.078	—	.078
Total through 1996	$10.523	$23.021	$33.544
Funds programmed, fiscal years 1996–2001			
Engineering/planning/ construction	$2.402	$4.633	$7.035
Total through 2001	$12.925	$27.654	$40.579

Budget Worksheet for Pinellas Trail, 1995–1996

Total personnel services	$248,980
Contractual services	
Miscellaneous	229,400
Hazardous waste	2,000
Intergovernmental services	24,690
Signage	2,000
Fleet operating and maintenance	15,690
Fleet (vehicle replacement)	7,880
Travel and per diem	830
Telephone	700
County water	600
Utility services	2,000
Solid waste	2,000
Rental and leases (equipment)	500
Repairs and maintenance (grounds)	1,000
Repairs and maintenance (equipment)	3,000
Printing and binding	500
Office supplies	500
Small tools	500
Clothing	3,000
Operating supplies (miscellaneous)	6,000
Total operating expenses	$300,790
Capital outlay (machinery and equipment)	12,083
Total capital outlay	12,083
Total budget	$561,853

Note

1. Most of this will be repaid by Pinellas County. Once it is repaid, the county will have paid 87.2 percent of all costs ($29,523,000).

---

sprucing up properties along the corridor, removing unsightly structures and junk, planting trees and shrubs—even, in one innovative program, using convicted graffiti artists to paint striking murals on blank industrial walls. Whereas roads seem to generate parking lots, asphalt, and sprawl, trails seem to spawn parks, picnic areas, and greenery.

Pinellas County, just 75 years old, is essentially built out and is now on the cusp of a challenging new phase of redevelopment. Pinellas Trail promises to become a focal point for much of that redevelopment.

Riverbank State Park
New York City

Gayle Berens

Norman McGrath

The 28-acre Riverbank State Park, located in West Harlem, is built atop the North River Water Pollution Treatment Facility and was paid for with public funds. While Chelsea Piers is a striking example of a recreational facility built with private funds, Riverbank State Park is an equally striking recreational facility built entirely with public funds. This state park represents the transformation of an unwanted but necessary facility—a sewage treatment plant—into a heavily used community resource—a state park and recreational facility—in Harlem, far from the gentrified Manhattan neighborhoods. Using innovative technology and developed with much community input, this publicly funded project was some 25 years in the making before it was finally realized.

The Ultimate NIMBY Project: A Wastewater Treatment Plant

In 1965, when New York City was given a federal order to treat its raw sewage before discharging it into the Hudson, the city began the process of identifying a site for a very unpopular facility. In 1968, after considering several alternatives, the city selected a site it owned on the Hudson River, at the west end of Harlem, between West 137th and West 145th streets.

The proposed North River Water Pollution Treatment Facility, which ultimately cost $1 billion to build, would process a billion gallons of sewage per week. Public projects of this scale typically have a percentage of total costs set aside for beautification—and this project was no exception. Although the community was not to be won over by promises of beautification, the state moved forward and secured an easement for the air rights above the plant to develop a park. The first effort to define the type of project to be located above the plant was a proposal commissioned from Philip Johnson in 1968, which involved flooding the roof and building a series of fountains that would spring from the pool. When community residents discovered that the pool was going to be using clean New York City water, they were outraged. Governor Nelson Rockefeller then committed the state to constructing a state park on the roof.

Numerous rooftop park and open-space development alternatives were evaluated; ultimately, in 1980, a committee of state officials and community representatives chose architect Richard Dattner to spearhead the design and development of a rooftop state park and recreational facility.

Between 1980 and 1993, when the park finally opened, the project was designed and redesigned and shown to every community group imaginable. According to Dattner, "The decision to locate in Harlem resulted in 25 years of community protest, political struggle, and a variety of efforts to assuage the community by balancing the pain of locating a sewage treatment plant in its front yard with the benefits possible from its construction."

Throughout the project's first year of design, planning sessions were held every other week with community residents; local elected officials; and representatives from the major federal, state, and city agencies that would oversee, construct, pay for, and operate the park. Ultimately, a steering committee was selected, composed of representatives from each of these three groups. The design team inventoried existing parks and recreational facilities, defined public transportation opportunities, studied adjoining community facilities and land use patterns, analyzed demographics, and studied the technical limits to construction at this difficult location.

"We met with the steering committee every two weeks," said architect Dattner. "We started with six schemes and a list of design criteria to use in evaluating and ranking the schemes. The design criteria included things like protection from north winds, orientation to the sun, energy conservation, proximity to access points, flexibility of use, views of the river, preservation of views from surrounding buildings, and so on. The steering committee and design team then ranked the six schemes against the design goals and assigned numerical scores. Based on their scores, two schemes were chosen for further development."

Building facades are wrapped in rust-colored brick tiles high-lighted with a bank of green and with red accents throughout. Fiberglass skylights cap four corners of all buildings.

Community members wanted several features that the state was unable to provide at that location. For example, putting in a large swimming pool with artificial waves would have been so expensive that the community would have had to forgo several other facilities. Another requested feature—a swimming pool deep enough to allow diving—could not be supported on the roof of the sewage plant.

Transportation and access issues were studied in detail, as the site is located 400 feet from Riverside Drive, a major traffic artery, and 58 feet above ground level, requiring a bridge across a railroad right-of-way and the six-lane Henry Hudson Parkway. After extensive studies and meetings with neighborhood groups, a 50-foot-wide, two-lane vehicular bridge with a wide pedestrian walkway was built at West 145th Street. A second bridge, a 40-foot-wide, single-lane bridge for emergency vehicles and pedestrians, was built at West 138th Street, providing access to the park at both ends of its nine-block length. Riverbank can also be reached via the 145th Street crosstown bus and a subway station at Broadway, one block east of Riverside Drive.

Construction of the park finally began in the spring of 1987. Of the two designs considered by the steering committee, the one chosen on the basis of large public hearings with renderings, plans, and scale models "was the one eventually built," said Dattner, "although not without continuing crises in the 13 years until construction was completed."

Development financing came from multiple public sources, of which 19 percent were federal, 45 percent state, and 36 percent city. Because the park was threatened by lack of funds at various stages in the eight-year development process, the state insisted that the project undergo value engineering, which resulted in significant design changes that lowered the overall cost. For example, the original design called for sophisticated continuous angled skylights, planned for optimum orientation to the sun. These were replaced by simpler roof trusses with skylights at right angles.

Most of the site's design and construction challenges were related to the limited amount of weight that the building below the park could support. Concerns included the load-bearing capacity of the plant's caissons, columns, and roof spans. Load equations also had to take into account expected live loads (people, vehicles, and snow). And much of the construction had to take place while the sewage treatment plant was fully operational, without interrupting its service, adding to the project's design and development complexities.

To comply with targeted load-bearing criteria, the park's buildings had to be made of lightweight steel with metal- or tile-faced panels. A honeycomb of en-

Norman McGrath

The swimming pool complex contains one 50-meter pool with two movable bulkheads, as well as a 25-yard outdoor pool, a wading pool, and large terraces located near the river to take advantage of summer breezes and views of the Hudson.

vironmentally friendly nonchlorofluorocarbon (non-CFC) Styrofoam panels was used to lighten sections of the park requiring soil for plantings.

The 28-acre roof, which is almost a half-mile long, consists of 14 separate sections that move independently as the roof expands and contracts with changes in temperature. To avoid damage from movement at expansion joints, each of the park's buildings is completely contained within one roof plate. Every column in a park building is located directly over a corresponding sewage plant column. Original plans called for the roof to carry 400 pounds per square foot throughout, but the design team was able to shave $10 million off the project by identifying only those roof plates that needed to support that much weight and designing other areas for lighter loads.

Weight limitations also made it necessary to limit the depth of the pool to four feet, to use wood instead of concrete for the walls of the handball court, and to clad the facade in prefabricated brick tiles (five-eighths of an inch thick) instead of whole bricks. Because the project's pipes, drains, and electrical conduits had to run over the plant's roof, utilities required special attention. Stormwater collected by the park's sophisticated drainage system is channeled through the sewage plant for treatment.

Designing an Urban Recreational Facility

Riverbank State Park, which opened in 1993, includes five major structures: a 50-meter pool with two movable bulkheads that allow it to be divided into three pool areas; a covered skating rink for ice skating in the winter and roller skating in the summer; a cultural center; a multiuse athletic building designed for basketball,

volleyball, gymnastics, and martial arts; and a 150-seat restaurant with a 100-seat outdoor terrace.

Outdoor facilities include a 25-yard lap pool; a wading pool 18 feet in diameter; four basketball courts; four handball/paddleball courts; four tennis courts; a waterfront amphitheater; a running track surrounding a football/soccer field; a community garden and greenhouse; picnic areas; and a children's playground.

Because of the treatment plant's location on the riverbank, decisions on how to site the park's buildings had to take into account a number of factors, including wind exposure and the potential for flooding. For protection against winter winds blowing off the Hudson, four major park buildings are clustered inward around a south-facing courtyard. In addition, the buildings needed to offer views of the river without blocking river views from nearby buildings.

Delineating the bridges are decorative entrance gates that echo Frederick Law Olmsted's design for Riverside Park, which abuts the entrance. At the 145th Street bridge entrance, the first visible building houses a carousel with figures commissioned from an artist. The nearby restaurant, encased by windows, features a large terrace with views up the Hudson River.

The cultural center, designed for maximum flexibility, has three wings radiating from a central stage area. Motorized bleachers can be retracted or extended to create performance space. The building also houses dressing rooms, lockers, storage, and the park's administrative office.

The covered skating rink is not fully enclosed and is maintained as an ice facility from late fall to early spring. It also has a concrete surface for roller skating during warmer seasons. The rink has bleachers, lockers, skate rentals, and a food concession area.

Over 80 percent of the park is landscaped for a variety of active and passive outdoor activities.

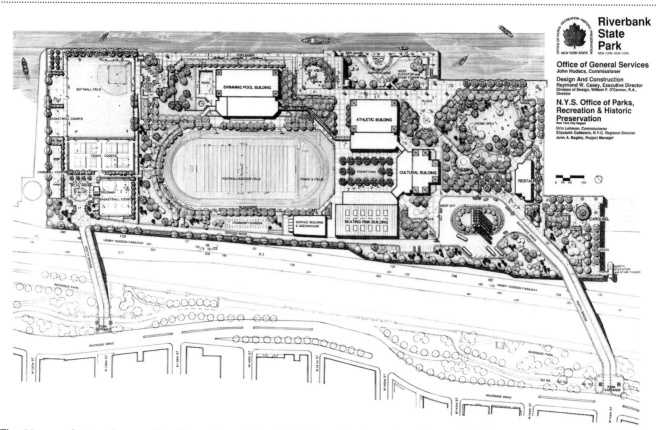

The 28-acre plant roof supporting the park consists of 14 independently moving plates, which limited the location of the park structures. Siting of the park's buildings had to take into account factors such as wind exposure and the potential for flooding. In addition, the buildings needed to offer river views to park visitors without blocking river views from nearby buildings. The four largest park buildings are clustered around a south-facing courtyard to shelter them from winter winds blowing off the Hudson.

A continuous promenade rings the entire park, providing seating, shade trees, and a sea-rail design that has become standard for much of Manhattan's waterfront.

Stanley Greenberg

"We designed the project to be as flexible as possible," said Dattner. "Everything is multipurpose to adapt to different sports trends." The park is ringed by a promenade high above the Hudson. Knee-high, striated concrete along the promenade discourages graffiti. To shield neighbors from noisy concerts and events, a boat landing and an outdoor amphitheater are located 50 feet below the athletic building, at the river's edge. From there, the sewage treatment plant is highly visible, but its design is inconspicuous. Clad in concrete, the plant has arched openings that reflect the form of a nearby bridge.

Operation and Management

Operated and managed by the state, Riverbank State Park has become the second most heavily used state park in New York: over 3.7 million users visited it in 1995. Security is provided by state park police, but has so far not been a notable problem. Closed-circuit televisions monitor the entrances and other areas of the park. Though not planned as such, the limited access to the park has proven to be a security bonus, allowing comings and goings to be monitored easily.

Project Data • Riverbank State Park

Land Use Information

Site area: 28 acres[1]

Gross building area: 196,900 square feet

Land Use Plan

Components	Square Feet	Acres	Percentage of Site
Buildings	196,900	4.5	16.1%
Athletic buildings	34,460		
Swimming pool	48,000		
Cultural center building	43,200		
Skating rink building	50,240		
Restaurant	9,000		
Maintenance	12,000		
Softball playing field		5.0	17.8
Children's playground		1.0	3.6
Running track and field		5.0	17.8
Community garden and picnic area		2.0	7.1
Amphitheater		2.0	7.1
Surface parking		0.5	2.0
Roadways		2.5	8.9
Miscellaneous walkways		5.5	19.6%

Financing Information

Funding Source	Amount (in millions)	Percentage of Total
Federal	$23.85	19%
Environmental Protection Agency Cleanwater aesthetic treatment		
State	58.17	45
Pure Water Bond Fund	4.77	
Parks	53.4	
Local	46.98	36
New York City Department of Clean Water	3.18	
Plant construction funds	43.8	
Total funding	$129	100%

Development Cost Information (in millions)

Site acquisition costs	NA[2]
Site improvement costs	
Sewer/water/drainage	$7.0
Paving/curbs/sidewalk	10.2
Landscaping/irrigation	6.3
Roof strengthening	16.0
Total improvement costs	$39.5
Construction costs	
Superstructure	$48.7
HVAC	3.3
Electrical	4.1
Plumbing/sprinklers	4.0
Graphics/specialties	0.2
Access bridges	20.2
Total construction costs	$80.5
Soft costs	
Architecture/engineering	$5.0
Project management	4.0
Total soft costs	9.0
Total development costs	$129.0

Development Schedule

Site purchased	1968
Planning started	1968
Construction started	1988
Park opened	1993
Project completed	1993

Notes

1. Not applicable. The entire park is located on the rooftop of a 2.2 million-square-foot sewage treatment plant.

2. New York State secured an easement from New York City for the air rights 59 feet above the site for the development of the park.

While the park is not always odor free, the occasional slight odor is of chlorine, not raw sewage. Although it was originally known as "the smelly park," the odor at Riverbank seems to have decreased as various adjustments to the treatment process have been made, and most of the open tanks have been covered. According to Gaspar Santiago, park director from November 1992 to November 1996, "The work the city did to cover some of the main tanks downstairs has resulted in a very positive situation for the park. Sometimes you get some odors—but not often, and they're not strong."

Conclusion

Although a recreational park and a sewage treatment facility are seemingly incompatible uses, the creative use of the rooftop provided a community with a much needed facility and helped neutralize the NIMBY (not in my backyard) attitude. Careful work with the community, although time consuming, resulted in a park that provided tremendous value to the neighborhood by meeting its recreational needs and becoming a popular meeting spot for children and adults.

Shreveport Riverfront Park
Shreveport, Louisiana

David Mulvihill

The Red River has been the economic lifeline of the city of Shreveport, Louisiana, since its founding in 1835, when the city's namesake, Captain Henry Shreve, cleared the river of more than 160 miles of logs and natural debris known as The Great Raft, making the river navigable and opening the city to commerce. For several decades, the city enjoyed steady economic growth, becoming a major cotton port of the South.

Shreveport eventually witnessed the decline of water transport, which gave way to the efficiencies of rail and motor transit. The discovery of oil in the region at the turn of the century led to the development of petrochemical plants and other industrial facilities on the riverfront, accelerating Shreveport's transformation into a major urban center of northwest Louisiana. Debris again gradually collected on the river, and in the 1970s the river was cleared once more to allow navigation of barge traffic from the Gulf of Mexico.

While river commerce continued to be an important part of the local economy, the quality of the riverfront steadily declined as it became a convenient repository for the by-products of the city's industrial growth. As the oil industry matured and moved westward into Texas and Oklahoma, Shreveport was left with a largely abandoned and neglected riverfront offering virtually no public use of the water. Beginning with Riverfront Park, Shreveport is once again pinning its economic hopes on its waterfront, this time with a focus on encouraging tourism and public use and enjoyment.

Bringing the River Back to the Community

In the late 1980s, economic development in Shreveport was stagnating, while crime and other urban ills began to plague the city. Inspired by successes in other cities, the city council, led by future mayor Hazel Beard and the Downtown Development Authority (DDA), decided that tourism development—specifically, the redevelopment of the riverfront—was key to the city's economic revitalization.

Two other coincidental developments turned the attention of city officials toward the riverfront. The legalization of riverfront gambling and its imminent appearance on Shreveport's waterfront alerted city officials to the need to formulate a comprehensive plan for development of the waterfront. At the same time, construction of five lock and dam systems on the Red River was nearing completion. Before the development of the lock and dam systems, the river's depth and speed varied greatly, and recreational use of the river was considered impossible; the new lock and dam systems would permit much greater control of the river's depth and flow.

The mayor at that time did not share the council's hopes for riverfront development and offered little official support. Undeterred, in 1989 the city council and the DDA spearheaded planning for the riverfront. The council and DDA officials felt strongly that for the project to be successful, the citizens of Shreveport would have to be actively involved in the planning.

To promote public involvement, the council and the DDA organized a public conference funded by the DDA. The nearly 600 Rivershape Conference attendees were asked for their ideas on the types of activities they would like to see on the city's waterfront. The DDA hired consultants and an illustrator to help facilitate the visioning process. Some of the major themes to emerge included a place to walk close to the Red River, an amphitheater, and a place to listen to music. More than anything, the public wanted access to the river. The ideas generated by this public forum were melded into a document that became the road map for the development of the riverfront.

In 1990, Councilwoman Hazel Beard was elected mayor of Shreveport on a platform of riverfront and tourism development. Having just completed a $20 million bond issue for streetscape improvements in the city's historic district, Shreveport lacked the funds to implement planning and development of the riverfront. Mayor Beard turned to the state legislature for help. Located in the northwest corner of the state, far from the capital in Baton Rouge, Shreveport had historically avoided pursuing state funding for city projects. But the mayor had observed that in other Louisiana cities, the state had helped fund many tourism development projects that could generate funds for the state as well as for the city.

The mayor and city council formed the Shreveport Riverfront Redevelopment Authority and began petitioning the state legislature for funding. Lacking experience with the legislature, the city was initially thwarted in its efforts, but eventually convinced state officials of the potential impact of legalized gambling and the importance of creating a well-planned and well-developed waterfront to encourage tourists to explore the city beyond the environs of the proposed casino. In 1991, the city finally received an initial commitment of $500,000 to develop a comprehensive plan for the riverfront.

To retain public support and involvement, the city formed the Riverfront Development Committee, comprising the city council, the Downtown Development Authority, the Metropolitan Planning Commission, the Tourism Bureau, Red River Revel Arts Festival officials, and more than two dozen citizens. Meeting once a month for two years, the Riverfront Development Committee was charged with transforming the ideas generated during the Rivershape Conference into an action plan for the waterfront. First on the committee's agenda was the imminent arrival of Harrah's Casino. The committee helped hammer out an agreement between the city and the casino, including the selection of a waterfront site for the casino that would be acceptable to all parties. The committee also helped set design and landscape standards for the casino that would support the city's vision for the waterfront. Final decision-making authority rested with the mayor and city council, but input from the Riverfront Development Committee was encouraged—and debated—throughout the process of planning and developing the park and casino.

To provide a tangible centerpiece for the redevelopment plan, it was determined that the first phase of the project would be development of the riverfront park. To ensure high-quality results, the city decided to limit

Lacking amenities, the previous park, built during the bicentennial, was eventually forgotten by the public and maintenance of the site declined.

Patrick C. Moore

A 72-foot-wide artificial waterfall serves as the park's centerpiece. The semicircular arbor at the top of the waterfall is a popular site for weddings and serves as the entrance to the park.

the size of the park to 5.5 acres, rather than to build a larger project of lower quality. While some residents questioned the need for a riverfront park, they offered no positive alternatives, and the city's ongoing efforts at community involvement managed to avert any serious opposition to the plan.

With plan in hand, Mayor Beard and the redevelopment authority again approached the state legislature. Encountering reluctance from state officials to provide further funding, they continued lobbying diligently to persuade state officials of the importance of the project. Through simple perseverance combined with more finely detailed plans and cost estimates, the city eventually prevailed upon the legislature to grant assistance. In 1993, the legislature awarded the city a $1.6 million tourism development grant. By this time, the city's coffers had been replenished by tax revenue generated by the newly built Harrah's Casino, located a few hundred yards upstream from where the park would be built. Mayor Beard placed all the tax revenue generated by the casino into a special tourism development fund. With this fund, the city was able to contribute more

than $182,000 toward the park's design and development. Contributions from the DDA of $20,000 and a federal Small Business Administration grant of $9,000 (for planting trees) rounded out funding for the park.

A Park Where the Park Was

Shreveport Riverfront Park is located on the site of an overgrown and abandoned park adjacent to the Barnwell Garden and Art Center. The park was developed as an extension of the Barnwell, a climate-controlled, geodesic, domed conservatory constructed in 1972. The central downtown location of the site puts it in close proximity to other entertainment-oriented developments such as the convention hall, the Civic Theater, the Spring Street Museum, and the Sports Museum of Champions. The park is also close to Harrah's Casino and to the future site of a Sci-Port Discovery Center. The park adds a complementary use to a section of the city already well established as an entertainment area.

The site was already owned by the city, as was the Barnwell Center. The original park, developed in 1976 in

Located near other entertainment-oriented facilities such as the convention center and museums, the park adds a complementary use to the area and gives residents another reason to visit downtown. The park has already generated interest in the development of new residential units nearby.

Neil Johnson

celebration of the bicentennial, was a substantially less ambitious endeavor than the current park, functioning only as a flat, open greenspace with sparse plantings and virtually no statuary or other amenities. A reflecting pool filled with Styrofoam logs, meant to imitate the historic clearing of The Great Raft, was designed to be an interactive element of the park but proved too complicated and poorly designed to operate and maintain. While the Barnwell Center continued to operate, maintenance of the park area declined as the space went unused by the public.

City ownership of the land precluded any acquisition costs, and its use as greenspace meant that no rezoning would be necessary. The casino had wanted to develop on the site, but according to Sharon Swanson, economic development director, "We knew the site wasn't right for the casino. . . . Its location near other family-oriented activities and former use made it a logical choice for the new park site."

The site's former use as a park also provided some assurance against potential environmental problems. Soil borings uncovered only some burned wood and glass, the remnants of a shantytown burned to the ground years earlier.

Designing a Park that would Set a New Standard

In February 1992, the city issued a request for qualifications from area landscape architects, and the contract was awarded to Patrick C. Moore Landscape Architects,

a firm based in Alexandria, Louisiana. The firm was already well known to city officials, having successfully redeveloped an urban petrochemical plant in another area of the city. The firm immediately began to work with the Riverfront Development Committee to solicit ideas on park design. Above all, the city wanted this first phase of the project to establish a new benchmark for quality, to encourage high design standards for further redevelopment efforts, and to signal a change in direction for the city. "Our landscape architect received input all along the way," said Mayor Beard. Despite the difficulty of managing so many varied opinions, "We felt it was necessary to involve the public through every step of the process." The firm's proposal was accepted in May 1992, and planning began for the park.

According to the park's designer, Patrick Moore, "the committee clearly wanted the park to reflect the unique characteristics of the region and the city's historical relationship to the Red River." A visual analysis of the region was conducted to identify the physical features most distinctive to the area. The terrain is marked by rolling, wooded hills of hardwood and pine trees; clear, sand-bottomed streams flowing over small, rocky outcroppings; sandbars; bluffs; and native vegetation spilling out along the riverbanks. The design concept incorporated each of these natural features. In October 1992, after significant input from the Riverfront Development Committee, the mayor and city council accepted a final plan and issued bids for construction, which began in December 1993 and took 11 months to complete.

The 5.5-acre park sits unobtrusively in a valley between the river and the Clyde Fant Parkway, sloping gently downward from the parkway to the banks of the Red River, a bit more than 240 feet away. At its longest, the park extends from the Barnwell Center beyond a South Pacific Railroad Bridge about 800 feet away.

The centerpiece of the park is a 72-foot-wide artificial waterfall that begins at the foot of an arbor located at the park's main entrance, just off the parkway. The water cascades over low stone terraces, interrupted by large rocks similar to those found in nearby Kisatchie National Forest, and gathers into a narrow pool ten feet below. From the arbor plaza above the waterfall, the sound of the falling water is nearly imperceptible. As visitors descend the steps alongside the falls, the sound of falling water steadily emerges. The terraced, grassy hills surrounding both sides of the fountain are anchored by five concrete segmental retaining walls, 18 inches high, that curve in and out along most of the length of the park.

A circular plaza from the previous park, surrounded by a 22-inch-high wall, sits to the left of the waterfall. The plaza originally contained a large steel abstract sculpture commissioned in the early 1980s, which was relocated to an open lawn area at the south terminus of the park. A flat granite seal, in the form of a compass and depicting the state bird, covers the center of the overlook plaza above the waterfall. After the sculpture was removed, it was discovered that a curious echo effect could be produced within the plaza. Because of this serendipitous discovery, the plaza is now incorporated into the sensory/fragrance garden tour that the Barnwell Center conducts for visually impaired visitors.

The free-flowing curves of the walls along the terraced hills are meant to emulate the sand and soil formations created on the riverbanks by the rise and fall of the waters. Each wall bears the color of one of the four soil types found in the strata of the riverbed: beige, sandy pink, light sand, and dark gray. The larger area of wide, terraced steps to the right of the waterfall is designed to serve as a natural amphitheater, giving audiences watching performances a view of the river. The original survey lines for the walls were altered during construction to retain many of the park's existing live oak trees.

A wisteria-draped, semicircular arbor at the top of the waterfall serves as the park's main entrance. The entrance is located at the intersection of Clyde Fant Parkway and Crockett Street, providing visitors with a view of the park and a new corridor to the city. The plaza beneath the arbor has become a popular spot for outdoor wedding ceremonies and group photographs (including the 1997 Miss U.S.A. Pageant). Arches at the top of the arbor are designed to match the city skyline that sits behind them.

Some of the park's plantings are annual, but most are ornamental evergreen shrubs and deciduous trees. Twice each year, under the direction of a professional horticulturist from the parks and recreation department, maintenance staff conduct seasonal changes in the park's flowering annuals. Surveys were conducted of other riverfront projects to determine which types of plantings do well in such environments. The trees and plants in the park include river birch, red maples, coreopsis, coneflowers, dwarf banana trees, sasanqua camellias, daffodils, azaleas, irises, and daylilies.

Terraced hills curve in and out through most of the length of the park, emulating the rise and fall of the river and providing a natural amphitheater with the Red River as a scenic backdrop.

Neil Johnson

Keeping the Park Safe and Accessible

Both the design and management of the park address safety and liability concerns. Lampposts running along the trail throughout the park and lining the steps on each side of the waterfall ensure that the park is well lit at all times. A conscious decision was made to include in the park's landscaping only plants that grow to a height of no more than three feet or that have a canopy beginning at no less than seven feet. This ensures an unobstructed view of the river and enhances security by providing a clear view of the park itself. But one of the best deterrents to crime is activity. The well-lit, well-patrolled park has become a popular site for families and couples taking an evening stroll. The park is patrolled regularly by city police; in addition, the DDA funds patrols by off-duty police officers on horseback. No serious crime or vandalism has been reported in the park to date.

The principal focus of the city's safety concerns has been the waterfall. At the behest of the city, the landscape architect surveyed parks with similar features in other cities and made minor adjustments to the waterfall to improve safety. For example, to discourage children from trying to climb on the rocks inside the falls, the rocks were moved away from the edges, and reflective tape was used to clearly delineate the area surrounding the falls.

Accessibility is a key feature of the park, which meets all requirements of the Americans with Disabilities Act. Beginning at the main entrance, a ten-foot-wide concrete trail runs the entire circumference of the park, connecting with the Barnwell and eventually passing below the waterfall. The trail anchors an existing six-mile-long, asphalt-surfaced jogging trail that runs along the river.

To address environmental concerns, the designers consulted with the U.S. Army Corps of Engineers. At the suggestion of the corps, the designers included a switching system on the riverbank that automatically shuts down electrical power to the park in the event of a flood. When the park did in fact flood shortly after it was completed, the switching system worked as planned. During construction, an unexpected environmental problem emerged when faulty drainage pipes running beneath the old park collapsed and had to be replaced.

Management of the park is under the supervision of the Shreveport Parks and Recreation Department (SPAR). A crew of four maintenance workers is responsible for upkeep of both the Barnwell Center and the riverfront park. In addition, some members of the Friends of the Barnwell, a volunteer organization, assist in the park's seasonal plantings. Park maintenance comes exclusively from the SPAR budget—all public funds. Except for special events, workers tend to the park five days a week.

Litter is swept and removed from the park each weekday, and the lawns are ordinarily mowed every ten days. In May and October, the park changes its annual plantings as an extension of Barnwell Center activities. A new underground sprinkler system was installed to keep the landscaping well watered.

The waterfall has been the most difficult and complex aspect of park maintenance. City personnel had to be specially trained to handle the sophisticated equipment and learn to administer precise amounts of var-

The park has become a popular site for musical events and festivals.

Neil Johnson

ious chemicals to keep the waterfall clean and in proper working order.

Ordinarily, admission to the park is free, but for special events, the park is temporarily fenced and an admission fee is charged. Although the park has no policy against pets beyond the city's leash ordinance, workers say that they have not experienced any problems related to animals.

Signage at the riverfront park is sparse and focuses mostly on the waterfall. Three small signs at the top and bottom of the waterfall and at a side walkway of the waterfall leading from the Barnwell Center clearly warn users not to climb on the waterfall.

The park is closed to vehicular traffic, but removable bollards at the southeastern end of the park allow entrance to service and emergency vehicles. The bollards are constructed of steel and must be unlocked and lifted to be removed, but in an emergency can be run over by a fire truck if necessary.

Passive versus Programmed Use

Because of its downtown location and the dearth of nearby residential development, the weekday users of the park tend to be joggers and downtown workers who come during their lunch hour to enjoy the scenery. The park does not have facilities for active recreation activities such as basketball or tennis.

To the surprise of many, one of the most popular uses of the park has been as a site for wedding ceremonies. The city charges a $150 usage fee for weddings, which has been a steady—if small—source of revenue for the park.

While no formal surveys have been conducted, maintenance workers have noted a steady increase in usage as more programmed events create a greater public awareness of the park. Programming for the park is managed by the Cultural Arts Department of the Shreveport Parks and Recreation Department. The three programming categories are city-sponsored, departmental, and rentals (e.g., for weddings). High attendance at some of the programmed events has led to considerable debate between those who view the park as primarily a passive open space and those who want to increase the park's use for public events.

Shreveport's annual Red River Revel Arts Festival is by far the most popular event held at the park. In 1995, a second main stage of the festival, which drew more than 200,000 people overall, was located in the park. The popularity of the park as a festival site has led to concern: some people, including the park's designer, question whether the park can tolerate such a high level of usage. Festival organizers argue that one of the goals of developing the park and adjacent river-

The park is rich in plantings that were chosen for their durability in the riverfront location.

front was to draw tourists to the city. "There is no way people are going to want to let the park just sit there," said Kip Holloway, director of the revel arts festival. In that regard, the park may become a victim of its own success.

As it seems unlikely that programming and use of the park will be curtailed, plans now call for some of the facilities to be upgraded to accommodate heavier usage. Electrical power is sufficient to handle large stage events, but water and sewage facilities have proved inadequate. And though the turf has so far been able to handle the large crowds, maintenance personnel caution that events must be scheduled far enough apart to allow time for the turf to recover. Careful management, combined with selective capital improvements, should ensure the park's continued viability for large-scale programmed events while protecting the scenic qualities that make the park attractive to passive users.

The park now gives the public access to the riverfront, but not to the river itself. Because the lock and dam systems have made the river safer, greater recreational use of the river and an increase in demand for public access points are anticipated. The park's master plan for the second phase of development calls for the construction of a dock on the waterfront. Plans are now in place for the development of a boat dock, a boat launch, and a stonework overlook. The city also plans to further integrate the park and other nearby attractions with the casino and a planned hotel development via a richly landscaped riverwalk. Funding for the second phase of waterfront redevelopment is now being put in place.

Conclusion

As the first phase of the city's riverfront redevelopment plans, Shreveport Riverfront Park was to set a new standard for development. The city attached high ex-

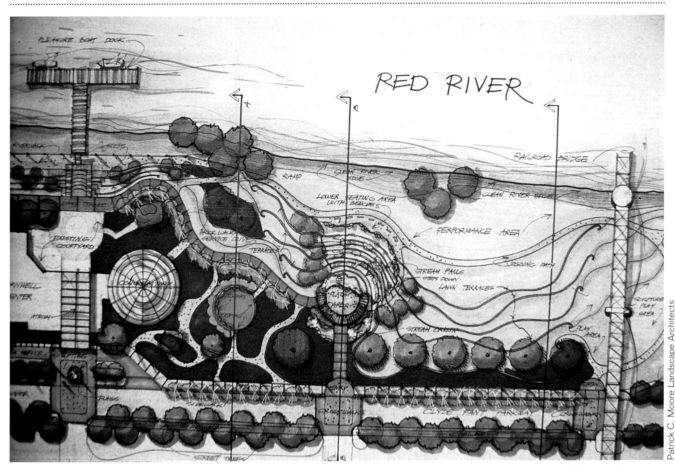

The plan for the park took advantage of the riverfront location: all activities face the river, including the amphitheater, the arbor, and much of the ten-foot-wide trail that encircles the park.

pectations to the project—expectations that have been exceeded, as the park has served as a catalyst for renewed interest in the waterfront. Featured prominently in tourism promotions, the park has become a regular site of riverboat tours. The success of the park in the mind of the public is evidenced by the passage of a recent bond proposal to acquire land for future phases of the riverfront development plan. The bond measure to acquire the land known as the Cross Bayou initially failed to pass; shortly afterward, the measure was renamed the Riverfront Park Extension Bond, and the $5 million bond issue gained easy approval.

Private investment has been slower to react to the park's success. Many business and property owners near the park were skeptical of the city's commitment to maintaining and upgrading the riverfront. The pending implementation of the second phase of the redevelopment plan and the continued success of programmed events have caused that attitude to change. There have been no formal studies of the park's impact on land values, but property assessments surrounding the park have increased. Some property owners have begun to plan improvements to their properties, and a new resi-

dential development near the park was recently approved. City officials admit, however, that it is difficult to determine how much of an economic impact the park is having and how much may be attributable to the presence of the casino.

The park has done more than promote tourism; it has expanded the public's perception of the waterfront. For the first time, debate is underway concerning the location of new commercial development on the river and the preservation of public access and greenspace. City officials involved in the development of Shreveport Riverfront Park attribute the park's success to the close involvement of the public and other community groups. As debate over further waterfront development continues, the city hopes to maintain that level of involvement.

The riverfront park is the first phase in Shreveport's efforts to reincorporate the riverfront into the urban fabric of the city. It offers a fine example of how a small city can use creative design and community involvement to turn an existing natural feature into a community asset, and has set a benchmark for quality for continuing redevelopment of the riverfront and the nearby streetscapes.

Project Data • Shreveport Riverfront Park

Development Schedule: Phase I

Request for qualifications	February 1992
Proposal accepted/planning begins	May 1992
Final master plan accepted/construction documents begin	October 1992
Bid for construction awarded/construction begins	December 1993
Construction completed	November 1994

Financing Information

Funding Source	Amount	Percentage of Total
State of Louisiana capital outlay	$1,645,000	88.60%
Small Business Administration grant (tree planting)	9,000	.48
Downtown Development Authority	20,000	1.10
City funding	182,597	9.80
Total	$1,856,597	100.00%

Development Cost Information

Site improvement and construction costs

Site acquisition cost	$0
General conditions	105,682
Allowances	22,275
Utility connection fees	2,129
Performance payment bond	17,650
Building permit	7,770
Demolition of structure	33,000
Site work	145,000
Irrigation	19,448
Plantings and lawn	122,116
Formed concrete structures	486,985
Reinforced steel structures	72,289
Concrete pavers	35,250
Site improvements	29,683
Fountain equipment	95,900
Damp proofing and waterproofing	17,200
Masonry, stonework	49,784
Miscellaneous metals	73,116
Building specifications	5,069
Painting	10,350
Plumbing/mechanical	99,750
Electrical	103,526
Total site improvement and construction costs	$1,553,972

Soft costs

Landscape architect (prime consultant)	$162,700
Structural engineer (subconsultant)	6,800
Electrical engineer (subconsultant)	7,800
Fountain engineer (subconsultant)	19,500
Total soft costs	196,800
Total improvement and construction costs	$ 1,750,772

Construction/Operating Costs

Amenity	Construction Cost	Operating Cost
Signage	$500	
Plantings	165,700	$4,000
Water features	562,600	42,300
Entrances	73,100	NA[1]
Land engineering	180,300	NA
Furniture	5,100	NA
Plazas	77,300	NA
Hardscape features	180,300	NA
Lighting	115,200	6,000
Special plantings	NA	7,300
Irrigation	19,500	4,600
Total	$1,379,600	$64,200

Operating Information

Annual operating expenses

Taxes	NA
Insurance	NA
Repair and maintenance	$35,250
Utilities	28,950
Total	$64,200

Annual gross revenues

Sources	
Special events rentals	$2,250
Total	$2,250

Note

1. Not applicable.

Turtle Park
St. Louis

Terry Jill Lassar

Motorists driving on Interstate 64 from their suburban homes to downtown St. Louis are treated to a vision of three monolithic turtles crawling across grassy mounds atop a highway embankment next to the St. Louis Zoo. Turtle Park is built on a sliver of land that is part of Forest Park, located in the heart of St. Louis. Forest Park, with 1,293 acres (one-third the size of New York's Central Park), is one of the largest urban parks in the United States. Dedicated in 1876, the park was developed in large part as a staging ground for the 1904 Louisiana Purchase Exposition (the St. Louis World's Fair), which drew more than 19 million visitors from around the world to St. Louis.

Forest Park continues to serve as a major tourist attraction, drawing some 12 million visitors a year. It houses many of the region's main cultural and educational facilities, including the art and history museums, the science center, the opera, and the zoo. The park provides a rich blend of passive and active recreational uses, serving as a center for golf, tennis, baseball, handball, cricket, bicycling, and more.

And now, thanks to the generosity of a local philanthropist and the efforts of the city, citizens, designers, and artists, Turtle Park provides a new use for a tiny bit of a grand park—a children's playground/sculpture garden where the play equipment is also art.

Forest Park's New Master Plan

For the past 20 years, Forest Park has been badly neglected. Faced with crumbling roads and curbs, antiquated facilities, and an aging infrastructure, in December 1993 St. Louis leaders convened a three-day summit to brainstorm strategies for refurbishing the park. Park managers from Chicago, New York City, and San Diego shared their experiences with park redevelopment efforts and master-planning processes. The summit underscored the importance of long-range planning and bolstered the city's decision to develop a new Forest Park master plan. The highly controversial two-year planning effort, under the leadership of Mayor Freeman R. Bosley, Jr., was designed to go beyond mere beautification and not just put "new carpet on a rotten floor." A previous master-planning program in 1983 had never been implemented, mostly because of inadequate funding and lack of political will.

In the early 1990s, the city passed a $1.8 million sales tax increase dedicated to capital improvements. This new funding source, which could potentially be used for park renovation, was an "important psychological boost that placed the city in a much stronger position," says Forest Park manager Anabeth Calkins. The city could now say "we're playing our part" and was finally perceived by the public as a serious player in the park restoration effort.

The Turtle Park playground was the first redevelopment project to implement the 1995 Forest Park Master Plan. The playground was also one of the few projects that managed to avoid controversy and escape the scathing criticism of park preservationists. Until the development of Turtle Park, a long history of controversy had surrounded Forest Park redevelopment projects, which were

Final touches are put on a turtle. The sculptures were created with plywood frames filled with concrete and then sprayed with a special, high-density concrete that had to be carved—quickly—by hand into recognizable turtle shapes. Zoo officials wanted the representational sculptures to be anatomically accurate and lent live turtle models to sculptor Bob Cassily and his crew for their work.

perceived by the public as intrusive invasions into the city's public living room. Over the years, several plans to build new playgrounds in the interior of the park had been scrapped. Environmental groups, including Citizens to Protect Forest Park and the Coalition to Protect the Environment, objected mainly to the additional parking areas that the new playgrounds would require.

Equally controversial were various plans to expand some of the cultural institutions located within Forest Park. In the early 1990s, the St. Louis Art Museum made an agreement with the city to lease parkland next to the museum to add more building space and parking. The lease, which had been approved by the board of aldermen, was recalled by a public referendum. The same environmental groups that had opposed the new playgrounds succeeded in combining forces to defeat the museum expansion.

An additional controversy revolved around the issue of privatizing public space. Forest Park Forever, a park friends group, had been established as an umbrella organization to raise funds for park improvements. In the early 1990s, Forest Park Forever was looking for funds for three redevelopment projects that would be paid for exclusively with private money. As part of the deal with the city, these three donor-driven projects would be privately developed; owned outright and managed by private entities; and administered separately from Forest Park.

"This was the catalyst," noted Anabeth Calkins, "for the 1995 Forest Park Master Plan." Important policy considerations were at stake. Was it appropriate for private donors to manage and operate facilities that were part of a regional park system belonging to the public? Were these new projects appropriate uses for the park? The initial proposals to privatize parts of Forest Park were eventually discarded, but the critical policy issues—including appropriate land uses for the park—were central to the master planning effort.

A 50-50 public/private partnership was adopted to implement the master plan, which will cost approximately $86 million. The city of St. Louis committed $43 million in public funds. Forest Park Forever, a private not-for-profit organization with a membership of 6,000, intends to match this with $43 million in private funds. The goal is to complete the majority of the work by the year 2004, to celebrate the 100th anniversary of the St. Louis World's Fair.

In the middle of the master-planning process, Sonya "Sunny" Glassberg, a philanthropist and longtime park patron, approached the city's parks department about donating a new children's playground in Forest Park. Glassberg had offered to fund another park project two years before, but the city delayed making a decision and Glassberg took her park pavilion to St. Louis County instead. Not wanting to miss out on this second opportunity, the parks department worked with Glassberg to develop an appropriate playground concept for Forest Park. However, it would be another year before the master plan was approved. Because this was the first "interim project" and no systematic approval procedures had yet been established, it was especially important to select a location that would not provoke controversy.

The 1995 master plan promotes the development of new active uses on the park's edges, so that the interior of the park can be preserved as a pastoral green oasis for more passive recreational activities. Thus, Glassberg was advised to look for a site on the periphery of the park that would strengthen the connection between the park and the adjacent community. She finally decided on a location on the south edge of the park, at Tamm and Oakland Avenues adjacent to the zoo.

The Site for Turtle Park

Most people never realized that the land proposed for Turtle Park, which had been bisected by Highway 40 in the 1960s, was part of Forest Park. That was one reason the location was expected to appease park preservationists, who would perhaps regard development of this vacant land strip as an addition to, rather than a detraction from, the park's open space network.

The 300-by-100-foot playground is bordered on the north by I-64 and on the south by Oakland Avenue and an older residential neighborhood. Oakland Avenue is lined with a dense mix of single-family homes, duplexes, and apartment buildings. Several commercial and institutional uses, including Deaconess Hospital, are located to the east.

Glassberg was drawn to this particular location, which had previously been a paved parking lot, in part because it was adjacent to Dogtown, an established resi-

dential community. "I liked the fact that it was a solid, middle-class, family neighborhood," she said. Because houses in this urban neighborhood were built on tight lots with small yards, residents welcomed a new neighborhood park as a valuable amenity. Park planners viewed the development of Turtle Park as an opportunity to better connect the south entry to the zoo with the adjacent residential neighborhood. Moreover, several proposals to widen the I-64 corridor had threatened to infringe on park property, and park staff viewed the playground development as a way to strengthen the southern edge of the park and protect it from further encroachments.

The 1995 Forest Park Master Plan established an advisory board to review all proposed land use changes to the park. Because Turtle Park was developed before the board was established, it was approved instead by the Forest Park executive committee. The playground was also reviewed by several city agencies—including the Department of Heritage and Urban Design, whose main concerns were parking and accessibility for people with disabilities.

The Department of Heritage and Urban Design has consistently advocated reducing parking and paved areas throughout Forest Park. The agency initially pushed to eliminate all parking at Turtle Park, assuming most visitors would be Dogtown residents who could walk to

The Dogtown residential neighborhood to the south is a mix of single-family homes, duplexes, and apartment buildings. Although the park's benefactor was given the option of locating the playground almost anywhere in Forest Park, she thought that Dogtown families with small homes and small yards might have a need for a neighborhood park and chose this spot within easy walking distance for many families.

the park. However, the park's designers argued that some parking would be necessary because the park was sufficiently unusual that it was likely to attract visitors from throughout the metropolitan area. A compromise was reached: half the original parking space allotment was provided in the form of some 24 on-street parking spaces, including several designed for handicapped visitors.

Meanwhile, future plans to extend MetroLink, the city's wildly popular light-rail line, could result in the development of several light-rail stations within the immediate vicinity, one of which would be a zoo station on Oakland Avenue across the street from Turtle Park. (One scenario calls for extending MetroLink west through the suburban city of Clayton, along the southern edge of Forest Park).

Why Turtles?

"There's just something magical about turtles and the way their shapes relate to the landscape," observed architect Richard Claybour who, along with local artist Bob Cassily, designed the sculpture garden. Glassberg added that "turtles were among the first sea creatures to crawl onto land, and the turtle has long been a symbol for peace." Moreover, the initial concept for the park called for a children's playground/sculpture garden where the play equipment was also art, and the smooth, curvilinear form of the turtle shell set low to the ground was an ideal shape for playground equipment.

Bob Cassily, who created the turtle sculptures, is known around town for his Brobdingnagian-scale animal creations—hammerhead sharks and squids at the St. Louis Zoo, crouching lions at the Gateway Mall, and a praying mantis at the Missouri Botanical Garden. Cassily originally envisioned a lone turtle emerging from the side of a grassy knoll, but the plan evolved into a group of seven turtles, the smallest seven feet in length and the largest measuring 40 feet from toe to tail. Unlike many philanthropists, Glassberg opted not to name the park for herself. But the large turtles are named after her three children—Tom, Dick, and Sally—and the four smaller ones after her grandchildren.

The zoo, which is a short walk to the park, did not directly participate in the project. However, zoo officials wanted the representational sculptures to be accurate and lent live turtle models to Cassily, who also served as the project's general contractor. While his workers shaped some 120,000 pounds of concrete into a 40-foot-long snapping turtle, the real thing rested in a trash can at the construction site. Workers periodically pulled out the turtle to study anatomical details.

Cassily's team started with mounds of dirt that were covered with structural steel rebar. To create the rough shape of the turtles, plywood frames were used as molds that were then filled with concrete. Cassily formed the final one- to three-inch-thick layers of skin and the shell texture by spraying Gunnite "shotcrete" at high pressure and then troweling it into the desired shape. This

Marilyn Zimmerman

Seven hatching turtles emerge from their eggs in the circular amphitheater. The 100-foot-long wall is molded in the shape of a snake and doubles as a bench.

Architect Richard Claybour notes that children sense that the turtle playground pieces are also art pieces, prompting them to be more focused and careful in their play activities than they are with more traditional playground equipment.

high-density concrete, which also contained sand, cement, and color, can be carved like sandstone. Cassily repeated this process three times to create the skin and the shell texture.

Each turtle represents a different species found in Missouri—a red-eared slider, three box turtles, a giant snapping turtle, a Mississippi map turtle, and a "stinkpot" turtle. The reptilian playground also includes a wall molded in the shape of a 100-foot-long snake that doubles as a bench and a clutch of hatching turtle eggs.

Cassily's original plan was to place the hatching turtle eggs in a sandbox, where children could play, but park staff were concerned that roaming animals would contaminate the sand with their droppings—in short, that the sandbox would become a giant kitty-litter box for the neighborhood, posing potential health risks. Instead of being used as the site for a sandbox, the area was turned into a circular amphitheater surfaced with rolled crushed rock.

Architect Richard Claybour designed the landscape setting for the sculptures—a series of gently sloping berms that look like the backs of turtles. The soil for these elevated earth mounds came from dirt stockpiled by the city parks department, which hauled the dirt to the site. The grass berms also function as sound baffles, muffling the sounds of traffic from I-64 below the park.

Turtle Park is a playground where the play equipment happens to be a collection of whimsical turtle sculptures. The fact that the entire park is a work of art makes it unique and raises some special issues. Although the artist had created many works of public art throughout the country, this was the first time he had designed an entire playground. Several times during the project, Cassily came up with new ideas that prompted changes

to the original park design. Unaccustomed to bureaucratic procedures, Cassily didn't realize that his artistic inspirations and alterations to the original plan were subject to a review process. At first, he couldn't comprehend why city staff weren't more flexible about accepting some of these alterations. "That's why," said Anabeth Calkins, "it is essential to have a straightforward review process to deal with the many project changes that will inevitably be proposed. One of the strengths of the 1995 Forest Park Master Plan is that it establishes a project approval process with detailed steps that must be adhered to."

According to Richard Claybour, children sense that the turtle playground pieces are also art pieces, and are prompted to be more focused and careful in their play activities than they would be with playground equipment that moves. This may be one reason, says Claybour, that there have been few accidents at the park. The 40-foot-long snapping-turtle sculpture was originally designed with a tunnel that children could enter through the turtle's open mouth. But after several children scraped their knees and cut their fingers on the rough surface, the tunnel was filled in.

Children seem to enjoy the simple play activities that the sculptures offer.

Turtle Park plan.

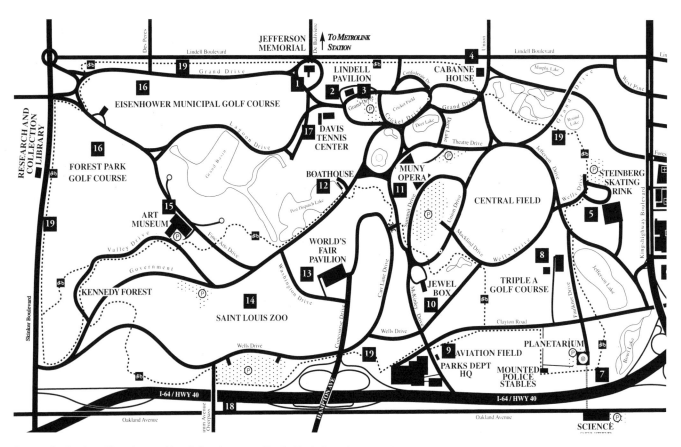

Forest Park plan. The sliver of land that became Turtle Park (number 18 above) is on the periphery of Forest Park. A 1995 master plan for the park promotes the development of active uses on the park's edges, so that the interior of the park can be preserved as a pastoral green oasis for more passive activities.

The grassy elevated mounds were kept low so that the entire playground is clearly visible from Oakland Avenue, which is heavily used. To encourage people to walk through the park instead of along the periphery, no sidewalk was built on the Oakland Avenue side.

Public/Private Collaboration

Turtle Park was a public/private collaboration between the St. Louis Parks Department and Forest Park Forever. These groups mainly contributed the soil that was used to construct the grassy berms. Donor Sunny Glassberg came up with $200,000 for planning and construction and an additional $10,000 for a park maintenance fund. Because Turtle Park was the first implementation project under the new master plan, it was important that it spark confidence and interest in subsequent park development, which it did. "The success of Turtle Park, along with approval of the master plan," said Anabeth Calkins, "has been the impetus for additional private funding." During 1996, St. Louis corporations contributed more than $12 million for improvements to Forest Park.

The unique techniques used to construct the playground drew public attention and generated much enthusiasm for the park. Large audiences flocked to the site to observe Cassily's crew creating the turtle sculptures. On I-64, equally curious motorists apparently slowed down to a turtle's pace to have a better look at the giant reptiles taking shape next to the road.

Now the playground is well used and much appreciated. During the summer, it's not unusual to see schoolchildren taking their lunch there, along with elderly residents who have come from the senior center to watch the young children play. Glassberg recounts that one day she spoke with an elderly woman who was sitting on top of one of the turtles and reading a large, heavy book. She told Glassberg that she frequently comes to read her Bible there because it feels like a spiritual place.

"The most satisfying thing for me," says architect Claybour, "is watching the people of all ages who come to use the park, especially in good weather."

Marilyn Zimmerman

Grass berms were shaped to look like the backs of turtles and also to serve as sound baffles to muffle the traffic noise from I-64 below the park.

Project Data • Turtle Park

Development Cost Information

Site acquisition cost	None (already parkland)
Site improvement costs	
Excavation/demolition/grading (in-kind contribution from parks department)	$30,000
Paving	10,000
Curbs/sidewalks	7,500
Landscaping (topsoil and rubber)	8,100
Fees/general conditions	5,400
Irrigation	6,000
Other (cleanup and miscellaneous)	7,000
Total site improvement costs	$74,000
Construction costs	
Turtle sculptures, snake bench, and wall	$151,000
Soft costs	
Architecture, landscape architecture, and engineering	$15,800
Total site acquisition and development costs	$240,800

Partnerships:
The Key to the Future for America's Urban Parks

Martin J. Rosen

A linear park is taking shape in Baltimore, as the city—with help from the Trust for Public Land—purchases former industrial sites, vacant lots, and old railroad property along the 14-mile Gwynns Falls stream corridor.

Until the early 1990s, the meandering stream corridor in the Gwynns Falls Valley, in Baltimore, Maryland, was scoured by floods, piled with trash, and all but abandoned by the residents of the middle- and low-income neighborhoods through which it passed. As early as 1904, the sons of Frederick Law Olmsted had envisioned the 14-mile-long stream corridor as a linear urban park to be anchored by the existing 1,400-acre Gwynns Falls/Leakin Park. But the vision was never realized, and by the 1960s, the downward spiral of the stream corridor was escalating. Even neighborhood children avoided Gwynns Falls—a vital open space resource at their very doorsteps.

In Mill Race Park, in Columbus, Indiana, what was once a swampy bottomland and toxic waste site has been brought to life with minimal public investment. Public and private funds and donated Job Corps labor and equipment helped create a community amenity that has drawn national attention for its design.

Then, in 1988, the late Dr. Ralph Jones, Baltimore's park director, challenged the Yale School of Forestry and Environmental Studies to help create a new vision for Baltimore parks. Inspired by this work, the city soon forged a partnership with two organizations—the Trust for Public Land (TPL) and Parks and People, a local nonprofit—to link that vision to a revival of Baltimore's neighborhoods. Residents were polled on their open space needs, properties were studied, and a master plan was created. As part of that plan, more than 70 civic organizations joined the effort to revitalize the Gwynns Falls corridor. High school students helped haul 70 tons of refuse from the park. Other young people cleared paths and removed invasive plants while learning job skills and earning wages. Funding for the acquisition of 35 acres of new land and for the park's construction is coming from local philanthropies, state and municipal government, and the fed-

eral Intermodal Surface Transportation Efficiency Act (ISTEA). Soon the Gwynns Falls Trail will link Baltimore's neighborhoods to the city's redeveloped harbor district—and, just as important, to a new spirit of urban possibility.

This park project and others detailed in this book reveal a major shift in the way parks and open space are being created and revitalized in U.S. cities. Since the early 1980s, federal government support for local parks and open space—through the Land and Water Conservation Fund state grant program—has been slashed, even in the face of rising need. A 1994 study by the National Recreation and Park Association showed that $30.7 billion of state and local recreational investment would be needed between 1995 and 1999 in order to meet public demand. With the decline in federal support and the tendency of cities to cut park budgets when money is tight, many of our urban parks are in dire need of repair and rejuvenation, and money is simply not available. Recognizing that the need for parks doesn't go away, cash-strapped states and cities are scrambling to raise local money and take advantage of private funds. At the same time, there is a growing belief that the most successful parks emerge from broad community participation and contribute bankable value to nearby residential and commercial districts. This confluence of forces is leading to new public/private partnerships to create, rejuvenate, and sometimes manage urban parks and open space.

In 1994, TPL created the Green Cities Initiative to help cities meet the need for more parks by providing assistance in real estate acquisition, finance, and negotiations, and by exploring new ways of involving communities in public finance strategies and park management. While every park is different, successful park efforts share two or more of the following characteristics:

- A formal planning and "visioning" process involving a broad spectrum of public and private stakeholders;
- Catalytic leadership from the public and private sectors;

- A strong connection between parks and open space and broader goals such as economic development, community identity, neighborhood renewal, and provision of needed services;
- A mix of private and public funding, with public funds often coming from state or local sources;
- The advice and assistance of nonprofit partners such as academics; urban planning groups; local civic, community gardening, and "friends-of-parks" organizations; and conservation real estate specialists such as the Trust for Public Land.

It is the premise of this chapter that such stakeholder-driven, public/private partnerships will be a primary force in America's future urban park efforts. The challenge of the modern urban parks movement is to ensure that these partnerships develop productively and equitably. We cannot know today what specific techniques will be used to create tomorrow's parks and open space. But we do know, from what has been accomplished so far, that successful parks will depend on visioning, team building, broad com-

During the summer of 1996, students from neighboring communities built two boardwalks and three observation decks at the south end of the Gwynns Falls Trail, just a stone's throw from Baltimore's acclaimed Camden Yards ball park and the new football stadium.

munity support, and creative financing and real estate skills. Just as important, we will have to forge new public/private partnerships to maintain and manage parks, so that the great parks created today will remain great parks tomorrow.

If there is a single danger in the public/private approach, it is the risk of sending the wrong message about the need for public sector funds and leadership. We must be clear that private money can no more bear the entire cost of park creation than public money can, and that in a time of rising need, governments need to appropriate more funds for parks, not less. Similarly, the public sector must take the lead in creating change. It is the public sector that must call for community investment in parks, create the visioning process, and invest in the master plans and documents that will get private partners involved. Healthy partnerships cannot be sustained without a substantial public commitment.

Downtown Park, in Bellevue, Washington, was envisioned as an organizing element for a growing suburban center. The tenacity of city leaders and the financial support and knowledge of the private sector created this crown jewel in the emerald necklace of the city's park system.

Successful Parks/ Successful Partnerships

A successful park is more than an island of greenspace marooned in the concrete of the city. Its success emerges from its relationship to surrounding development and from the special features that attract users and make the park central to a city's image and personality. Its success is also related to the value it provides to the community—be it economic or qualitative value. Success depends not only on good planning and sound execution of park design, but also on continued public/private support for and involvement in park programming and management. In most cities, the era when a simple purchase of land by the city would lead to the creation of a city-envisioned and -designed park is gone. Instead, park creation and redevelopment involve putting together a development team, assembling land (often from multiple

and diverse owners and users), raising funds from sources outside the city budget, and ensuring participatory planning every step of the way.

As is evident from the case studies in this book, significant strides have been made toward building productive partnerships. In communities across the country, committed and visionary leaders are beginning to understand the power that parks have in knitting together the frayed urban fabric. Leadership may come from politicians, as in Bellevue, Washington; from neighbors and special-interest groups, as was the case with Minneapolis's Cedar Lake Park and Trail; or from businesses, such as those near Boston's Park at Post Office Square.

But no matter where the impetus comes from, the most successful partnerships include the widest range of stakeholders. The most obvious of these are government, business, and charitable foundations, who may together provide the major financial support for a park project. One significant national foundation partner is the Lila Wallace–Reader's Digest Fund (LWRDF), which has invested $15 million to create and improve urban parks in 11 cities and to share lessons with public and nonprofit leaders about best practices in the field. The LWRDF supported the Trust for Public Land's research on urban park needs in the early 1990s. In 1994, with the foundation's continuing support, TPL launched its Green Cities Initiative to bring its deal-making, fundraising, and park-planning skills to a wide range of public and private urban partners.

But the most important partners in any park plan may be nearby residents and neighborhood groups. The time should be long past when political leaders and professional park designers create parks for—instead of with—neighborhoods. The success of any park depends on how it is used; to ensure neighborhood involvement and support, professional designers and facilitators can use community meetings, written surveys, and individual interviews to lead local residents—the ultimate users—through the visioning process.

What is sometimes not understood about the park visioning and planning process is the extent to which it can transcend creation of a specific park or open space and deal with larger questions about community identity and purpose: What kind of city do we want to become? What role will parks play in our community? How do we want open space resources to be distributed in our city? What social and economic benefits do we want parks to provide? How will park programs serve city residents? And how will residents resolve conflict over these issues?

So it is that the creation of Cedar Lake Park and Trail in Minneapolis reveals a city that prizes nature, bicycle transportation, active recreation, and citizen initiative. Similarly, the process that created Downtown Park in Bellevue, Washington, reveals a city that has chosen to use a park to create a sense of place and encourage a pedestrian-friendly, densely populated center. Mill Race Park, in Columbus, Indiana, shows that the city prizes volunteerism and cooperative effort. And in Spartanburg, South Carolina, Flagstar Corporate Plaza and Jerome Richardson Park reveal a city committed to downtown revival.

In some instances, a major park project simply cannot get off the ground until a community answers larger questions about how the park might shape and confirm its future. In Seattle, voters have twice rejected efforts to create an 86-acre "commons" in a lower-income, light-industrial neighborhood north of downtown. Seattle Commons has been supported by the mayor and city council, generous corporations and philanthropies, and enthusiastic volunteers and professional staff. But other Seattle residents have worried about gentrification, rising

Doyle Bussey

rents and land prices, and the diversion of city resources from smaller neighborhood parks. If and when this worthy park is created, it will be stronger and more successful because the process has addressed these issues to the satisfaction of most residents.

Whether Baltimore would become the kind of city that links its neighborhoods to larger community resources is a question to be answered, in part, by the creation of the Gwynns Falls Trail. For two decades Baltimore had been working to rejuvenate its downtown harbor district as a cultural, recreational, and retail showplace. In this context, Baltimore officials and residents began looking toward the western neighborhoods, which are joined to the harbor by the lush—though trash-strewn—ribbon of Gwynns Falls. The visioning process took more than four years and included contributions from 16 community groups, 11 nonprofit organizations, and eight city agencies. In 1995, TPL helped produce a master plan that assigned tasks to specific groups. Since then, trash has been cleared, boardwalks have been built, and a schedule for major trail construction has been set—all to

answer the larger question about what kind of a city Baltimore would become.

The Complexity of Assembling Urban Parkland

Assembling land for today's urban parks is complicated by the involvement of various stakeholders and multiple jurisdictions, complex ownership patterns, and the frequent need for extensive environmental assessment and cleanup. Razing abandoned buildings and cleaning up contaminated "brownfield" sites can turn economic sinks into economic engines for a city, but such projects are also complicated by myriad federal, state, and local regulations that can make the politics of a project as complicated as the economics. Rarely do city park departments have the staff or financial resources to take on assemblages and cleanups. Completion of these new parks often requires interdepartmental teams within a public agency and the support of nonprofit and for-profit development partners.

In Winston-Salem, North Carolina, for example, civic leaders have long despaired of salvaging the city's southeast gateway district, a blighted patch of abandoned warehouses adjacent to the Old Salem historic park—Winston-Salem's major tourist attraction. An eyesore at the very doorway of a bustling downtown, for years the southeast district has offered no shopping, lunch spots, or gathering places for Old Salem visitors—or for students from the four surrounding prep schools and colleges. And easy access to a greenway along Salem Creek and a "strollway" along a former trolley line was blocked by a public road (which is now slated for closing).

In the early 1990s, local business leaders, educational institutions, and civic

Working with Nonprofit Real Estate Partners

The Trust for Public Land (TPL) is a national nonprofit organization that works with government agencies and landowners at their invitation to safeguard land for conservation and public use. TPL's capital funds for land acquisition allow it to move quickly to take land off the market, enabling TPL to in essence "hold" the land for a public agency or conservation group, which will then raise the funds to buy the land from TPL—typically, at or below the fair market price.

Landowners who sell to TPL may deduct the difference between fair market value and the selling price as a charitable contribution. About 60 percent of TPL's financial support comes from landowners who are willing to sell property to TPL at below-market value, allowing TPL to apply the additional land value to future land purchases and operating costs.

TPL's capital funds for land acquisition come from a reserve fund of grants, loans, and other income made available to TPL by foundations, individuals, banks, and other institutions specifically for interim financing needs on projects with a public land preservation component.

Third-party partners like TPL provide valuable assistance to public agencies and landowners in the following ways:

- Buying time. Because of budget cycles, limited staff, and legal and political constraints, government agencies often find that they are not able to act quickly when important parcels of land become available. Since timing is critical in active real estate markets, TPL can make up for such constraints by responding quickly and securing properties through options or purchase contracts, protecting the land until public purchase is possible. Third-party negotiators like TPL can structure transactions to meet both landowners' and public agencies' needs.
- Solving complex acquisition challenges. TPL's staff of real estate, finance, and legal experts specializes in complex real estate transactions such as those arising from land assemblages, exchanges, title and survey problems, disputed water rights, zoning uncertainties, hazardous waste contamination, and litigation.
- Assisting with public finance. TPL's public finance program provides technical assistance to local governments and citizens' groups seeking new public funds for open space protection, including evaluating and managing ballot measures, and provides support for developing other local funding and financing vehicles.

groups joined to forge the Southeast Gateway Council, a private nonprofit organization dedicated to renewal of the southeast district. In 1992, The American Institute of Architects sponsored a two-day design workshop to envision a plan for the area, which involved a land assemblage. But as a relatively small city, Winston-Salem lacked the staff and expertise to complete the ambitious project. At the request of the city, TPL researched the feasibility and costs of assembling almost nine acres of commercial properties west of Main Street for a proposed public plaza and retail village. TPL contracted for title searches, environmental audits, appraisals, and an economic feasibility study. TPL also negotiated with the eight area landowners to secure options to purchase their properties. Working together, TPL, the city, and a group of civic leaders came up with a financing package for the project: approximately $1 million will come from the site's developer; several million more will come from the county; the city; and private donations from individuals, foundations, and corporations. Plans call for a new visitors' center for Old Salem, a pedestrian shopping plaza, and completion of the two greenways.

Creating parks from urban sites often requires such multiple and complex partnerships. Sometimes a development component is built in to support the park, and the developer becomes part of the partnership. Outside planning and design groups may donate their expertise; an example is the work undertaken by the American Society of Landscape Architects to help create a vision for a greenway along the Los Angeles River. Private funding for the planning stage may come from local philanthropic foundations that hope to leverage a public commitment in the form of a bond act or tax measure, as was the case in Los Angeles County, where a bond measure—the Los Angeles County Park, Beach, and Recreation Act —was passed in 1996 that will provide

about $319 million for acquisition and capital improvement projects, including $9 million dedicated to improving and restoring the Los Angeles River with a greenway. This is at a cost of about $7 per year for an average household.

Other models are emerging, particularly in urban areas where vacant, underused, and often contaminated urban lands and buildings offer cities key resources for the revitalization of their waterfronts and neighborhoods.

The Trust for Public Land, with seed funding from the James Irvine Foundation, recently launched the California Center for Land Recycling (CCLR), whose mission is to foster land recycling as a way to redirect growth away from the fringes of metropolitan areas and to revitalize the urban core. To assist in the development of new policies and strategies for rejuvenating urban centers, CCLR supports and documents model projects that incorporate community participation, economic development efforts, and brownfield remediation.

Understanding the assets and roles of public and private partners is key to building successful and strategic partnerships. Nonprofits may bring short-term efficiencies to a project, taking advantage of the dynamic real estate market on behalf of a public agency that cannot move quickly; flexible funding and financing from creative and entrepreneurial sources that can leverage public sources; organizational flexibility to build staff around projects, hire consultants, and track down the expertise needed; and community credibility, through their contacts with broad constituencies and their goal of working on behalf of the public's interest. The public sector can add stability and legitimacy to a project, grounding it with a stable base of funding, a long-term commitment to public use and management, and the ability to link the project to a broader city vision or plan, which can support and leverage the project.

Raising Money and Forging Transactions

Usually, the first question park advocates and public officials ask about any park or open space project is, how will we pay for it? An analysis of nearly 100 land acquisition cases that TPL has completed with local public agencies showed close to 20 different sources of acquisition and development funding, including sources at the state and federal levels. And these numbers showed few projects with single sources of support: 58 projects relied on at least two sources of funding.

The cases in this book demonstrate that funding sources are as varied as the projects themselves. Sometimes private stakeholders bear all or most of the costs of park development, as was the case for the Park at Post Office Square in Boston and the Flagstar Corporate Plaza and Jerome Richardson Park in Spartanburg, South Carolina. More often, private stake-

holders such as businesses and foundations provide capital grants, indirect capital (through fundraising campaigns), management assistance, and publicity—or, in the case of developers, an influx of residents or workers to use and support the park. In exchange for these private contributions, governments may contribute free or discounted land, tax and financing concessions, and city support services for the park or open space.

In 1995, officials and residents of Santa Fe, New Mexico, hoped to buy a 50-acre former railyard—the last major open parcel in the city's booming downtown. The Catellus Development Corporation—the successor of the Atchison, Topeka & Santa Fe Railroad—did not lack prospective buyers for the land, which was appraised at $29 million. The city of Santa Fe wanted at least a portion of the parcel for a park and other public use, and it wanted some control over how the balance of the property was devel-

Barton Springs and Barton Creek, meandering through Austin, Texas, have been symbols of Austin's well-being since the turn of the century, providing the city with recreational opportunities.

Eric Swanson

• 213 •

Austin has the opportunity to serve as a model for other cities by demonstrating how trails add to a community's quality of life by providing close-to-home recreation.

oped, but it wasn't sure how it would pay for the land. At the city's request, TPL stepped in to bargain with Catellus. By offering a tax benefit to the corporation, TPL acquired the land at an $8 million discount. As part of the arrangement with TPL, the city agreed to dedicate at least ten acres of the property to a public park.

Funding and support for a single park project may come from many sources: federal, state, and local governments; foundation funds; corporate grants; developer concessions; and donations of land value by landowners. Often a nonprofit partner serves a coordinating and brokerage function—raising funds, combining funds, and structuring the final transaction. A nonprofit partner may also be able to maximize funds, reducing the cost of a property by offering a tax break to a landowner—as in Santa Fe— or accepting a donation of land for a city. In Boston, TPL accepted the donation of a 1.2-acre rail corridor from Consolidated Freight Corporation (Conrail) for a new greenway in East Boston, one of the city's most densely settled neighborhoods. To enable the city to accept the property,

TPL agreed to have an environmental assessment and clean-up performed.

New Public Funds for Parks

Nonprofit partners can also help by building community support for open space protection. One of the most heartening developments in recent years has been the public's willingness to help fund new parks and open space acquisition. As is the case in all aspects of park creation, effective public fundraising is based on effective team building: when enough stakeholders show enthusiastic support for a project, a community will often commit new funds to parks and open space.

In the late 1980s, Austin, Texas, faced a serious open space crisis when development west of the city began to pollute Barton Springs, a downtown swimming hole that is one of the city's best-known natural and recreational features. Austin environmentalists had been trying to protect the creek corridor for decades, but the pollution of Barton Springs sparked wider community concern. In 1991, TPL began working with government and community groups to quantify Austin's open space needs. Questionnaires distributed to residents revealed that a majority would support new local taxes for recreation and park facilities. In 1992, in the wake of a TPL-organized campaign for the measure, voters approved a $20 million bond act to establish the Barton Creek Wilderness Park.

It is no accident that Austin's support for park facilities coalesced around a specific place. Citizen support for well-conceived financing measures with explicit goals for land acquisition continues to have good outcomes in cities. The "market share" of parks and recreation bonds in the municipal bond market increased in recent years from 1 to 1.5 percent. The municipal finance industry has noted the public's willingness to pay for parks. Voters are also more likely to approve new spending for parks if a property or properties have already been designated and optioned for acquisition. This not only protects a valuable park property while funds are being raised, but also provides a tangible focus for voters evaluating an open space tax or bond measure. While governments are usually prohibited from risking public funds to option properties in advance of voter approval, a nonprofit partner is not, and TPL has been asked to provide up-front financing in many communities.

Nonprofit partners can also help government and community groups by polling voters on open space needs and conducting funding and direct-mail advertising campaigns. Using such techniques, TPL has helped pass funding measures in Portland, Oregon; King County (Seattle), Washington; Dade County (Miami), Florida; Los Angeles County; Austin, Texas; and Pima County (Tucson), Arizona.

Even after a measure is approved, a public agency may ask a nonprofit partner to hold land until funds accumulate, structure a special lease-purchase agreement, or arrange for the land to be transferred in several phases to meet budgetary

or legal requirements. A lease-purchase agreement can be particularly helpful if a city has decided to acquire land and does not have up-front funds. For a new park in Lakewood, Colorado (pop. 121,000), TPL structured a 30-year lease-purchase transaction. The lease is renewable year by year, and the city has reserved the right to purchase the property before the 30 years have passed.

In other instances, a public agency may ask a nonprofit partner to assemble properties for a planned unit development (PUD), so that park or conservation lands can be transferred to the public agency and the remaining land can be sold to private developers for cluster development. After voters in Austin, Texas, approved a $20 million bond initiative to acquire land along Barton Creek, TPL used a portion of those funds to purchase a 1,000-acre historic ranch for the Barton Creek Wilderness Park. The city's PUD ordinance allowed TPL to sell 240 acres to private developers for cluster development; the remaining acreage was sold to the city for the wilderness park. The subsidy provided by the development purchase allowed the city to acquire the conservation land for approximately a quarter of what city planners had expected.

Partnerships in Ongoing Management

Public/private partnerships have proven highly effective in generating vision, creating public support for new parks, raising and maximizing funds, and structuring workable land-acquisition transactions. The greatest need for the future is to enlarge the focus of partnerships to include park management. In uncertain budgetary times, some cities hesitate to create parks because of the ongoing obligation to manage and maintain them. But there is no reason to assume that the creativity and energy that partnerships bring to park creation cannot also be applied to park management and maintenance. The public sector, which can no longer run the nation's urban park systems alone, must call on the ideas, skills, and strengths of private partners, not only to create parks, but also to guarantee their long-term health and usefulness.

As the case studies in this book illustrate, many successful park projects continue to depend on private support. In some instances, this support is monetary. In Spartanburg, South Carolina, the Flagstar Corporation pays to maintain the plaza and park it largely created. Management of Manhattan's Bryant Park is funded mostly by proceeds from the park's restaurant and café and from assessments of a business improvement district—an increasingly popular way for businesses to return to the public some of the wealth generated by urban open space. And at the Park at Post Office Square in Boston, fees for private parking support park management.

But just as important as financial support are the energy and vision private partners bring to parks. In the most successful park processes, the same partners who help envision and build parks stay involved to help fund and manage them. Through continuous evaluation, planning, programming, and use, these committed private partners seek not only to create but also to sustain valuable parks. At Cedar Lake Park in Minneapolis, park neighbors organized as the Cedar Lake Park Association have continued their involvement—not only by raising more than $1.2 million for the park's support, but in hands-on efforts to restore natural ecosystems absent for 100 years. In Pinellas County, Florida, groups and communities along the Pinellas Trail have raised money for plantings, benches, water fountains, and other amenities, and have also donated greenery and planted demonstration flower boxes. One community along the trail has created a bicycle and pedestrian plaza, organized musical perform-

ances where the trail passes through downtown, and is making it possible for its segment of the trail to be used at night. Such measures draw users to parks, who come to value them in a whole new way. Through such efforts, the real meaning of a park emerges, one user-day at a time.

Several other examples are particularly worthy of consideration. Established in 1980, the partnership between the New York City Parks and Recreation Department and the Central Park Conservancy is the largest and most productive public/private park partnership in the nation. In its first 15 years, the conservancy raised $110 million to restore and reclaim Central Park from decades of declining maintenance and increasing vandalism. In addition, the conservancy contracts with the city to help develop programs for the park. And the nonprofit's 175 staffers bear many responsibilities traditionally borne by city employees. Not only has Central Park been largely rejuvenated through the conservancy's ministrations, but the effort has freed the city parks department to devote funds and staff time to smaller neighborhood parks.

In Philadelphia, declining public monies and a venerable philanthropic tradition have led to a three-way partnership between the Philadelphia Recreation Department, the Fairmount Park Commission (manager of one of the nation's largest urban parks), and Philadelphia Green, the inner-city division of the Philadelphia Horticultural Society (a chapter in this book details Philadelphia Green's work developing community gardens on abandoned inner-city lots). The organization also assumes broad responsibilities often borne by a city parks department: it plants, prunes, and removes trees; beautifies boulevards and neighborhoods; fights graffiti; and organizes environmental education programs. Some of the more than $3 million the horticultural society spends on such projects each year is raised through its annual flower show;

Proposals for the Sante Fe railyard site include a plaza with a park, commercial areas, and a cultural center. The development of this historic site, anchored by a depot founded in 1608, was the subject of intense local debate.

the balance is from traditional philanthropic sources. Although staffing remains half of what it was in the early 1980s, the city recently responded to this private energy by incrementally restoring staff to the Philadelphia Recreation Department.

The experiences in New York and Philadelphia bear important lessons for the urban parks movement. The first is that great parks are not created once, but are re-created over and over again, as is happening in New York City. The experience in Philadelphia teaches us that, despite the worries of some observers, private efforts can be solidly democratic, can forge strong community partnerships, and can create important open space resources in low-income neighborhoods.

The time ahead holds lessons for all of us. Perhaps the most important of these is that public/private partnerships are not a new solution to any single problem, but

rather a doorway through which we discover new solutions to many problems. For years we have been too inflexible, thinking that great parks must be created and paid for in a certain way and serve a certain purpose. In the area of maintenance and management, we have believed that if we mowed the lawns and repaired the picnic tables we could keep a great park great. But greatness cannot be "maintained" like infrastructure. Greatness emerges through use and must be re-envisioned by each generation.

The promise of the new public/private partnerships is that they will remain flexible and open to new approaches— constantly reinvigorated by their mix of governments, businesses, charitable and stakeholder groups, and nonprofit consultants. Such partnerships present the greatest hope of the urban parks movement.